With the Royal Garhwal Rifles in the Great War 1914–1917

D. H. DRAKE-BROCKMAN

The Naval & Military Press Ltd

Published by
The Naval & Military Press Ltd

BRIG.-GENERAL C. G. BLACKADER, C.B., D.S.O.

Commandant 2nd Battalion Leicestershire Regiment in winter, 1914. Commanded the 20th (Garhwal) Brigade in 1915. Later promoted to Major-General and command of a Division.

BRIG.-GENERAL H. GORDON, C.B., C.M.G., D.S.O.

Commanded the 2nd Battalion Leicestershire Regiment in succession to the late Major-General Blackader, C.B., D.S.O.

DEDICATED

TO THE MEMORY OF

The gallant British Officers, Garhwali Officers, Non-Commissioned Officers and Riflemen of the Regiment who laid down their lives on the Field of Honour and Glory in the service of King and Country during the Great War—1914 to 1918.

" Happy is he o'er whose decline,
The smiles of home may soothing shine,
And guide him down the steep of years :
But oh ! how grand they sink to rest,
Who close their eyes on Victory's breast ! "

MOORE'S MELODIES.

Elliott & Fry.

BRIG.-GENERAL D. H. DRAKE-BROCKMAN, C.M.G.

GRAND OFFICER CROWN OF ROUMANIA.

Commandant 2nd Battalion and Commanded 1st and 2nd Battalions "The Garhwal Rifles" in France and Egypt.

Foreword.

WHEN the 2nd Leicesters went to the War with the Garhwal Brigade very few of us knew anything about the Garhwal Rifles. They were definitely not an advertising Regiment. But we were soon to find out what sort of stuff we had along side of us. They tackled their job very quickly and seemed to shake down to the strange conditions of fighting and climate much sooner than most Indian Units of the Indian Army Corps. After a considerable experience of soldiering in foreign climes, I think I may safely say that these two Battalions of Garhwal Rifles were more like a British Regiment than any other native troops. For one thing, they never lost their form though they had their full share of casualties both in officers and men. No doubt this was largely due to the fact that they were commanded by two first-class C.O.s in Colonels Swiney and Drake-Brockman, backed up by as good a set of British Officers as one could hope to find anywhere. In the second place they never had a bad show, and so kept their original morale and prestige: and what a lot that means!

Even to this day, after so much has been written about the War, comparatively few English people, whether soldiers or civilians, realize what a burden of responsibility fell on the shoulders of the twelve British Officers of an Indian Battalion. An officer of a British Regiment was surrounded by N.C.O.s and men whom he knew intimately and whom he could trust implicitly, and of whom a large proportion were fit to become officers themselves. But a British Officer in an Indian Battalion was nearly always entirely on his own, with no one of his own race and kind to look to for the help and backing which mean such a lot in a tight place. It must have been a terrible strain on that handful of white officers in an Indian unit.

In two actions of their campaign in France the Garhwalis made history by original and clever tactics new to the whole of the British Army. And it is remarkable that each Battalion was concerned in one of these historic occasions.

During the first battle of Festubert in November, 1914, the 2nd Leicesters and 1st Garhwalis were told off to retake a section of trench which had been captured by the Germans. For this purpose we were lent to General Egerton's Brigade. It was a terribly cold night, with snow lying thick on the ground. Most of the Officers were assembled in the Brigade H.Q., a broken-down farmhouse in Festubert. The troops were lying down outside snoring and coughing and swearing.

We were getting so tired and bored that it was almost a relief when the Brigade Major came in with the orders for the attack.

I pushed off with two Companies of Leicesters to one flank of the trench and Colonel Swiney with the 1st Garhwalis went to the other flank. The Leicesters, with some loss, got into the trench, but were held up there by machine gun and rifle fire. The 1st Garhwalis did better, for they got into their end of the trench and bombed their way along the whole length of it, capturing over 100 prisoners. This was an important occasion, because it was the first time that the systematic attack of a trench by bombers and bayonet men was put into practice, and, with certain modifications, this form of attack became a standard in the British Army. The name of Lieut. Robson, R.E., who accompanied the Garhwalis, should long be remembered as the originator of the plan. The other incident concerns the 2nd Battalion at the battle of Neuve Chapelle. This was our first big battle, and all of us had made most careful preparations, and officers and men were all on tiptoe of excitement as Zero hour approached. For the first time in history British and Indian soldiers were to hear the roar of a tremendous barrage of our own Artillery. Colonel Drake-Brockman had an important rôle, and it was essential that his Battalion should get off the mark at once and keep the correct line of advance. To ensure this, Colonel Drake-Brockman got his men out into No-Man's Land before our Artillery opened fire, and, taking advantage of a fold in the ground, his assaulting Companies lay down and waited there for the signal to advance. One can imagine the feelings of these brave Indians right in front of the line lying out for over two hours waiting for Zero hour. By this plan many casualties from our own "shorts" were saved and the men had the best chance of a good start. What fine advantage they took of it is recorded in the many histories of the battle. They put up a magnificent show and captured nearly 200 prisoners. This was the first time in the war for our troops to form up on the enemy's side of the assembly trenches and is thus of peculiar historic interest.

In conclusion, I would like to say that there is no one more fitted to write the history of the Royal Garhwal Rifles than the author of this book. I refer specially to their campaign in France, where we were brigaded with them all the time. Brigadier-General Drake-Brockman commanded the 2nd Battalion and then the amalgamated Battalions during the whole time they were in France without missing a day from wounds or sickness. This is a wonderful record for a Regimental Officer. He knew his men and his officers, and, what is more, he knew his soldiering from A to Z. He was a man who was never deaf to the call for strenuous endeavour. To me it is a thrilling tale of the firing line. simply told by a front-line Officer.

H. GORDON,

LONDON, 1934. *Brig.-General.*

CORRIGENDA.

1. Page 11, column 2, lines 22 and 33—For " Leicester " read " Leicestershire."
2. Page 18, column 2, line 3—For " Leicester " read " Leicestershire."
3. Page 21, column 2, line 26—For " 29 " read " 40."
4. Page 23, column 1, line 7—For " Ralputs " read " Rajputs."
5. Page 29, column 1, line 21—For " Dut-out " read " Dug-out."
6. Page 34, column 2, line 11—For " her " read " here."
7. Page 45, column 1, line 25—For " XVI." read " VI."
8. Page 52—For objective " A-C-K-D-G-H " read " A-C-K-O-G-H."

Preface.

IN undertaking to write this narrative of my regiment in the Great War, I make no pretensions to any particular qualification for the task. It was my good fortune to have been present at all the battles except the first and second battles of Ypres in which the Indian Army Corps took part, and therefore I was enabled to acquire by personal observation a first-hand knowledge of the events herein recorded as well as of important localities described. My main object is to furnish a complete and authentic record of the regiment's doings for the period which the narrative covers for future reference, as unless such events and impressions gained at the time are recorded at once by someone having first-hand knowledge of the events, much is lost by recording them years afterwards and compiling them from sources which cannot be considered so reliable. Such as it is, therefore, I publish it, as it contains some original documents, accurate maps and orders issued which should suffice to give it some interest, should it possess no other, especially to the regimental officer.

It was originally intended that this book should embody the two diaries of both the battalions up to the date of amalgamation, each diary being produced one under the other, day by day, exactly as written in the field by the Commanding Officers and thereafter the single diary of the combined battalions, styled "The Garhwal Rifles." As however, the book with all the appendices and illustrations proved a rather long production, and the publication cost high, I have re-written the whole story, reducing it in length, but have kept the orders, reports, &c., in their original form. The appendices, I consider, form a most interesting and important part of the book. Up to the date of amalgamation at the end of March, 1915, the story is chiefly that of the 2nd Battalion, of which I was the Commandant, and thereafter the story is that of the combined battalions which also came under my command from that date to their return to India in the spring of 1916. I have added a brief account after that date up to the time of my giving up command of my battalion on completion of my five years' tenure of command in November, 1917.

The official document giving all the battles and actions on all fronts has now been published, and from this it will be seen that the regiment took part in the following battles and actions in France :—

(1) OPERATIONS IN FLANDERS — 10TH OCTOBER TO 22ND NOVEMBER, 1914.
 (a) Battle of LA BASSEE — 10th October to 2nd November, 1914.
 Battle of Armentières — 13th October to 2nd November, 1914.

(2) WINTER OPERATIONS — NOVEMBER, 1914, TO FEBRUARY, 1915.
 Defence of Festubert—23rd to 24th November, 1914.
 Defence of GIVENCHY—20th-21st December, 1914.

(3) SUMMER OPERATIONS—MARCH, 1915, TO OCTOBER, 1915.
 (a) Battle of NEUVE CHAPELLE—10th to 13th March, 1915.
 (b) Battle of AUBERS RIDGE—9th May, 1915. Attack at Rue du Bois.
 (c) Battle of FESTUBERT—15th to 25th May, 1915.
 (d) Battle of Loos—25th September to 8th October, 1915. Action of Piètre—25th September, 1915.

Eventually the Battle Honours were sanctioned in the "Gazette of India," No. 194, of 1926, and the Regiment was awarded the following :—

LA BASSEE, 1914.
Armentières, 1914.
FESTUBERT, 1914-15.
NEUVE CHAPELLE, AUBERS,
 FRANCE AND FLANDERS, 1914-15.
EGYPT, 1915-16.
MACEDONIA, 1918.
KHAN BAGDADI, SHARQAT,
 MESOPOTAMIA, 1917-18.

Those printed in capitals may be borne on Colours and Appointments.

Application was made by the Commanding Officers of the four battalions to the War Office Battle Honours Committee asking that the regiment might be allowed RAMADI in place of KHAN BAGHDADI, and also to have LOOS as an honour. But the request was not granted.

The points put forward in support of the application were that at Ramadi the 2nd Battalion took part as a battalion and were sufficiently prominent to obtain special mention in the Commander-in-Chief's despatch. Moreover, at this battle, the battalion took about 2,000 Turkish prisoners, the Divisional General and his Staff, and captured three field guns, whereas at Khan Baghdadi but some 300 men of the regiment participated and that only in the interesting, but bloodless, pursuit to Ana after the battle, and, generally speaking, that Ramadi was a far more strenuous affair and one that will long be remembered in the regiment.

At Loos the amalgamated battalions took part in the holding attack and suffered heavy casualties, but it seems that they were serving beyond the area defined for the grant of this honour.

In the "Gazette of India," No. 193, of 1926, the regiment was included in the list of units entitled to bear the distinction AFGHANISTAN, 1919, on their appointments, in recognition of its services during the campaign known as the 3rd Afghan War.

Though this book is intended as a record of my regiment in France during the Great War, I was forced, owing to the prominent part I was called upon to play throughout the period covered by the narrative, to introduce more of the personal element than I otherwise would have wished to do. Although I am alone responsible for the opinions and criticisms expressed in these pages, I have done my best to give a real and complete story of the events.

The maps may be relied upon for absolute accuracy, as they were made by me on the ground and while everything was fresh in my memory. The photographs might have been more numerous, and some highly interesting ones could have been taken, but the possession of cameras, though sanctioned at one time for a very short period, was afterwards cancelled. Those of the two churches and concrete dug-out for field gun were taken by me during my visit to the battle fields in the spring of 1921.

As the authors of "The Indian Corps in France" say: "But the piety and industry of individual students may shed a tiny ray of light upon the small segment of ground where their comrades lived and fought and died." Being one of those humble students I have tried to do so in this short narrative.

My best thanks are due to the following :—

Messrs. Elliot & Fry, for their permission to reproduce my own photo ;

The Editor of the "Illustrated London News," for permission to reproduce the two pictures of (1) Naik Darwan Sing Negi, 1st Battalion, winning the Victoria Cross ; (2) The 2nd Battalion at the battle of Neuve Chapelle ;

Captain (now Lieut.-Colonel) Etherton for the photographs of Egypt.

Brig.-General H. Gordon, C.B., C.M.G., D.S.O., for so kindly writing the Foreword and for his kindly encouragement.

To my publishers for all the trouble taken in publishing this book.

I have left the text as originally written in 1922, though some of the reforms suggested have since been carried out.

D. H. DRAKE-BROCKMAN,

Brigadier-General,

Late Commandant 2nd Battalion Garhwal Rifles.

LINDFIELD,

SUSSEX, 1933.

CHAPTER I.

IN 1914, when the Great War broke out, there were only two battalions of Garhwalis in the Indian Army. The 1st Battalion was raised in 1887. Up to this time Garhwalis had been freely enlisted in Gurkha Battalions, and for this reason, and owing to their uniform and equipment beng similar, they had invariably, by the uninitiated, been confused with Gurkhas. In Gurkha Battalions they had invariably done well and showed themselves good soldiers.

This war soon proved what excellent sodliers they were, truly *nulli secundus*. General Sir James Willcocks, who commanded the Indian Army Corps in France, says on page 57 of his book, "With the Indians in France": "The Garhwalis as a distinct type were being tested for the first time in class corps. The 1st and 2nd Battalions of the *39th Garhwal Rifles did splendidly on every occasion in which they were engaged. In fact they surprised us all; not that we did not expect them to do well, but they suddenly sprang into the very front rank of our best fighting men. At Festubert in 1914, and at Neuve Chapelle, nothing could have been better than their elan and discipline, and they at once established a reputation which will live in India."

The 2nd Battalion was raised in 1901, and both battalions were permanently located in their own country at a hill station called Lansdowne, 6,000 feet elevation, in the Garhwal district of the United Provinces of India.

Garhwal, or British Garhwal, is a district in the Himalayas under British administration. The word "Garhwal" means 'the land of forts," "Garh" meaning a fort. It is bounded on the north by Tibet, from which it is separated by a magnificent range of snowy mountains stretching as far as the eye can see from east to west, and with no peak under 20,000 feet in height. On the south by the plains of India, the Bijnor district of the United Provinces. On the east by Kumaon, which stretches away on to the Nepaul border. And on the west by the River Ganges. To the west of the Ganges lies Tihri, or foreign Garhwal, a native State which also furnishes recruits for the regiment.

Both Battalions were in the Garhwal Brigade, as it was then called, of the Meerut Division, and which consisted in peace time of the following four regiments:—2/3rd (Q.A.O.) Gurkha Rifles, 2/8th Gurkha Rifles, and the two Battalions of the 39th Garhwal Rifles, which, together with the G.O.C. and Brigade headquarters, were all situated at Lansdowne, which was 19 miles distant by the bridle path and 26 miles by the cart road from the railhead at Kotdwara.

For active service, however, a Brigade in India is always formed with one British Battalion and three Indian Battalions, and so the Garhwal Brigade, when it mobilised for service in France in August, 1914, consisted of the following four battalions:—

2nd Battalion Leicester Regiment. O.C., Lieut.-Colonel C. G. Blackader, D.S.O.
2nd Battalion 3rd (Q.A.O.) Gurkha Rifles. O.C., Lieut.-Colonel V. Ormsby.
1st Battalion 39th Garhwal Rifles. O.C., Lieut.-Colonel E. R. R. Swiney.
2nd Battalion 39th Garhwal Rifles. O.C., Lieut.-Colonel D. H. Drake-Brockman.

The 2/8th Gurkha Rifles were transferred to the Bareilly Brigade to complete that formation.

We had not met the 2nd Leicester Regiment, "The Tigers," before, but we had heard of their reputation and that it was a splendid regiment. We soon found this out, and it was not to be wondered at considering what a splendid commanding officer it possessed in Colonel Blackader, as well as a first-rate set of officers. We soon became great friends with them all, and always felt glad when they were alongside us in the trenches or any attack—a compliment which I am glad to say they reciprocated. We were very fortunate in getting them into our Brigade. They had a hard time of it during the war, for after all the time they spent in France with us they went off to Mesopotamia and suffered many casualties in all the many actions there, while we went to Egypt. It was very nice for me meeting the same battalion again afterwards when it came under my command in the Delhi

* In the subsequent reorganisation and numbering of units of the Indian Army the Regiment was given the number 18 and is now the 18th Royal Garhwal Rifles.

MAJOR H. M. MACTIER,

Second in Command 2nd Battalion. Killed at the Battle of Neuve Chapelle, 11th March, 1915, while temporarily commanding the 1st Battalion.

Brigade in 1919. It was then commanded by Lieut.-Colonel (now Brig.-General) B. C. Dent, C.M.G., D.S.O. Colonel Blackader shortly afterwards received a Brevet-Colonelcy, and in January, 1915, was appointed to command the Garhwal Brigade when our Brigadier was promoted to the command of the 3rd Lahore Division, which caused us great joy, as we all knew what a sound man he was. He turned out as good a Brigade Commander as he had been a regimental one. The command of the Leicesters then devolved on Lieut.-Colonel (now Brig.-General) H. Gordon, D.S.O., another fine soldier.

The 2/3rd Gurkhas were old friends of ours. Originally the 39th was raised as the 2/3rd Gurkhas, but later, when the late Lord Roberts was Commander-in-Chief in India and decided to have a whole class regiment of Garhwalis, all the Gurkhas remained on as the 2/3rd Gurkhas, and the Garhwalis were all transferred to form the 39th again, as this number was vacant then owing to the disbandment of the old 39th Infantry.

The 2/3rd Gurkhas is a good regiment, having been properly organised by a first-rate commanding officer. Thank heaven we, too, had been well and soundly organised and good ideals inculcated from the beginning by the C.O., Lieut.-Colonel J. Evatt, D.S.O. (now Brig.-General), and this standard had been kept up by the British Officers who, in Indian regiments especially, must set the highest example. The fruit of this from the firm discipline established was seen when the regiment was eventually weighed in the scales in the fiery ordeal of this great war, and it was, I venture to say, not found wanting. This is half the battle, for a regiment will always do well where the officers make it their business thoroughly to understand and "identify" themselves with their men, show themselves possessed of a strict sense of duty, and look after their men and their interests without any pampering. With Indian troops, as long as you are just, you may be as strict as you like. Where the officers know their work and show themselves good men to follow, know the characters and dispositions of their men and gain their confidence, a firm and rigid discipline can always be maintained. But when the reverse is the case, then, as sure as there is a sun in the heavens, that regiment will fail when the real ordeal comes. I have seen it on more than one occasion in this late war, and the greater the hardships to be undergone the greater will be the failure. For, after all, good discipline is the basis of everything. Discipline is just as necessary in the home, though in a lesser degree, and in every walk of life, but especially in the Services, where it is the foundation of all good work. It means good marching, good fighting and good everything. It is like the foundation of a house. If you wish the house to stand in all weathers you see that it is dug on firm soil, or on a rock. What did the greatest captain of all time, the great Napoleon, say? I quote one of his maxims: "A good General (or Commanding Officer), a well organised system, good instruction and severe discipline, aided by effective establishments, will always make good troops." That is like other maxims of his relating to strategy, and the truth of it is eternal. To add weight to what I say I mention the remark made to me by the old Subadar Major of my Battalion when I was leaving on the expiration of my command. "Sahib," he said, "we always had confidence in you, and you never let us down. We see now the benefit of all the strict discipline that you upheld." I consider this the greatest compliment ever paid me by anyone, high or low, coming as it did from one who had shared with me all the privations of that trying time in France.

As mentioned above, there were only two Battalions of Garhwalis at the outbreak of war, and to send both to the front meant that there was no other Battalion left in India to furnish sufficient reinforcements, but only the two small depôts which, though they both enlisted extra recruits and trained hard at once, they could not at first, nor for some time, furnish sufficient reinforcements to replace the large number of casualties and keep the two Battalions up to full strength, as very heavy casualties were naturally to be expected in a war of this magnitude. This was an error on the part of the military authorities in India which had to be rectified shortly after arrival in France by making the experiment of attaching men of another class, *i.e.*, Dogras, from other units, in order to keep up our strength. They, however, only remained for a very short time, and were all transferred to Dogra units immediately after the battle of Neuve Chapelle. Both Battalions were then amalgamated temporarily, which was a much more popular expedient. Still, it was nice for us all that both Battalions did go to the front together, as it enabled most of us to get to France straight away.

When both the Battalions had left the depôt, Commanders set to work to recruit and train hard, and right good work did they do. Recruits came in splendidly, especially after two men of the regiment, one in each battalion, had gained the coveted distinction of the Victoria Cross. All through the war the little district of Garhwal responded nobly to the call for recruits, so much so that in the number of recruits enlisted, Garhwalis stood at the head of the list of percentages of the Indian Army, and two extra Battalions, the 3rd and the 4th, were eventually raised. These two extra Battalions still exist, and have not been disbanded like others which were raised for the war. It is hoped that they will be able to be kept up to full strength, as His Majesty the King Emperor possesses in Garhwalis soldiers who are intensely loyal and grateful to the British Raj, and whose discipline and valour have now been well tried and put to the test. And there could have been no better test than the fiery ordeal of the Great War.

The work done by the two Depôt Commanders was very heavy. They, with others, formed a most important link in the chain, and notwithstanding the usual lack of preparation and of material on the part of the Indian Government, the link stood the strain well. The work was most monotonous. Day after day the same eternal drill, musketry and other training, coupled with all the accounts of the whole regiment on service and extra reinforcements sent from time to time. When men returned sick or wounded and invalided they had to be settled up with, their pension papers made out either for them or the heirs of those who had been killed. This added to the already great burden of work.

CAPTAIN E. R. P. BERRYMAN.

2nd Battalion. Adjutant in France, also of "The Garhwal Rifles" in Egypt. Later Brevet Major and D.S.O. in Mesopotamia. Wounded at the Battle of Aubers, 9th May, 1915.

It is not to be wondered at then that the accounts of some depôts got into great confusion. This was most noticeable where the officer in command was not possessed of a strict sense of duty, or where the organisation of that particular unit to which the depôt belonged was faulty.

Of course some Commanding Officers were very short-sighted, and in order to have all their best officers with them on service generally left a less competent officer behind to command the depôt, which required a senior and very experienced officer. In addition, some took their best clerks with the unit and left the unfortunate depôt commander inadequately staffed for his heavy work. Where this happened the best cure would have been to have sent that particular C.O. back to the depôt to stay there until he had unravelled all the accounts.

One has also to take into consideration the system of accounts in Indian units and the Military Accounts Department. No doubt the original confusion was due to that Department's incapacity. It was not equal to the strain. The Indian Establishment was not quick or smart enough to cope with the tremendous amount of work, nor were there a sufficient number of really good clerks. Those taken on temporarily during the war were generally not only new to the work but untrained and unable to write really well and neatly, with the inevitable result.

To add to the confusion, the authorities chose, on the eve of mobilisation, to introduce in our division an entirely new system of accounts. This was eventually found quite unworkable in practice and had to be abandoned. These accounts took months to get straight in some units, and in others they never got straight. Deficiencies had to be struck off, which was the most common-sense way of dealing with them where there was no fraud. Otherwise the Indian "Babu," or clerk of the Pay Department, would have been delighted to have gone on issuing "objection" statements to the crack of doom and wasted enough postage stamps which, in time, would have almost paid up the deficiencies.

The Indian "Babu" is a queer individual. From my own pay lists I can speak from experience. In some cases he would insist on paying the same man twice over in the same pay roll, and when such errors were pointed out to the office, and special typed lists sent to help him by showing him exactly what men were actually present and on leave, &c., he would have none of it, but went on paying them twice over, thereby increasing our work, as it would eventually be discovered on audit and a refund asked for. He is a slave to his god "dastur" or "custom." In some of my pay lists he would give, say twenty men's names on one side and opposite only 18 amounts, and you were left to guess what

GROUP OF OFFICERS 2ND BATTALION 39TH GARHWAL RIFLES.
CAMP LA-VALENTIN, MARSEILLES.

Capt. H.R.B. Reed. Lt. A.E. Clarke, Q. Master. Lt. Wilcox, Capt. A.G. Lyell. Capt. A.W. Robertson-Glasgow. Capt. D.A. Blair.

Major J. Woods, Med. Officer. Major H.M. MacTier, 2nd in Commd. Lt.-Col. D.H. Drake-Brockman, Comdt. Capt. E.R.P. Berryman, Adjutant. Major G.H. Taylor. Capt. G.W. Burton.

CAPTAIN G. W. BURTON, D.S.O.

2nd Battalion. Killed at Givenchy 12th October, 1915.

the other two men were owed, or vice versa. The amounts were written almost illegibly and slanting across the page instead of being written neatly and straight opposite each man's name. However, he did his best in most instances, I suppose. The fault lay with the system, which only allowed an inadequate number of clerks in the pay office or regiment, which might have been sufficient in the old days when one had about an hour's office work at most, but quite inadequate to-day. I suppose Government departments will always be full of red tape!

Notwithstanding the good and hard work done by some depôt commanders year after year, hot weather after hot weather in the dust, heat and flies, not one, I believe, ever got a reward, not even in the shape of some minor decoration. Some never had the good fortune to get off on service, where, at any rate, one has some excitement and change of scene and air. Some depôts, I know when I was Inspector of Depôts, were in splendid order, accounts were all square, no losses, and yet they got no recognition. Only perhaps some general remarks in the way of mild praise issued in some training memorandum to all—good, bad and indifferent alike. Surely some who could have been specially recommended merited a little extra reward as much as other minor officials sitting snugly out of the heat at Army headquarters! But the basket was always empty long before it ever got so far down as the humble depôt commander! "They also serve who only stand and wait" said the immortal Milton, and as General Robert Edward Lee, the American General Commanding the Confederates in the American Civil War, one of the finest soldiers that ever lived, said to his war-worn and ragged veterans who crowded round him on his horse when he was obliged to surrender to the Federal General at Appomattox Court House: "Soldiers, you go to your homes with the consciousness of duty well performed." In this, then, lies the Regimental and Depôt Commanders' reward, though no such stirring words were ever addressed to them, in the consciousness of having done their duty well in the majority of cases, and they can say with the poet :—

"The same our failure or our glory
If conscience says our best was done,
Whether the name be told in story
Or buried in oblivion."

CHAPTER II.

Outbreak of War—Orders for Mobilisation—Mobilisation of the Meerut Division—Departure of the Battalion from Lansdowne—Orders to Stand Fast at Railhead Kotdwara—Leave for Karachi—Long wait there—Finally leave for an "Unknown Destination."

TOWARDS the end of July, 1914, events were moving somewhat rapidly in European politics. The air was charged with electricity, and one could not help feeling that it would not be long before war broke out. Naturally, we all wondered if any Indian troops would be sent to Europe. However, we were not left long in suspense, for after war had been declared by Germany, our Government also declared war upon her because she refused to abide by her treaty to respect the neutrality of Belgium.

First the 6th (Poona) Division was mobilised and sent to the Persian Gulf, and five days after the declaration of war, on the 9th August, 1914, came the orders for the mobilisation of the 7th (Meerut) Division. The 3rd (Lahore) Division had received orders to mobilise a day or two before. Thus the Indian Army Corps, for service in France, was to consist of these two Divisions with the usual complement of Artillery and Divisional Troops and administrative departments.

The Meerut Division, of which our Brigade, called the Garhwal Brigade, formed part, was commanded by Lieut.-General C. A. Anderson, C.B. (afterwards General Sir Charles Anderson), a thoroughly sound and good soldier. He took us to France and commanded us the whole time that the Division was there till he took over the command of the Indian Army Corps in September, 1915, from General Sir James Willcocks.

The Indian Army Corps consisted of the following :—

3RD (LAHORE) DIVISION.

Lieut.-General H. B. Watkins, C.B., Indian Army, with three Brigades, &c.

7TH (MEERUT) DIVISION).

Lieut.-General C. A. Anderson, C. B., late Royal Artillery.

Dehra Dun Brigade (Brig.-General C. E. Johnson, Indian Army).—1st Batt. Seaforth Highlanders, 1st Batt. 9th Gurkha Rifles, 2nd Batt. 2nd Gurkha Rifles, 6th Jat Light Infantry.

Garhwal Brigade (Major-General H. D. O'Keary, C.B., D.S.O., Indian Army).—2nd Batt. Leicester Regiment, 2nd Batt. 3rd (Q.A.O.) Gurkha Rifles, 1st Batt. 39th Garhwal Rifles, 2nd Batt. 39th Garhwal Rifles.

Bareilly Brigade (Major - General F. Macbean, C.B., C.V.O., late Gordon Highlanders).—2nd Batt. Royal Highlanders, 41st Dogras, 58th Rifles (F.F.), 2nd Batt. 8th Gurkha Rifles.

There was the usual complement of Artillery, Divisional Troops and administrative services.

Later, in France, a third battalion was added to the Garhwal Brigade, making five altogether, the 1st Batt. 3rd London Regiment (Royal Fusiliers), T.F., a smart, good regiment, which remained with us the whole time we were in France.

The system in India was that those Battalions that were in the Field Army, *i.e.*, "mobilised battalions," were supposed to have on hand certain articles of field service equipment and also all their mobilisation orders and indents ready and checked so as to save time when mobilisation was ordered. Both our battalions were in the Field Army, so we had everything ready. When orders came to mobilise they were conveyed to all men on leave or furlough in the usual yellow mobilisation envelopes telling them to rejoin headquarters at once. However, the postal arrangements in the hilly district of Garhwal were somewhat primitive, as from Pauri the chief civil station of Garhwal, where the Deputy Commissioner lives, and 36 miles from Lansdowne, all letters had to be sent out by means of the local "chitti rasan," or postman, who had many miles to traverse over hill and dale. So telegrams were sent to Pauri and the two other places where there was a telegraph office, and the aid of the Deputy Commissioner invoked. He at once dispatched his chaprassies, or messengers, to the various Pattis and Pergunnahs (sub-districts and districts), and thus got the news round quicker. But it is extraordinary how news does travel in the East. Men heard of the

CAPTAIN A. W. ROBERTSON-GLASGOW.

2nd Battalion. Killed at Richebourg L'Avoué 13th November, 1914.

news to mobilise some time before they received the yellow envelopes through the medium of the post office. In a week or more the greater number had arrived. To complete our numbers the first squad or two of recruits was sworn in, *i.e.*, attested and took the oath of allegiance, after which a man is considered no longer a recruit and receives the balance of his clothing and equipment. This still left a very few men short. As the reserves had been called up or mobilised, too, the best of them were selected to complete the Battalion.

At that time the Indian Army Reserve was not on a satisfactory basis. Men were allowed to join the Reserve if they had done three years' service with the colours and were not more than 32 years of age provided there was a vacancy. The strength of the Reserve was 200 per battalion. Each man received a retaining fee of Rs. 3 per month and full pay and any allowances to which he might be entitled, during the period of two months' training, which took place every two years.

Men could stay on up to 25 years' total service if not discharged in the meantime as medically unfit, when they became entitled to a small pension. Naturally, as many as could stayed, or tried to stay on, for the pension if possible, with the result that there were not many of them whom one

LIEUT. J. T. C. WILCOX.

2nd Battalion. Killed at the Battle of Festubert 12th May, 1915.

could consider fit for such a strenuous campaign. The two months' training, moreover, which they went through every second year was quite inadequate to make up even the lee-way they had made through going back to their villages and civil life, as the Oriental ages much quicker than an European and soon loses his martial bearing and knowledge once he gets back to his civil occupation. What he regains at the training he soon loses again after he has left. Instead of two months' training every second year he should have had two months every year, as a man could not make up in so short a period all that he had lost in addition to the large amount of training and musketry, &c., he had to cram into the two months. So it was not many men who were fit enough to accompany the Battalion. The youngest and best were selected and the remainder were left at the depôt, some eventually to come to Marseilles, where they remained only to go back again as being quite unfit for the front line. This was a great waste of money, but all due to the parsimonious methods of the Indian Government in their dealings with anything military. They never gave enough to do things really efficiently. In matters military their principle was not "whatever is worth doing is worth doing well." It would have been far better to have had a less number of men in the Reserve and the terms of service such that would have ensured the men being fit and not too old or decrepit. The Indian soldier is at his best from five to ten years' service, that is as a private. After that, he might go on in the Reserve up to fifteen years' service, and that is the limit of his real usefulness if the Reserve is to be of any real value to supplement the active army. If only intended for garrison duty such as butt markers and garrison guards to relieve fitter troops, of course they could go on longer. Eventually all the Reservists were formed into companies for such duties in India during the war, when it was found that the majority were too old and unfit for the strenuous work in the field.

The Indian Government has always been noted for its parsimony towards the military, and yet when it likes it can spend money like water for any civil ceremonial. An Indian army officer always had to pay for his rations in the field, whereas his British confrère got his free, with good allowances in addition. The Indian Government was somewhat fond in its dealings with military matters of giving paltry and inadequate allowances for any particular purpose, such as office and so forth, and so washing their hands of any further responsibility, saying, in the language of the vernacular, "Bandobast Karo" (you arrange). It is now, I think (and hope), abolishing this pernicious system, and carrying out the recommendations of the Esher Committee.

Following their usual practice it was first proposed to make officers pay when in France, but owing to the representations made, this was cancelled and whatever had been cut from our pay was refunded. Again, our horse allowance was Rs. 30 per mensem at that time—scarcely equal to £2. Now it may have been increased or free rations for a charger given, but then the cost of hire for our Government charger which it was proposed to cut from us came to £5 a month, or £3 more than our allowance! This was, I am glad to say, also cancelled, and the privilege given free.

Another instance of the parsimony of the Indian Government is shown when an officer retires from the Indian Army after long and faithful service. The British service officer, should he retire when out in India, or go home on leave to retire, gets his passage home free, but not so his confrère in the Indian Army, who, as the Indian Army Regulations (always delightfully ambiguous and generally only interpretable by a Babu) then stood, could only get a free passage home by committing himself and getting dismissed from the army! The officer of long proved and faithful service is left to find his own way to the home country 6,000 miles away. It is hoped that this anomaly will cease and a passage home, after either a certain number of years approved service or rank, be granted.

The orders were to take with us at first 10 per cent. reinforcements, in addition to our full field service strength. The Indian Army is really only organised for small frontier expeditions in India, and when we were launched into this huge war the military authorities in India at the time could not "think large enough" or imagine what huge requirements in men and material would be needed.

The full field service strength of an Indian Battalion was 752 of all Indian ranks, with 13 British Officers extra, which included a medical officer. This total of 752 was made up as follows:—17 Garhwali officers, which included the Garhwali Adjutant, 40 havaldars (equivalent of sergeant), 29 naiks (equivalent of corporal), 14 buglers and 640 riflemen, with one ward orderly. So with the 10 per cent. extra reinforcements the total came to 827 of all ranks. These latter 10 per cent. reinforcements were left at Marseilles on arrival to come up later to replace casualties.

Everything was soon ready and orders having come shortly after, the battalion marched out of Lansdowne as part of the 20th (Garhwal) Brigade, 7th War Division, Indian Expeditionary Force, at 10 a.m. on the 21st August, 1914.

The first camp out was at a place called Dogadda, ten miles distant. I had intended doing the whole march to Kotdwara, our railhead, 19 miles, in one day, as we generally did, as the road was all down-hill, though on the way up we generally took two days on account of the transport, which could not well do it in one day.

It was fine when we started, but just as we arrived at the camping ground it began to rain, and very soon it was pouring heavily, so much so that the ground was soon flooded, as it was in August, the height of the rainy season, when generally the heaviest rainfall takes place. It was impossible to do anything, and shortly after arrival a message was received by orderly from Lansdowne ordering us to halt at Dogadda that night. All our tents had been sent on to Kotdwara, so as to be ready for us on arrival there, but something always turns up to mar the good plans that one makes, or tries to make. Luckily, there were some tents already pitched at Dogadda belonging to the 8th Gurkhas, which they kindly lent to us, so half the battalion

SUBADAR MAJOR NAIN SING CHINWARH, SARDAR BAHADUR, M.C.

2nd Battalion. Subsequently granted rank of Hon. Captain.

occupied these while the other half battalion I sent on that same afternoon to Kotdwara, to be joined by the other half the next morning. It poured heavily during the night.

The following British Officers accompanied the Battalion :—Lieut.-Colonel D. H. Drake-Brockman, Commandant ; Major H. M. MacTier, Second in command ; Major J. H. K. Stewart ; Major G. H. Taylor ; Captain A. W. Robertson-Glasgow ; Captain E. R. P. Berryman, Adjutant ; Lieut. A. E. Clarke, Quartermaster : and Major J. Woods, I.M.S., Medical Officer. The total was eight British Officers, 17 Garhwali Officers, 14 buglers and 734 rank and file.

On arrival at Kotdwara the next day (22nd August) we received orders to entrain for Karachi at 6 p.m. on 23rd August, but these orders were cancelled by wire later in the evening and we were ordered to "stand fast till further orders." While here we took over and issued our field service warm clothing, which I had arranged to be kept instead of being sent up the road to Lansdowne. Also we received a draft of 62 rank and file, including 40 reservists, which made our complement of 827 complete, including the first 10 per cent. reinforcements. Captain Bunbury, of the 13th Ralputs, also joined in order to complete our complement of British Officers. All the others were on furlough in England and would join us en route.

This delay at Kotdwara in the middle of the hot season and rains was unfortunate and quite unnecessary. It was a malarious place, and at this time of the year alive with mosquitoes. It is situated at the edge of the "Terai," or "Bhaber," as it is called in those parts. Living for the men in single fly tents and for officers in 40lb. tents was therefore no joke. Altogether we were nine days in this delightful spot and, considering the further long wait we had at Karachi, it was quite unnecessary for us to have been sent out of Lansdowne till practically three weeks later, if just a little forethought and common sense had only been exercised by the authorities in Simla. As it was, the men began to get fever, notwithstanding the administration by the medical officer of five grains of quinine daily. The long stay at Karachi, coupled with the sea air and voyage, got rid of most of this fever. Why the authorities at Simla were in such a great hurry to get us out of Lansdowne it is difficult to imagine. One would have thought that nothing would have been easier for them than to have enquired first whether the transports were ready for us or not, and then sent us off just in time to embark on them and so avoided these long waits in tents during the monsoon.

We left Kotdwara on 30th August at 6.15 p.m., and arrived at Karachi on 2nd September. En route we had a minor accident which fortunately was not worse. Our engine went through a small low culvert, derailing a couple of carriages. As we were going dead slow at the time, being close to Lahore, no one was hurt. Another engine and carriages were soon obtained and we continued our journey.

At Karachi we were again detained for fifteen days in camp, so there could not have been any real urgency to get us out of our station in such haste. We could have remained comfortably and with considerable advantage.

Captain Burton joined us here. He had been left to command the depôt temporarily but as Captain Holland had arrived from England he took over the command of depôt and released Captain Burton. Captain Bunbury also left to join his own unit.

Eventually the Battalion embarked in the hired transport S.S. "Coconada" on 16th September. We had on board with us half a battalion of the 2/3rd Gurkhas, with some Ordnance details. After we were on board, the ship's captain got orders to "stand fast till further orders," so we remained alongside the jetty till 20th September, when the ship went outside the harbour and anchored. Other transports did the same and took up positions prior to sailing the next day. Other troops of the Indian Army Corps embarked at Bombay, and their ships were to meet ours at pre-arranged rendezvous in the Indian Ocean. Our convoy was escorted by H.M.S. "Dartmouth," and on 23rd September we sighted the other portion from Bombay. It was a curious sight, for at first only small puffs of smoke were visible all along the horizon, and gradually the ships themselves became visible and joined us. The whole convoy, being now complete, proceeded on it way to the "unknown destination," which everyone knew was Marseilles, under escort of His Majesty's ships "Swiftsure" and "Fox."

CHAPTER III.

Voyage to France—Arrival at Marseilles—Change of Rifles and Ammunition—Camp La Valentin—Muddy Camp—Leave for Orleans—Six days in Camp—Finally leave for Lillers—Billeted at Calonne sur la Lys for the night before marching for the trenches to relieve troops of the British Expeditionary Force.

THE voyage to France was uneventful. The submarine menace had not developed as it did later, so there was not much danger en route except from a chance enemy cruiser. An escort was therefore necessary the whole way, till almost in sight of the French coast. During the voyage the men did running and physical drill daily to keep fit. Our ship arrived at Suez at 3 p.m. on 3rd October, and we entered the Canal at 12.30 a.m. next morning. Captain Reed joined the Battalion here, and the others, Captains Blair, Lyell and Wilcox, joined us at Port Said the next day, all having been recalled from furlough in England. Port Said was reached at 3 p.m. on 4th October. All our ships were cheered by the French sailors belonging to the French men-of-war there as we steamed up to our anchorage.

After coaling, the convoy assembled outside in the roadstead on the 5th, and all 18 ships left Port Said the next day, 6th October, at 2 p.m., escorted by a French man-of-war, the "Jaure Guiberry." It was calm the whole way in the Mediterranean except for one day, which made some of our men rather seasick. Some stood the motion of the ship wonderfully well considering none of them had even so much as seen the sea or a ship in their lives.

Malta was passed at 7 a.m. on the 10th, and Sardinia the next day at the same time. When we neared the French coast and no further danger was to be apprehended, the ships' captains got orders from the man-of-war to steam on independently to Marseilles, and the man-of-war dropped astern. We were not in a very fast ship, but she cracked on steam and went ahead for Marseilles, where we arrived at 1 p.m. on 12th October. We got orders to disembark on the 14th and be ready to furnish fatigue parties up to 500 men to help unload other ships. These orders were, however, cancelled in the early morning of 13th October, and our ship went alongside at 12.30 p.m. the same day, and we commenced disembarking at once and unloaded the ship and furnished at the same time fatigue parties to unload other ships. All the rifles that we brought with us were exchanged by the Ordnance Department, which had established their stores in a hangar at the docks. The Battalion filed into the hangar, and each man, after handing in his rifle and receiving another of the latest pattern in exchange, filed out at the other side. Our ammunition also was exchanged for the Mark VII. pattern for use with this rifle. Machine guns were also exchanged. All kit was unloaded from the ship and immediately loaded up on ten large two-horsed wagons supplied us to take it to Camp La Valentin, about ten miles out of Marseilles, and left escorted by Nos. 7 and 8 Platoons. As the ship had been loaded at Karachi by cooly labour to save time and the men, there was a terrible mix-up of kit in the hold. Some things got left behind, to be brought out next day by the right half battalion under Major Taylor, who was left behind in command. Battalion headquarters with the left half battalion marched off to Camp La Valentin at 8.15 p.m. The route lay for a part of the way through Marseilles town, and the inhabitants, notwithstanding the lateness of the hour, opened their windows and clapped and cheered us all the way. The journey was mostly uphill, and the cobbled streets made one's feet rather tired towards the end of the march. Camp was reached at midnight. After some difficulty our exact part was located, camp pitched and kits sorted out, and such arrangements made as were possible in the darkness. Luckily, though it was rather threatening, it did not rain on the way, but at 5.30 a.m. it began to come down and rained heavily, with the result that the camp, which was situated a bit low in some meadows, soon got terribly muddy. It was wet and miserable all next day, the 14th, and the day after. An intermittent drizzle made it very cold and damp.

The G.O.C. 15th French Army Corps, with the Governor of Marseilles had intended visiting the camp, but, owing to the inclement weather, their visit was postponed. The G.O.C. Indian Army Corps came round the camp about 1.30 p.m. on the 15th. Each battalion had three interpreters

M. BREE.

10th Regt. Foot Artillery. Interpreter to 2nd Battalion.

attached to help in arranging billets. &c. Some time later, one was considered sufficient. Two joined us here at camp, Messieurs M. Brée and Richaud, of the 10th Regiment of Foot Artillery. The third, Lieut. Watney, joined a day or two later.

The camp got into a very muddy condition owing to the continuous rain and the number of men walking about. It cleared up for a time on the 17th, and we got a little sun up to mid-day, which we took advantage of to dry our kits.

The Division began to leave this camp on 17th October, the Dehra Dun Brigade being the first to depart. We received our orders on the 18th to entrain at the Gare d'Arenc, Marseilles, on the 19th, at 2 a.m. Captain Wilcox was sent into Marseilles to arrange for the carts, some of which arrived at 2 p.m., and were loaded up at once and sent off to the station. Heavy rain began to fall at this time and the camp was flooded out. It continued for two hours, and the camp became a quagmire. Owing to our Brigade and the 21st (Bareilly) Brigade moving off at the same time, there was some difficulty at first in getting all our carts, but they eventually turned up, and the last lot left camp at 6 p.m.

A good deal of confusion occurred with all this transport going out of camp at the same time, owing to the lack of staff arrangements to control it. The battalion left camp at 8.30 p.m., and reached the station at 12.30 a.m. The train was marshalled at 2 a.m., and loading began at once. British and Garhwali Officers were accommodated in first-class carriages and the rank and file in wagons, which on French railways do either for troops or animals. The train left at 6 a.m. on 19th October. The route taken was *via* Cette and Bezières, along the south coast to the west, arriving at the latter place at 4 p.m., where the men had a meal. We left again at 6.30 p.m. Cahors was reached at 8.30 a.m. next morning, and a halt was made for the men to cook a meal. The train left at 12 noon, and travelling all that night we arrived at Les Aubrais station at Orleans at 10.30 a.m. on 21st October. The Battalion detrained at once and went into camp at Les Groues.

All throughout the journey the inhabitants had been most kind and hospitable, giving the men sweets and cigarettes, &c., and cheering them at all halts. The French railway authorities also were most polite and obliging, and ample supplies of wood and water were available at each "halte repas," or cooking station.

All kit in excess of the scale laid down had been packed up in bundles and left at Marseilles at the base depôt with our 10 per cent reinforcements. Each man carried a blanket wrapped up in his great coat on his back. Officers were allowed weights as follows :—

Commanding Officer, 50lbs. All other British Officers, 35lbs.

The kit for each man was as follows :—

Per man—

- 1 waterproof sheet
- 1 blanket
- 1 log line
- 1 pair of socks
- 1 towel
- 1 Balaclava cap
- 1 holdall

Per follower—

- 1 waterproof sheet
- 1 blanket
- 1 set of cooking pots

Garhwali Officers were allowed 10lbs. in addition to that allowed for rank and file.

The weather was cold in the mornings and evenings, but mild in the day time. Although cloudy, there was no rain.

LIEUT. C. WATNEY.

Interpreter to 2nd Battalion.

More warm clothing had to be drawn here from the Ordnance Department for issue to the men, consisting of one shirt, one vest and one pair of drawers, but as the men had already received an issue of field service clothing on the winter scale when in India, this extra issue was quite unnecessary, so only one article was taken, *i.e.*, the pair of drawers. Nine bicycles were issued to the battalion and our machine guns and mountings were returned to the Ordnance in order to have new mountings fitted. Such is the extraordinary way we do things, that on the moment we go into field some most important things have to be altered, or changed, at the last moment!

We had received our 1st Line Transport at Marseilles, and this consisted of nine Army transport carts and 34 mules. At Orleans we received in addition two water carts, six G.S. wagons, and one cook cart for the Train or 2nd Line Transport with 18 draught horses. We had to supply drivers from the Battalion for all these, and it was ludicrous to see our men trying to drive these huge 16 hand horses when none of them had ever seen a horse beyond perhaps a small hill pony in his life! However, they made a remarkably good job of it. Eventually, R.A.S.C. drivers weregiven us.

The next morning, 24th October, the Division went for a route march in full service order with all transport. It was a fine morning, and the march of six miles was very pleasant. A billetting party, consisting of one British Officer, one Garhwali Officer and four non-commissioned officers, was despatched to " an unknown destination " at 5 a.m. this day, to arrange billets for the Battalion.

Companies practised route marching again the next day under Company Commanders. Eight horses were received for those British Officers who had none. In the evening orders came for us to entrain the next day, 26th October, at 11.30 p.m., as the whole Division was being moved up into the front line. Kits were packed on the G.S. wagons, which were placed loaded on to the train. All tents were handed over to the Ordnance Department at the camp before leaving, including officers' tents, which were valued by a Committee, for which they later received compensation.

Two days cooked rations for the men were carried on the train and one day in supply wagons. Our train left at 1.35 a.m. and took on 40 men and one wagon of the 1st Battalion, who had got left behind. It was a cold journey in the train. The route was *via* Rouen and Abbeville which latter place we reached at midnight on 27th October, two hours late. Calais was reached at 4.30 a.m., six hours late. After a short halt, we proceeded *via* St. Omer and Hazebrouck to Lillers, which was the Indian Army Corps railhead, where we arrived at 2 p.m. on 28th October.

After detraining, we marched at once for our billets, which were at a place called Calonne sur la Lys, seven miles distant, where we arrived a bit tired at 7.15 p.m. and were comfortably billeted in a mill and other buildings. As the men had to set to work and cook their food, it was not till late—1 a.m.—that they finally got to rest, to dream and wonder what the morrow had in store for them.

CHAPTER IV.

Brigade Marches to Les Glatignes—Halt in fields near Les Facons—Conference at the British Brigade Headquarters—Sounds of firing audible—Arrive at Rue de l'Epinette—Commanding Officer with Adjutant and representative of the British Regiment to be relieved proceed to trenches to be taken over—Battalion arrives later and trenches are taken over—20 days' spell of trenches without relief.

NEXT morning the Battalion paraded at 7.10 a.m. to march with the rest of the Brigade to Les Glatignes, in the following order: 2nd Leicesters, 1/39th Garhwal Rifles, 2/3rd Gurkha Rifles, 2/39th Garhwal Rifles. Train in same order of march as units. The roads were good as far as Locon, which we reached at 11 a.m. Sounds of heavy firing were heard all the way. After leaving Locon we proceeded to Les Facons on the road parallel to Les Glatignes, where we halted in some fields while the G.O.C. went to the British Brigade Commander's headquarters, which were situated about a mile further on in a large farm called Cse. du Raux. Aeroplanes were busy in our vicinity all day. The weather was cloudy and rather cold. At length at 2 p.m. Commanding Officers were summoned to the Brigade headquarters, where we learnt that we were to relieve the 14th Brigade, 5th Division, British Expeditionary Force, which consisted of the following four regiments—Worcestershire Regiment, East Surrey Regiment, King's Own Scottish Borderers and the King's Own Yorkshire Light Infantry. The line that we had to take over rested with its left on the main Estaires-La Bassée road and ran about 100 yards in front of or to the south of the village of Richebourg L'Avoué and parallel to the Rue du Bois for some distance, and thence it took a deep curve southwards towards Festubert and Givenchy. Our G.O.C. was informed that the left was the most important part of the line where the main Estaires-La Bassée road was crossed by the Rue du Bois leading to Neuve Chapelle. These cross roads were later named "Port Arthur," where a salient was formed encircling them. The 2nd Battalion was specially selected by our G.O.C. for this important part of the line. At this period the Germans were about 200-300 yards off, but were digging hard and gradually getting nearer.

At 7 p.m. the Battalion was called up to an estaminet, or inn, at the Rue de l'Epinette, where it was halted. One of the British regiments had their headquarters established at this estaminet, and I remember they gave us a good dinner off a very fine goose, which I expect had once formed one of the occupants of a neighbouring farmyard! Here extra ammunition was issued, making each man up to 200 rounds. Also extra entrenching tools were taken over from the Brigade reserve. Our 1st Line Transport was sent back to where their billets had been apportioned and was joined by the 2nd Line, or train, which had been halted well in the rear.

At 7.30 p.m. very heavy firing was heard, and continued for half-an-hour. At 8 p.m. all Commanding Officers were sent for to interview the G.O.C., and immediately after each, accompanied by a representative from the regiment that was to be relieved, proceeded to the portion of the line held by it to see the situation and arrange the relief with the Commanding Officer, while the Battalion remained at the Rue de l'Epinette. It was a long way down the Rue du Bois to get to our part of the line. We arrived at length, my Adjutant, Captain Berryman, and myself, with the representative of the King's Own Yorkshire Light Infantry, which was the unit we were to relieve, and found their regimental headquarters in a ruined farmhouse close behind the trenches. Having arranged matters, I remained with their Commanding Officer while Captain Berryman returned with the guide to order up the Battalion, which arrived at 12 midnight, and came down a side road which led down to the farm from the Rue du Bois, where we met them. Companies then immediately commenced taking over their part of the line that had been portioned off to them. While this was proceeding, heavy rifle fire broke out. It lasted half-an-hour, and we had five men wounded.

Our left, which rested on the La Bassée road, linked up with the Dehra Dun Brigade and the Seaforth Highlanders, who held their extreme right.

I kept our Battalion headquarters in the vicinity of the ruined farm in a sort of dugout. In reality it was one of those brick pits in which they store beetroots. It was quite a new one, and had evidently been used by German cavalry when they were in occupation of this part of the country and before they were driven back, for I found stuck in the roof a nice pair of their jointed tent d'abris poles. The farm house, or what remained of it, formed a too conspicuous object, and though the dut-out was shallow, it did us for the time very well. The cellar in the house had evidently been occupied by the headquarters signallers of the relieved regiment, and apparently a heavy howitzer had made a direct hit, for the walls were covered with the poor fellows' brains and blood. There were still the owner's cows and other live stock at the farm roaming about the ruins. The owner turned out to be a woman, who came up daily to feed them. I had to get our interpreter to tell her to take them away and not come up again as the farm was only about 80 yards from the front line. One of her fine cows was lying dead in the stall, killed by a shell. She took the cows away at night, but left the pigs, which roamed about disconsolately. Eventually they were killed one by one by shell and rifle fire. At night, even when it was bitterly cold and a heavy frost on, the pigs were happy as long as their snouts were covered up. They poked them under the straw at the bottom of a stack in the yard. They did not mind their bodies being exposed to the frost and cold!

The 1st Battalion continued our line on to the right. Then came the 2/3rd Gurkhas and the Leicesters, whence the Bareilly Brigade took on the line to Festubert and Givenchy, where our line linked up with the French.

The trenches we took over were very shallow, hardly deep enough to cover a man kneeling. I remember well, when going round with the Commanding Officer of the King's Own Y.L.I., that we had to go round over the ploughed fields, as there was no room to go round inside the trenches. It was a misty moonlight night, and the stacks of tobacco on stakes stuck in the ground looked like men advancing in extended order—so much so, that on more than one occasion later I was deceived by them swaying in the breeze. Shortly afterwards they were blown to smithereens by shell fire. As we went round, one of their N.C.O.'s looked up and said: "Thank God, the relief's come!" But it had not, at that moment, but did soon after. How glad these poor fellows must have been when they were relieved and able to get away and obtain the rest they so much needed! They had done magnificently, despite the terribly hard time experienced in stemming the onrush of the German hordes in the first days of the war.

Immediately the relief was complete, all companies commenced digging like moles and got through a lot that night. Work on the trenches never really ceased, as in that clay soil, with frosts and thaws, apart from the shelling, they were always cracking and crumbling and needed repair daily. We soon made them in first-rate condition, so that everyone, Staff and all, who came round, invariably complimented us upon them. At that time we had no material, such as sandbags, &c., for revetting, but had to go every night to the ruined houses in the village just behind and take all the doors and wooden beds for this purpose. These answered better than sandbags, which rotted quicker in that damp, wet soil.

We had a long spell in the trenches for our first "go"—twenty days without relief! It soon initiated us into the work. One thing struck us all, and that was the remarkable steadiness of our men under artillery fire. Considering that neither they, nor in fact any of us, had ever been under heavy artillery fire before, it was marvellous how well they stood it and how steady they were.

Rations, of course, had to be brought up at night. The ration carts could come up the road and shelter behind the ruined houses along the village street while the men, so many from each Company, were sent up by communication trenches to take over and carry their share back to their companies. Similarly, water came up in the water carts, and we supplemented this by drawing water at night from the few pumps that were still intact in some of the houses. There were one or two enormous shell holes in the road which the drivers had to try and avoid, and which they did for a time, but at length one of the carts, rather unwieldy vehicles, especially for our little men to manipulate, fell into the biggest of them, never to be got out till later, when the holes were filled up.

The worst of a long period in the trenches without relief is that you cannot get clean and the men are apt to get verminous.

Later, as more troops arrived, reliefs were made quicker, and the men, when in billets, had good, hot baths and a change of underclothing.

The evacuation of the sick and wounded had to be done at night. This meant for us on the left a long trek down the road to the aid post and field ambulance wagons, as these could not come so far, as they would have been exposed.

As a rule the Germans did not waste much ammunition by shelling at night, so we were left in peace, though their snipers were hard at it day and night. In any attack, of course, they used plenty of ammunition and also had searchlights. In regard to the quantity of ammunition available, and all other kind of war-like material, we were far behind them in these early days of the war, and so could not effectively reply to their "hate." If one telephoned up to the gunner officer for a little ammunition to be expended on some bomb gun or minenwerfer that was annoying us to "straf" (using a very expressive Boche word) them a bit, the reply generally received was: "Sorry, but I have used my allowance!" This was, at that time, 18 rounds daily per battery. We had no bombs, consequently we had to grin and bear it.

We had some days of severe shelling. On 5th November they started shelling our Battalion headquarters hard. We were obliged to take refuge in the support trench, as there were too many of us for the day-time in a small ruined hut and dug-out where we were concealed, so we all cleared out into the support trench in rear, which was screened from view by the remains of the hut and the hedge, except the guard of one lance-naik and three men, whom I ordered to remain where they were. Unfortunately, for some reason the lance-naik did not understand and came after me to enquire if he was to remain or come along, too! As I was talking to him from the end of the trench and he was under cover at the foot of a large walnut tree just above us, and close to the trench and farm building, a large shell came over (you could always hear them coming) and struck a bough of the tree straight above our heads and exploded. If it had not struck this bough it would have gone on some 30 yards further and exploded on the ground. A large piece of the shell came straight down and struck the poor fellow on the chest, making a hole large enough for one to put one's head into. He expired in fifteen seconds. He was a nice young fellow, and I regretted his end. If he had remained where he was he would have been safe, as that small ruined building was not touched.

The daily routine thus went on. The Germans were gradually getting nearer to our front line by sapping till they reached a point and made their permanent front line about 50 yards from ours—a little closer in some parts and a bit further off at others. This life exacted daily its toll of casualties. One, two or more every day, and so gradually increasing the weekly total.

For some time it was thought that there were spies behind our line. One night, when one of our men was drawing water from a house on the road, he was accosted by a man dressed like a British soldier. When he was spoken to and challenged by our man, he suddenly fired his rifle at him, then threw it away and fled in the darkness. Luckily he missed our man, who picked up the rifle and brought it to battalion headquarters. It was marked K.O.Y.L.I., and had evidently belonged to that regiment and taken from one of those killed. Our man, I must admit, looked a weird sight, wearing his Balaclava cap drawn down with no other head-dress. In other parts, too, there seemed to have been spies behind our front line, especially at Festubert. They probably got left after an attack, either accidently or (most probably) purposely. In time they were all rounded up or killed.

During this first spell of our trench life we had several minor attacks. The first one took place on 4th November by the Germans, and was directed at the left of our line, just where we linked up with the Seaforths. It was a misty morning, and about 10 a.m. shrapnel and howitzer fire opened, being specially directed at our extreme left trench and the Seaforth's trenches. Then musketry fire broke out. At 12.15 p.m. the Seaforths sent over asking for reinforcements, and Captain Reed, with two platoons, Nos. 3 and 4, were sent to help them. One platoon was then directed to take their place in the front line. As Nos. 9 and 10 platoons had already been sent in to form a Brigade reserve, this left only one platoon in my battalion reserve, so short-handed were we at that time.

The total length of the line held by the battalion was about 1,100 yards, for which we had barely 600 men. The enemy's fire continued all day, but no infantry attack was pressed. The farmhouse by battalion headquarters suffered much from shell fire. The night, however, was quiet, except for the usual sniping. Our two platoons remained with the Seaforths all that night, as they had suffered severely from the enemy's artillery fire and needed reinforcements. The next day fire was again opened on the same trenches, continuing till 2 p.m., but not much damage was done. We also had to vacate temporarily our headquarters dug-out. German aeroplanes were busy all the afternoon. The 6th was a quiet day. Our guard, which was stationed in a ruined house on the main road in order to point the way to Battalion headquarters and, at night, patrol the road and search other houses in our area, was shelled that morning and the sentry killed. The men had foolishly lighted a fire, the smoke of which was seen by the enemy. This always drew artillery fire if coming from a house.

On the 7th very heavy shelling again took place, the left flank being again the object of the attack, which this time was pressed right up to our trench on the left flank and that of the Seaforths. We were able to help them by enfilade fire. The attack was repulsed. Close up in front of the Seaforth's trenches a German officer lay wounded. He covered himself with his cloak, but the Seaforths later brought him in and sent him to the aid post. Again at 6 p.m. heavy fire broke out, and it seemed as if they intended attacking once more, but nothing resulted. That night our scouts sighted some transport with its escort on the La Bassée road and opened fire. The enemy must have suffered some loss. Our patrol returned intact.

The 9th of November broke misty, but fine. Heavy shelling of the right flank trench of the Seaforths, and also our left flank company, again took place. In the meantime, I had gone in to Brigade headquarters for an interview with the G.O.C., as steps were being taken to organise a raid on the German trenches opposite our right flank where it ran into what we called the "gap," which was a portion of the ditch which ran along our front at this part and into which our right and the 1st Battalion's left ran. A raiding party of 25 men from each Battalion was at first arranged, the whole to be under the command of Major Taylor, of the 2nd Battalion. This was increased later to 50 men each—total, 100

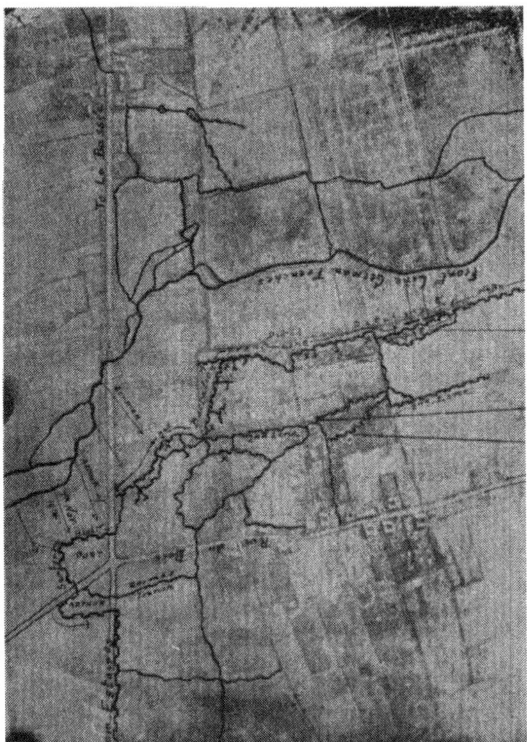

Aerial Map showing British trenches (section held by the 2nd Battalion Garhwal Rifles during the winter of 1914-15) with opposing German trenches before the Battle of NEUVE CHAPELLE, and to illustrate night attacks of the 9th and 13th November, and German attack of 7th November, 1914. Firing Line and supports—3 Companies. Reserves—1 Company.
x x x x—Machine Gun Emplacements.

men. The 50 from the 1st Battalion had no British officer. The time fixed for the raid was 6 p.m., but owing to unforeseen delay it did not take place till some time later. The whole party was lined up in the ditch on the right flank, and when all was ready the signal to advance was given. The special feature of a night attack is the imperative necessity for absolute silence till you are actually ready to charge and close up to your objective. Otherwise cheering too soon only gives the enemy notice of your intention and time to meet your attack. Our men crawled right up to the German parapet in silence and lay unnoticed under it. Major Taylor lay there himself, and when he considered the psychological moment had arrived, he gave the signal to charge into the trench by firing his revolver at some grey-coated Germans whom he could just see walking by below him, and all immediately jumped into the German trench with a yell. I don't suppose men were ever scared so much as these Germans were. for they bolted down every handy communication trench as if all the demons in Asia were after them ! I think it must have been this incident that gave rise to the yarns and pictures which one saw in the illustrated papers of men dressed like Gurkhas with drawn kukris in their mouths crawling up to the German trenches.

The operation was excellently carried out by Major Taylor. He deserved great credit for its success. It cannot be ascertained exactly what amount of damage we did. We took six live prisoners. one of whom was wounded. Two it is known were killed, but the great thing was the moral effect which it must have produced on the enemy. The prisoners, after having all their documents taken from them, were sent into Divisional headquarters through the Brigade. They afforded good information as to what units were in front of the Division. this being of much use to our Divisional General. It was intended that the German trench should be filled in and destroyed before returning, but it was found too deep to carry this out effectually without further help. So after trying to fill it in a bit, it was abandoned and a retirement ordered by Major Taylor, as by now a heavy fire had broken out from the German support trench and searchlights began to play all over ours.

It is not known what happened to the 1st Battalion party, but they appeared to have lost touch in advancing and gone off a bit to the right. It turned out, however, that they had several casualties, including the Garhwali officer. It would seem that they kept more upright and could not have been close enough to the hostile trench when they cheered and charged, the result being that the Germans were able to meet and repulse their attack and inflict some loss on them. Our party only had four wounded, and this was due to the able manner in which Major Taylor had led his men. I am glad to say that he got a mention in despatches for his work, while three men he brought to notice also got decorations. A full report, both Major Taylor's and mine, will be found in Appendix VII.

The same morning, when our scouts were retiring early at daylight, one of them got wounded badly, and Rifleman Ganesh Sing Sajwan gallantly brought him safely in under fire. For this he was awarded the Indian Order of Merit.

On 12th November each Battalion sent in representatives for inspection by F.M. Lord Roberts at Locon.

The next attack we made was on 13th November, and was on a slightly larger scale. Commanding Officers were called into Brigade headquarters to discuss the arrangements to be made. On returning from this interview I walked back with Colonel Swiney. We were not, then, well acquainted with the lie of the land, but as far as Chocolate Menier Corner (a name given to designate the cross-roads there, owing to a large advertisement of that chocolate being on the wall of a house at the corner) the road was well screened by houses, orchards and trees. but on passing the cross-roads there was a large stretch of road lined with tall trees without cover on the south, or the side towards the enemy, up as far as the large factory. We were accompanied by two gendarmes, to whom I explained the necessity of examining the houses of Richebourg L'Avoué for possible spies. Both were mounted. As soon as we emerged from the shelter of the trees on to the open stretch of the Rue du Bois the Germans opened a brisk fire from their trenches, which were visible on our right hand (though we at first did not realise this) some 300 yards away. The gendarmes turned round and galloped off, pursued by the German fire, while Colonel Swiney and I sought cover. he wisely by going to the left of the road behind some small houses there, and I by trying to do a record sprint to the houses by the factory. But this I found too much, and stopped to take breath under cover of one of the tall poplars lining the road there and then diving suddenly into the ditch alongside the road, where I was under good cover and whence I could get along all right. I think the Germans must have devoted most of their attention to the flying mounted gendarmes, as they afforded such a good target! One, I

MAJOR G. H. TAYLOR,

2nd Battalion, killed Richebourg L'Avoué, 13th November, 1914.

heard later, did get a graze on the neck from a bullet.

This time the assaulting party was to consist of 250 men of the 2/3rd Gurkhas, with 50 men of the 2nd Battalion under Major Taylor, the whole being under the command of Lieut.-Colonel Ormsby, of the 2/3rd Gurkhas. The artillery had been ordered to co-operate, and when their first gun fired at 9 p.m. the advance took place. Shortly afterwards a cheer was heard on the right, where the 2/3rd were, and this was immediately followed by heavy firing on the enemy's part. Heavy casualties appear to have been caused to the assaulting troops. Some managed to reach the hostile trenches, but some retired to their own trench. Several wounded came in, but could give no news. In the meantime Lieut.-Colonel Brakspear, of the 2/3rd Gurkhas, came back for more men, as some had successfully got into the German trench. There were several wounded, including two British officers. Nothing was known as to what had happened on the left to Major Taylor's party. Meanwhile, the enemy's searchlight began to play all along our line, making the place as light as day. Accompanied by Captain Berryman, I went up the ditch to see if anything could be ascertained, but no information could be gleaned. On our return, the situation was explained to Colonel Ormsby, who asked me to arrange another party under a British officer to make another advance in conjunction with his men and try and bring in the wounded. All this time a heavy fire was being kept up by the enemy—both rifle and shrapnel. I arranged for another party, under Captain Robertson-Glasgow, to advance, and brought up the detachment of the Poona Horse (dismounted) to replace these men. They had been placed at my disposal as reinforcements. The trenches were now getting full of wounded men, and a hail of bullets kept coming over, making an advance very difficult. As many wounded as possible were sent off to the aid post in the rear, and scouts were sent out to try and ascertain what had happened to either party of ours, but they could not now get out far enough. In the meantime, a company of the 9th Gurkhas had been sent up as reinforcements, but were not employed, as it was found hopeless to try and do anything further under the circumstances. A full report of this action will be found in Appendix VII. Our casualties were two British Officers killed—Major Taylor and Captain Robertson-Glasgow—one Garhwali officer—Jemadar Khusal Sing Danu—and 10 rank and file killed and 26 wounded out of the total of 72 of our Battalion employed. The enemy were now fairly on the "jump" after our former successful raid, and this second larger one, but it was not to be supposed that he would be caught napping twice. Having an excellent searchlight made things so much easier for him and increased our difficulties tenfold. The orchard just behind our line and our front trench was as light as Piccadilly at night. He continually used his searchlight night after night after this.

On 15th November we had an unfortunate accident from our own artillery, who, usually so accurate, for some reason put a few lyddite shells within 15/20 yards or less of our right flank trench, one of which fell right into our trench, killing four men and wounding one. News was telephoned straight away to Brigade headquarters and the Artillery informed, and the officer commanding the Royal Artillery apologised for this accident afterwards. Among those blown to bits was a nice young bugler, Narain Sing. The only thing about him found was a portion of the leather letter bag he used to carry. This day, too, about 2.30 p.m., a short, but severe, shrapnel fire was opened again on our headquarters near the farmhouse and buildings close by, necessitating a hasty evacuation temporarily to the support trench. Unfortunately a fine stack of straw was set fire to and burnt up. This had supplied us with lovely straw for our men in the trenches and ourselves for lying down on. Underneath all this straw was a lot of loose ammunition, which, owing to the great heat, went off "pop, pop," like a miniature action. Our own reserve ammunition in boxes was got out of danger by Major MacTier. The day was a miserable one, and a slight fall of snow occurred. It continued wet and cold now day after day. We had been just on twenty days in the trenches and were soon to be relieved. The officers of the 2nd Gurkhas, who were to relieve us, came up to see the trenches, and all information was given them. They came up by night, and the relief was carried out without any hitch, though it was a slow business, as the trenches were narrow and muddy owing to the rain. The ground round about her was low and the water level could not have been much more than one foot below the surface. This, as will be seen later, was to drive us out of our trenches to build a breastwork farther back nearer the road. While the relief was being carried out, the enemy continued to play his searchlight and opened fire, which caused a little delay.

Before the relief actually commenced, our machine guns got an opportunity to open fire on a party of the enemy who were trying to creep up the ditch lined with willows perpendicular to our front and parallel to the main La Bassée road. They were spotted by means of one of the flares the enemy were sending up. We handed over our telephones to the relieving regiment, as they had not yet had their own replaced. The Battalion marched off at 9.30 p.m., when the relief was complete, independently first by Companies as far as Rue de l'Epinette, whence it marched as a whole to billets at Le Touret, which was reached at 10.45 p.m. Thus ended our first experience of trench warfare, which was to last the whole time we were in France and for some time after, till eventually we had trained sufficient men and amassed sufficient ammunition, when the last big "pushes" resulted in the Germans' final overthrow.

The men needed their rest very much. They had done extremely well, and they had occupied the most important part of the Brigade front, the Battalion having been specially selected for this important part of the defence. Several gratifying complimentary messages were received from the G.O.C.'s Brigade, Division and Army Corps. (See Appendix III.).

During this and other spells of trench warfare I invariably instructed our scouts when going out that if they shot any of the enemy, or found any dead out in "No Man's Land," such as their patrols whom we had shot, that they were always to take off them any documents they might find. Some rather interesting letters, &c., were thus brought in. After perusal I sent them in to Brigade headquarters, as they afforded useful information as to what unit of the German Army was opposite us.

I remember reading a letter from a wife to her husband, in which she was very bitter against the British. One remark was: "Ha! Herr Krupp, with his 42 centimetre guns, will utterly destroy them!" Another, "Be sure you bring me a souvenir from Paris." This request, I am glad to think, was never fulfilled, or was possible of fulfilment, as the German hordes were stopped almost at the gates of Paris and hurled back.

It was extraordinary, too, how superstitious some were. Wives or sweethearts had sent charms to their fiancés to wear. One wrote "Be sure you don't forget to wear that charm I sent you. If you wear that you won't get shot."

I remember seeing in one of the illustrated papers pictures of some of the charms that the Germans used, having been sent them by their relations. The mentality of the Germans was hard to understand. Extremely thorough they are in everything. How neat their knapsacks were with "a place for everything and everything in its place." Besides all those things necessary as equipment, I noticed that they always had a small book of prayers, presumably a Government issue to each man. Yet they could commit, at any rate in the early days of the war, atrocities against innocent civilians which staggered the civilised world!

CHAPTER V.

Billets at Le Touret, Rue du Bois and La Couture—Action at Festubert—Relieve the 1st Battalion in the trenches at Festubert—Second longer spell of 26 days in the trenches without relief.

THE Battalion only spent two days at Le Touret when it moved into other billets near by, and further up the Rue du Bois towards Richebourg L'Avoué, to make room for the 1st Battalion, which had been relieved after us. On 23rd November the Brigade moved to La Couture, a short distance further back, which we reached at 3 p.m., and waited on some open ground by the village, which was covered with snow, while our billets were being arranged. At 4.15 p.m., however, the other three Battalions of the Brigade suddenly got orders to proceed at once to Festubert to reinforce the Brigade there, which had been heavily attacked and a portion of their trench captured, The Germans were still in possession of a portion of the captured trench, notwithstanding they had been attacked two or three times. In this attempt two Battalions had been decimated in making frontal attacks piecemeal against the trench, which was full of machine guns in position. There was not a vestige of cover, and the snow made matters worse for the men. Attacking like this without heavy artillery support, which at that time we could not give owing to shortage of ammunition, and in piecemeal and not in sufficient depth, was a suicidal policy. If such an attack had to be made over such open ground it could not be done successfully with less than three Battalions distributed in depth and not in a line. The situation could not have been properly appreciated by the Brigadier of that Brigade, the Ferozepore Brigade, who had taken over charge of the operations from G.O.C. Bareilly Brigade. It is very easy to say that " the trenches must be retaken at all costs," and that " the attack must be carried out immediately," and so forth, from a comfortable brewery well in rear, with warm fires and a good dinner. These were favourite expressions of the Higher Command at that period of the War. A *personal* reconnaissance by the Brigadier is very necessary, as well as by any Commander, before he launches his troops into an attack. Their strength has also to be considered. As this was a most interesting and well-executed attack by the 1st Battalion I give the details in full, together with an accurate sketch of the same.

The Battalion arrived at the point " A " shortly after 7.30 p.m. and halted. Colonel Grant, of the 8th Gurkhas, commanding the centre section of the defence, was sent to point out to Colonel Swiney, commanding the 1st Battalion, a certain road on which the left of the Battalion was to rest while attacking. At first he apparently put them on the wrong road, *i.e.*, " D," which runs down to Festubert but did not go on any further towards the enemy's trench. With their left on this road they were then to attack frontally over the level snow-covered ground, with another battalion, the 107th Pioneers, which they replaced in the trench marked " C," and which was to prolong their right. The front on which they were to attack was about 300 yards, which at their strength meant little or no depth. While the battalion was at " A," the C.O. reconnoitred forward as far as he could from the points " B " and " C." The Brigadier had told the C.O. that he had reason to believe that the enemy had left the captured trench, but another officer, Lieut. Orchard, of the 2/8th Gurkhas, who had been in the previous attacks, gave quite a different story and said that the Germans were still in force in the captured trench and had several machine guns. He strongly urged oblique attacks on the right and left of the lost trench from rear of the inner flanks of the Battalions on its flanks. The General was then asked to reconsider his previous orders, but shortly after Colonel Grant came again with the order that the attack was to be carried out immediately as originally directed.

Three Companies were then moved up into the trench " C," and one Company was in support in rear in ditch " B." Eventually this rear Company was ordered to go to the left of " C," and to follow up the attack on the right of the road there,

SKETCH to illustrate the Action of FESTUBERT
on 23rd–24th November 1914.
Compiled from details furnished by a German prisoner
to I. A. Corps. Hd. Qrs.

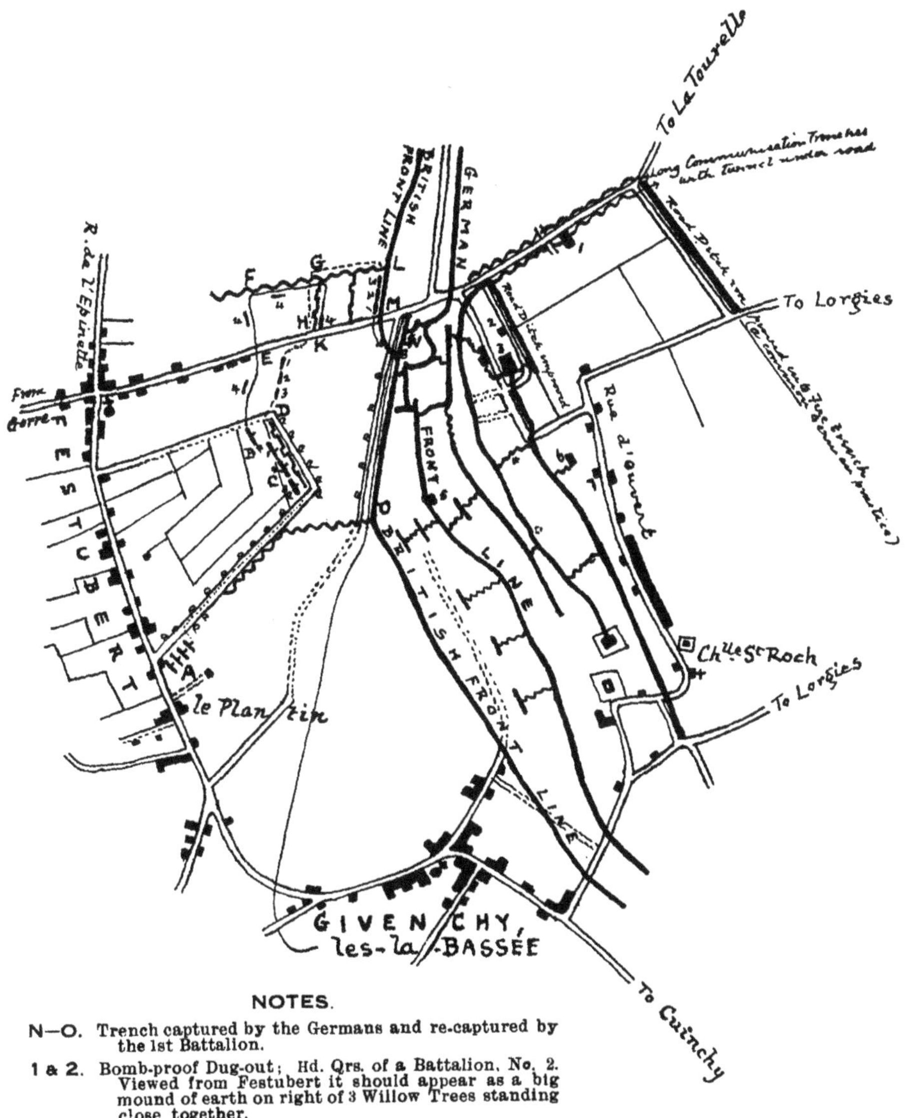

NOTES.

N—O. Trench captured by the Germans and re-captured by the 1st Battalion.

1 & 2. Bomb-proof Dug-out; Hd. Qrs. of a Battalion, No. 2. Viewed from Festubert it should appear as a big mound of earth on right of 3 Willow Trees standing close together.

3. Observation Post, 10—15 yards loophole.

4. Communication Trench, much used.

5. Observation Post.

6. Battalions Hd. Qrs.; damaged House.

7. Damaged Farm, possibly occupied by Medical Staff.

8. Barricade made here by Capt. Lane.

which was then believed to be the one on which the left of the Battalion was to rest and which was said to lead up to the enemy's right. However, it was soon discovered that this road ended abruptly at "D," so evidently they were not in the right place. Further information was then asked for, and, if possible, a guide to show them the exact and correct road, for the battalion was unacquainted with the geography round this village, having arrived in the dark. Colonel Grant returned as guide. He was informed that the road on which they then were ended at "D," and a search was made for the other road, and shortly after it was struck at "E." The Battalion then moved, less one Company, up the ditch along the right side of this road as far as they could to "K," and was then to deploy to the right and attack. The fourth Company was ordered up by the communication trench to the point "M," and to stand by there ready to move as soon as the objective was taken.

This Company (which I presume was the headquarters Company and Battalion Reserve) struck the communication trench at "F," and moved on to "G," where the headquarters of the 129th Baluchis, under Colonel Southey, was. With him a consultation took place, and he expressed the opinion that so weak a frontal attack under the circumstances had no chance of success. After further negotiations with the Brigade on arrival at this point, and it being urged that such an attack could not possibly succeed with so few troops in the manner it had been ordered to be carried out, and suggestions made, orders were received that the attack was to be carried out immediately, but that it might be carried out by the Commanding Officer as he thought fit. On receiving this fresh order, which gave him the latitude he wished for, the Commanding Officer decided to make a flank attack from "M" down the trench and not frontally. The supporting company was then ordered to the point "H" ready to move up the road, while the rest of the Battalion moved *via* "H," "G," and "L" to "M." It was now 2.30 a.m., and the attack was begun from "M." First for a few traverses a Sapper officer, Lieut. Robson, with some bombs, advanced with the leading Company and drove the enemy back by bombing round each traverse. This was then discontinued, and the leading company, under Major Wardell, gallantly drove the enemy back traverse by traverse, killing some and capturing prisoners. In the meantime the second Company, under Captain Lumb, which had been following, diverged slightly to the right up a ditch, alongside the road which, as they advanced, they found getting shallower and shallower, and finally affording no protection or cover,

HOW NAIK DARWAN SING NEGI,

of the 1st Battalion, won the Victoria Cross at Festubert, 23rd-24th November, 1914. The Victoria Cross was also gained by Rifleman Gobar Sing Negi, 2nd Battalion, for a similar action at the Battle of Neuve Chapelle, 10th March, 1915.

so Captain Lumb, with a section and half (the remainder being blocked in the communication trench by prisoners and escort, who came on shortly after) left the ditch and pluckily jumped into the enemy's trench at the head of Major Wardell's company and continued the advance. Finally the whole trench was recaptured by daylight, together with 105 prisoners, a trench mortar, two machine guns and much equipment, and hands joined with the 107th Pioneers at the other end.

So ended this smart little action, for which the 1st Battalion deserves great credit, especially Major Wardell, Captain Lumb and the Sapper Officer Robson, who were the leaders in this attack. The last-mentioned officer, unfortunately, was killed in my left flank trench on the La Bassée road by a sniper in December, when inspecting the rising of the water in the trench and considering the means of combating it. The 1st Battalion lost Major Wardell (killed) and Captain Orton (wounded), and was awarded one Victoria Cross to Naik Darwan Sing Negi, who led round each traverse. Captains Lumb and Lane each received the Military Cross for their gallantry in this action, and several men got other decorations. Colonel Swiney received a brevet colonelcy.

I do not think that it has ever been definitely decided how Major Wardell was killed. He was wounded in his attack and was, I believe, able to get back to the first aid post. On his way back in the dark he took a wrong turning and so went up a trench held by the enemy. This was not surprising, as Major Wardell was short-sighted, and the trenches at that part were intricate owing to part having been captured and the many saps which ran up to our trenches. As his body was never found I fancy that this is what happened. He was a great loss to the regiment, being a capable and keen officer and one intensely interested in his men.

Meanwhile the 2nd Battalion remained at La Couture, where we received some warm clothing. All of it had to be returned, as the chest measurements were much too small. The next day, 25th November, we received orders to proceed to Festubert, presumably to relieve the 1st Battalion. We were directed to rendezvous at Gorre Church, where we would get orders. We arrived there at 1.45 p.m., and naturally expected to be met by some staff officer to give us orders. After waiting some time, and no one turning up, I set out with my adjutant, Captain Berryman, to search for the missing staff officer. After inquiries, we eventually ran the Brigadier and his Staff to earth, ensconced in a comfortable brewery with warm fires. Nobody then deigned to take any notice of us, and after waiting some time, we got orders what to do. We then went to the front line to see the situation and arrange matters, leaving the Battalion resting in the rear under cover of a large farm. At dusk we moved up and relieved our 1st Battalion in the same trench that they had recaptured, with three Companies, the fourth Company remaining behind at La Couture, under Major Stewart. A description of the trenches at this place and our work there will be of interest at this juncture.

The trenches, whoever they were made by, were very bad ones. Too wide for one thing, and the front parapet wasn't bullet-proof. Shelters had been scooped out underneath without any support, which weakened it very much, and afforded no protection at all from shrapnel fire. Also the whole bit of the line we occupied was one huge grave, for some unit had buried all their own and some German dead in it, instead of throwing the corpses over the parapet and burying them under cover of darkness. This unsavoury job of exhuming the dead we had to do, as it had to be done, and we buried them all at night. It was also a very dangerous job, as the opposing trenches at this part were extraordinarily close, in some parts as close as five yards, where the Germans had sapped up close. For this work the Army Commander was pleased to get the men some decorations, including the Order of Merit. Others, as recommended, were given pecuniary rewards. When one walked down the trench one felt the ground very springy, due to corpses being covered only by six inches or less of earth. Immediately opposite the small dug-out that I occupied I noticed that British soldiers who came along always stopped and wiped their feet. On inspecting this spot to ascertain the reason, I found the side of a dead face and the black hair of a head just visible. Unwittingly the men had used this to wipe the mud off their feet! However, this job was at length satisfactorily finished and the trenches made more healthy and habitable.

On 26th November our other Company, under Major Stewart, came up to relieve the detachment of the 41st Dogras. There was a great mix-up of units in this front. On the extreme left there was a small lot of a British regiment, first from the Connaught Rangers, and then from the Black Watch. Then we came, then more of the Black Watch, and then the 41st Dogras Detachment, which our 4th Company relieved. So it will be seen that we were unnecessarily split up, which is bad for command, but I suppose they were a bit too "gabraoed," or upset, at Brigade headquarters after the late attacks to worry about such things.

The extreme left and right were rather ticklish places. There was a lot of bombing going on there on the left, as it was very close. Also where our No. 3 Company was on the right there was a lot of bombing, too, to which we replied, as we had received a good supply of bombs. When the bombing became rather hot on the left and the officer of the Black Watch reported this to me, I directed him just to quietly withdraw his men a few yards, half to the left and the other half to the right, towards my men, so that a short bit of the trench where the bombs were falling would be left vacant for a time till they stopped. The men remained in view of it and were ready to go back at once if necessity demanded. This was done, but the few that went towards the left, instead of remaining there within sight, apparently misunderstood and went right on into the next unit's sphere and eventually down a communication trench and so got back to Brigade headquarters. What yarn they told there goodness only knows, but it upset Brigade headquarters very much, for I received a hysterical memo. asking why the trenches had been evacuated, and that they were to "be retaken at all costs"—the same old phrase! All this time it must be remembered that we had been lent to another, the Ferozepore, Brigade, and were not with our own just then. I, however, reassured them by telling them that as the trench had never been evacuated there was no need to retake it. It just shows the state of nervousness they were in, as, instead of first quietly inquiring of me what had happened before issuing such a memo., they apparently took what the men had told them to be true.

The 2/8th Gurkhas were now sent to relieve the Black Watch, and their C.O., being senior to me, took over command of this section. News came on the 28th that we were to be relieved by the Leicesters of our Brigade. Their officers came up as usual to arrange what they could in daylight, and during the night the relief was completed. Our last Company to reach billets at La Couture was No. 3, at 1.15 a.m. Here we remained for three days only, when we again had to go into the trenches in our old original section to relieve the 59th Rifles. While at La Couture on 1st December we received orders to send 100 men to Locon to be inspected by the King. They went there under Captain Burton. The 1st Battalion also sent a like number, and it was here that the man of theirs, Naik Darwan Sing Negi, who had been awarded the Victoria Cross for gallantry at Festubert on 23rd November, received it at the hands of His Majesty.

We took over our old bit of the line on 2nd December, and this time we were destined not to be relieved till 27th December—a spell of 26 days. This time Battalion headquarters had a much better dug-out and mess. It had been made by the 59th Rifles, I believe, in the middle of the orchard by the farmhouse. As an addition to our forces, the Indian cavalry were now being given a spell of trench life by detachments, as there was nothing else for them to do at this period of the operations. The machine guns of the 4th Cavalry were sent up to our line, and they occupied the extreme right in what we called the "gap," just between the two battalions, situated in the ditch that ran along our front and into which our trenches ran at this point. Our line, owing to taking in this gap, was of considerable length. Beyond the usual sniping the time was uneventful, except for the mud and water, which seemed to be rising. Being on a slightly lower contour than the German trenches, all the water that they pumped out of their trenches ran down the ditch alongside the La Bassée road into ours. It was very misty at times during this month. It was most uncomfortable having to walk round the trenches in liquid mud and water, especially in the communication trenches. The other trenches were more or less kept clear by constant attention, but in parts it was impossible to cope with the rise, as the water level was only a few inches below the surface. The enemy was active in sending up flares and searchlights at times during the night. We had no such things as these, and when we did get them they were never nearly as good as the German ones while we were in France.

On 9th December Captain Harbord, 44th Infantry, reported his arrival, and also Captain Parkin, 113th Infantry, in command of 158 Garhwali reinforcements from the depôt in India.

On 14th December we got orders to carry out a fire attack on the German trenches from 10 a.m. to 5 p.m., with a view to assisting the advance of a Division to the north of us, the object being to hold the enemy to this front and prevent him sending reinforcements away from it. We gained fire superiority all along the line and rendered his loopholes useless. One of our machine guns was put out of action here by having the water jacket in front perforated by a bullet. The German ones always had a bullet-proof steel front to the jacket. However, this was only one of the many improvements and dodges we were to learn from our foe. The next day we made again another fire attack at the same hour, and again the next day, 16th December, to aid the Lahore Division, which was attacking to the south. Later we heard that they had captured two of the enemy's sap-heads. Our Brigade Major, Major Young, of the 4th Gurkhas, was wounded by a sniper on his way home after visiting our line; and died shortly after. He was a good fellow and an excellent Brigade Major. Major Stewart, commanding No. 3 Company of our Battalion, was taken to replace him. In the evening the enemy maintained a continuous fire, which damaged our loopholes considerably. The next day at 7.30 a.m. the enemy again suddenly opened a hot fire on No. 1 Company's trenches. Apart from destroying some loopholes, no damage was done. This was in retaliation for what we did to them the morning before. Up to this date we had never had a visit from our Brigadier, or even a glimpse of him in the trenches, but on the 18th we received intimation that he would be coming round. However, he never got so far as our part of the line. At 12.30 p.m. all Commanding Officers were called to see the G.O.C. Brigade at a house in the Rue des Berceux, not far behind our line. Here we received instructions, in conjunction with the 1st Battalion, to keep up a heavy fire on the opposing trenches while the Leicesters, supported by half a Battalion of the 2/3rd Gurkhas, attacked the enemy's trenches to their front. This was carried out successfully at 3.45 p.m. on the 19th December, a good length of trench being captured with some prisoners and two machine guns.

On the 20th a German aeroplane came over our line, and immediately after the enemy opened a heavy fire attack on us, while apparently they made attacks elsewhere on our front. The result of this was we heard the next day that the 2/2nd Gurkhas had been driven from their trenches, as also some of the Sirhind Brigade, all of which, except those of the 2/2nd Gurkhas, had been recaptured. We again kept up heavy rifle fire while an attempt, presumably, to recover the lost trenches was being made. Our artillery shelled the enemy heavily at dusk. Our right flank trench was bombed for a time by the enemy, but no material damage was done. The water in the trenches was now rising quickly, and we could hardly keep it down. The Germans were pumping their trenches and were presumably more or less dry, but we had no pumps. The water in any case would have been too much, so another portion of trench was dug behind the flooded-out bit, as damming it was of no use. The water washed the dam away. We asked headquarters to arrange for some artillery fire to knock out the pump which a Sapper Officer, Lieut. Robson, said the enemy were working opposite our left flank. Poor Robson was killed here in the evening of 23rd December. So a gunner officer came up to arrange and put a telephone line back to his battery. However, nothing could be done that day, as his guns were required to fire elsewhere. The next day, 25th December, Christmas Day, he came again, and this time for business. The range given was taken from the map, and 300 yards added, he told me, to make sure, as his guns were old and much worn. He signalled down "all ready." Bang, we heard in the distance, and over came the shell. It fell just a yard or two over our parapet. Fortunately it was a "dud." The look of astonishment in the gunner's face was most amusing. The range was at once rectified, the object got on to, and shells dropped in its vicinity. But I don't think any hit it. The water was as bad as ever, and our men worked hard at night bare-legged in the icy-cold water to clear the ditches to make the water flow off more freely.

The same day we heard that we were to be relieved at last, as the C.O. and officers of the relieving regiment came round with their G.O.C. to see the trenches, though nothing official had then come. They belonged to the Worcesters, of the 5th British Brigade. I showed them round, and had just seen them off at the entrance to the communication trench by the Rue du Bois about 3 p.m., and got back to my dug-out when Captain Berryman came running up with the news that "the Germans were out of their trenches." "The devil they are!" I replied, and went up with him. Sure enough I found a number sitting on the parapet of No. 2 Company's trench, and also out in front of No. 1 Company. They were trying to converse with our men and giving them cigarettes, biscuits and boxes of cigars. As I could speak German I conversed with them. They all belonged to the 16th Regiment, and it is a strange coincidence that at the battle of Nueve Chapelle later in March, 1915, among the prisoners that the Battalion took were these identical men who came out on Christmas Day at this informal "armistice." They seemed very jolly, as if they had had a good feed with plenty to drink. In fact, they told me that they had had a good dinner. One of them said to me that there must be "Friede auf der Erde" on this day, being Christmas Day. They seemed convinced that they were winning, and one of them said, with a wave of his hand, that the Russians were quite out of it. He gave me a bundle of his newspapers to corroborate his statement.

This "armistice" was of short duration.

Strictly speaking, it should not have taken place without permission. Both our and the German headquarters (we saw from captured documents later) were very angry about it when it became known, and rightly so. At 3.45 p.m. a whistle sounded from their trench, and they all, driven by their neat, dapper N.C.O.s, or "unter officiers," scuttled back to their trench. The men were not so neatly turned out as the N.C.O.s, naturally, as they have harder and more fatigue work to do. One man, I noticed, had on a pair of civilian corduroys over his uniform ones.

The truce was well kept for all that night. Not a shot was fired. The silence, so different to the usual crack of rifles and spluttering of machine guns, was almost uncanny.

The way that they came out was amusing. First, the evening before, they put out small Christmas trees with lighted candles on them on the top of their trench. Our men were astonished, as it looked, they said, like their own "Dewali" festival in India. During the morning singing and shouting were heard. After a time heads appeared, and finally their whole bodies—and out they came! It shows what confidence they had in our men. We could not have trusted them in like manner. We took the opportunity to search for poor Taylor's and Robertson-Glasgow's bodies. They were killed on 13th November. Only the latter's body was found. Taylor and the Garhwali officer must have got right into the German trench and been killed there. Robertson-Glasgow's body was found close to the parapet. He was buried in the military cemetery between Epinette and Le Touret on the Rue du Bois.

It was a strange feeling being able to wander up above ground after being so long below the surface. A couple of dead Germans were close to the side road. They looked so quiet and lifelike in the attitude they were lying in, so opportunity was taken to have a look at them. They were mere skeletons inside their uniform! One had no head. Both must have been killed by a shell.

On the 27th we received orders that the Worcesters would relieve us at 4.30 p.m. It being winter, and the days closing in early, it was possible to get up to the trenches in relief earlier. They arrived soon after 5 p.m. and took over, and the relief was completed by 8 p.m. I am afraid that the trenches we handed over were rather a poor legacy, owing to the amount of water, which kept rising. This eventually caused the line to be evacuated during the winter and a breastwork constructed behind near the Rue du Bois. Companies marched as soon as relieved independently to billets at La Couture, which the last company reached at 9.30 p.m.

So ended our second and longest spell in the trenches at any one period. The Battalion of the Worcesters that relieved us was the Battalion that the Commander-in-Chief had singled out especially to praise for their good work in the early days of the war.

The 2nd Battalion casualties had been very heavy all this period of trench warfare. Though not many in any one day, the total mounted up quickly, so that from the commencement up to the date of relief on 27th December, 1915, it came to two British Officers and one Garhwali Officer killed; two Garhwali Officers wounded; 53 rank and file killed; and 242 rank and file wounded. Grand total, 300 casualties.

CHAPTER VI.

Brigade after relief marches to Lillers and vicinity for a longer spell of rest—Battalion is billetted at Hurionbille—Short leave to England is opened—All Officers proceed in turn—Training continued while in billets—Leave again for the Trenches after 22 days' rest.

AFTER relief on 27th December, 1914, the Battalion, with the rest of the Brigade, left La Couture for billets in the vicinity of Lillers, which was the Indian Army Corps Commander's headquarters at that time as well as our railhead. Our route was *via* Paradis and Robecq to Hurionville, where our billets were, and which we reached at 2.30 p.m. on 30th December. On the way between La Couture and Paradis we were met by General Anderson, commanding the Meerut Division. He stopped and said some nice words to the Battalion and congratulated us on the good work done. The roads were very muddy and, at parts, flooded. The weather was inclement and cold. The village of Hurionville was only a small mining village and situated about a mile-and-a-half beyond Lillers, so that the billets were not very good. However, we all (men included), made ourselves quite comfortable—the men in barns, with plenty of straw. We had our mess in the inevitable estaminet. We received news soon on arrival that short leave was open to England for all officers, and hastened to take advantage of this privilege. I went the same evening with two others, as one never knew when such a privilege might suddenly be stopped, owing to the exigencies of the service. We went to Boulogne, on the homeward journey, by train, arriving there in the early morning, getting free passes the whole way and back. The return journey was not quite so comfortable, as from Boulogne we returned in motor-buses, and it was a long 50-mile drive back all night. We arrived at our billets about 1 a.m. a bit tired, as the buses were fully packed with returning officers. We all snatched a little sleep leaning against each other! A few reinforcements from Marseilles were received out of those men we had left there on arrival.

The Army Commander held an inspection of the Brigade on 4th January, at 11 a.m. He saw each Battalion and said a few words of congratulation to each. Meanwhile each day we were busy training and practising different kinds of work, such as digging trenches, live bomb throwing, capture of a hostile trench by bombing and with the bayonet, laying out a line of trench, disposal of captured prisoners, night work, &c,

It was announced in the "London Gazette" about this time that His Majesty had instituted a new decoration styled the "Military Cross." The Subadar Major of the Battalion, Subadar Major Nain Sing Chinwarh, was awarded this decoration in the same "Gazette," and Rifleman Ganesh Sing Sajwan was awarded the Indian Order of Merit for his gallantry at Richebourg L'Avoué on the early morning of 9th November—the day of our successful raid on the German trenches.

On 7th January, 1915, our Brigade, with the Sirhind Brigade of the Lahore Division, marched to a village called Burbure, two miles off, for inspection by Field-Marshal Sir John French, the Commander-in-Chief. It was a rainy and blowy day. After arrival at the rendezvous we lined the road and were kept waiting in the wet for some time. At last the Commander-in-Chief arrived and walked slowly down our line, followed by his motor-car. He never said a word as he went along each unit, not even to the Commanding Officers, who were mentioned to him by name as he passed, not even a shake of the hand, which I thought very strange. Not knowing the language, of course he could say nothing to the men, so this was done at the end of the inspection through the Corps Commander. Unfortunately, owing to the length of the line, little or nothing was heard except by those who happened to be close up at his end of the line. We thought he might have said a word or two of welcome to each Regiment direct by addressing himself to each C.O. as he passed. It would have been much more appreciated, as we could then have told our men afterwards what he had said, but he just passed stolidly down the line without saying a single word and hardly looking at the men. A few words of welcome or appreciation given personally are worth much more than written complimentary orders issued later through the usual channel. In the case of Indian troops, who had come some 5,000 miles or more to fight in a strange country, it would have been doubly appreciated.

At the conclusion of the "inspection" we learnt that our Brigadier, Major-General Keary, had been promoted to the command of the Lahore Division, the vacancy having been made by the necessary and ruthless pruning out of some incompetent Generals. He took advantage of our all being together to say "Good-bye," and shook hands with all British and Garhwali officers. The command of the Brigade then devolved upon Lieut.-Colonel C. G. Blackader, D.S.O., the Commandant of the 2nd Battalion Leicestershire Regiment of our Brigade. He got the command of the Brigade permanently shortly after, with a brevet colonelcy, at which we were very glad, as he was a sound soldier, a splendid commanding and regimental officer. He proved himself a first-rate Brigade Commander.

The weather, during the time spent in these billets, was wet and stormy, with only a short spell of sunshine occasionally. Sapper officers were busy improving our bombs, and one with a friction fuse was being tried and issued. This was a boon, as now, by a sharp turn, the fuze could be lighted without any lighting up of a slow, or ordinary, match, with the disadvantage of probably giving oneself away.

So the time in rest passed quickly and pleasantly, combined with a lot of work fitting ourselves for future trench warfare, which was quite novel in its way.

Kind people at home started making gifts of warm clothing. This was in addition to that issued by the Government and what relatives sent us. In fact, what we received was much too much, and I had to ask that no more be sent, as we had more than enough. One article people were very fond of sending was body belts. I suppose kind ladies thought that we were so likely to get chills. When the belts were issued to the men they never by any chance used them as intended—round the stomach. They invariably put them round the neck as a sort of comforter! Socks and cigarettes were always welcome. Socks wore out quickly, and the men smoked a lot of cigarettes. On leaving Hurionville I sent back to store nine bundles of warm clothing which we could not possibly issue, owing to the men having so much of it.

We left Hurionville at 10.15 a.m on 21st January *via* Lillers—Busnes—Robecq to Calonne, where we arrived at 2.30 p.m. The next day, which was cold and frosty, we marched to Vielle Chapelle, arriving at 4.30 p.m. It was a trying march, as the roads were flooded in parts, causing numerous blocks which we, being the rear Battalion of the Brigade, felt most. Here we received orders that the Brigade would go into the trenches, two Battalions in front line on the Rue du Bois and two in reserve behind in the village of Richebourg St. Vaast. It was a frosty night, and the next morning was also frosty and very cold. We left Vielle Chapelle for billets at Richebourg St. Vaast at 2 p.m., as it was only a short march. The billets here were not so good, as the village was not very far behind the line and had suffered much from shell fire, especially the nice old church, whose steeple had been fired at many times but as yet had not fallen in. It was eventually to get a few more direct hits and come down with a crash. I remember it had a fine old organ, which had been ruined by the shell fire. When

THE CHURCH, RICHEBOURG ST. VAAST.

I went over in April, 1921, there was only a bit of one wall standing, and it was a big church, too. All the graves had been blown up and contents blown to bits and scattered over the churchyard. Every vestige of the village was gone. Our transport went back to a large farm called Cour St. Vaast, a short distance off. The Leicesters and 1st Battalion were in the trenches and we and the 2/3rd were in billets to start with. The line we took over was along and in front of south of the Rue du Bois, where a breastwork had been made instead of the trenches which we had occupied at first, owing to their being flooded out. The original front line was held by picquets, while all the rest were in dug-outs behind and under cover of the ruined houses along the Rue du Bois of the village of Richebourg L'Avoué, ready to man the breastwork. While in these billets we supplied working parties to make

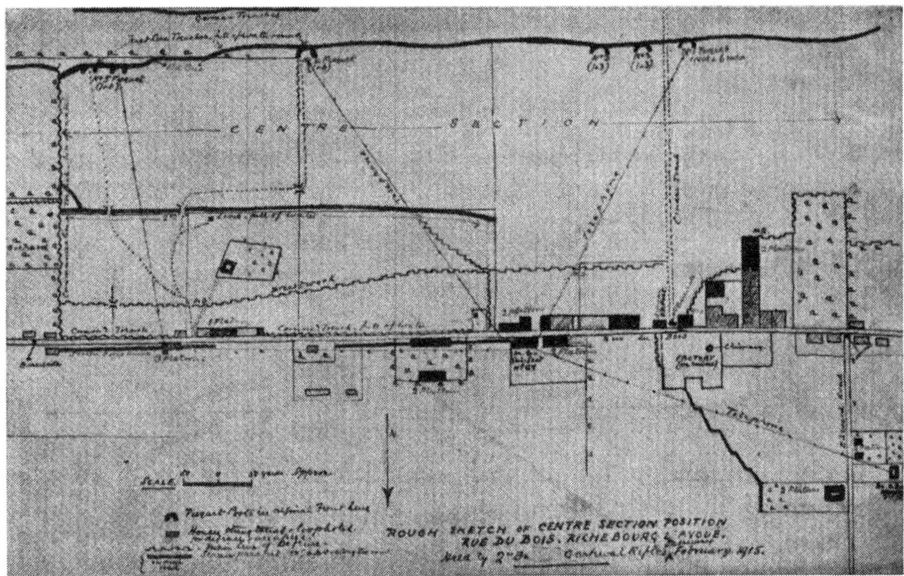

redoubts in the Rue des Berceaux and, after dark, to improve the trenches on the Rue du Bois. The Battalion relieved our 1st Battalion on 26th January. (See sketch of picquet line as held here and Appendix VI. for the orders issued to them). Our spell of trenches now was much shorter, arrangements being made to relieve us every week or so. We left the trenches again on the evening of the 29th, being relieved by the 6th Jats, and we went back again to Vielle Chapelle. Here we did close order drill and smartening up work generally. This is most necessary, as otherwise the best men are apt to think such things as smartness and saluting are not necessary on service, which is a great mistake. Also it is most necessary in billets and in the trenches to have a strict and good arrangement just the same as in peace time in barracks, for cleaning and inspection of rifles and accoutrements every morning, else men are apt, the best of them, to get slack and neglect these most important things. (See Appendix XVI). In this trench warfare it occurred more than once with some units, owing to the neglect of these most obvious precautions, that the rifles got dirty and the bolt worked with difficulty, a fatal thing, as upon the rifle depended the safety of the owner. It was with this object that a bolt cover was eventually issued. Until such was issued we found that the upper part of an old, worn-out sock answered the purpose very well. Fatigue parties were now supplied regularly for work on redoubts and communication trenches, the latter by night, being closer to the firing line. Sometimes the whole battalion was out.

On 4th February we moved up again to Richebourg St. Vaast, the Battalion being in Brigade reserve while the remainder were in the front line. The next day we came in for some shelling, so that we had to clear the men outside the houses into whatever cover that could be found. The shelling lasted about an hour, about 50 shells coming over. A good many houses, including the church, were struck. Here the Corps Commander visited us in our billets on 7th February. He was specially struck with the cleanliness and smart turn-out of the men, notwithstanding the poorness of the billets and the hard fatigue work they had to do every night. He said, as he was leaving, " Aren't they clean ! "

On 8th February we again relieved the 1st Battalion in the front line, the Battalion moving off at 8 p.m. The relief was completed by 10.30 p.m. The same stretch of trenches along the Rue du Bois was taken over, picquets being put in the original front line connected by telephone, so that the remainder behind on the road could, if necessity demanded, move up to the breastwork while the picquets retired upon it. The ground was very sticky, and going up any communication trench nearly took the heel of one's boot off at every step. Walking over the ploughed fields one's boots got so covered with earth that one could hardly lift them up.

Here we had attached to the Battalion a Lieut.-Colonel Johnstone, commanding the 8th Battalion West Riding Regiment,

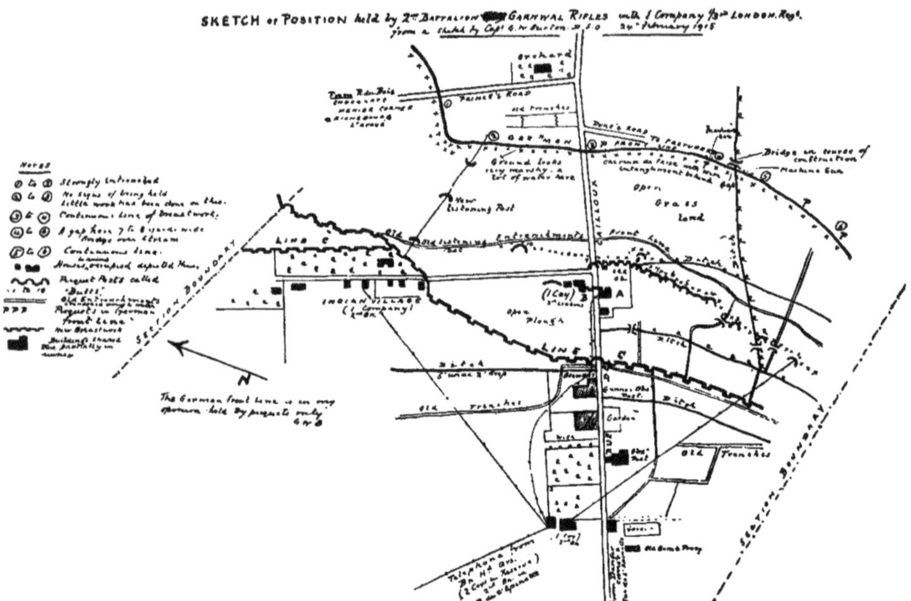

for initiation into the mysteries of trench warfare for three days. He stayed at my headquarters and accompanied me round whenever I went up to the trenches daily to inspect.

All this time the weather was cold and frosty.

We were relieved on the 10th by the 15th Sikhs, who came up at 8.45 p.m. The relief was soon got through. We went to our old billets at Vielle Chapelle, where we were this time for ten days till we went into another part of the line near the Rue de L'Epinette. At Vielle Chapelle, like at Lillers, there were Corps baths in a brewery, where the men went by detachments for a clean up and issue of clean underclothing. The 3rd London Regiment, T.F., was now being attached to the Brigade and joined us on 17th February The Battalion relieved the Highland Light Infantry in the trenches on the evening of 21st February and occupied the trenches in front of a village, which had been given the name of "Indian Village," in the deep bend where the line curved round to Festubert southwards. A portion of the line here consisted also of isolated picquets in small separate breastworks which were styled "butts," as they were like grouse butts. These were eventually linked together. A Company of the London Regiment was attached to the Battalion and commanded by a Captain Moore. I gave him this portion of our line as he was attached for instruction, being new to the work. Their companies were all in turn attached to different units for this purpose.

Nothing of any great importance occurred while we were here. The so-called "Indian Village" was in a dirty condition, the ruined houses, such as they were, having been used by some unit, or units, as latrines in default of a more suitable place. This was a legacy left for us to see to, so I had all the battalion sweepers, and applied for a lot of others, which were sent me from the Division, and had the whole place cleansed.

We improved very considerably the breastwork and defences of this part of the line while we were in occupation. We endured some heavy shelling while here.

For the first time our machine guns were to be brigaded under a machine gun officer. Eventually they were formed into companies, which was a sounder way of working them. Even now we were a long way behind the Germans in the number of guns we possessed and efficiency of working them. The German machine gunner was an expert in the use of this weapon. It was a most efficient arm. The bomb guns were likewise brigaded under a special bomb gun officer. Though this system made for efficiency, it took away officers from a regiment and generally one of your best, too. Captain Lodwick, of the 2/3rd Gurkhas, was our brigade machine gunner, and Captain Parkin attached to us became the brigade bomb gun officer.

We were relieved by our 1st Battalion in the front line and occupied some houses behind in the Rue de l'Epinette as reserve for three days when we were relieved there by the Scots Guards, whose Commanding Officer was good enough to say the billets we handed over to him were the cleanest that he had ever taken over. He also wrote to our G.O.C. to this effect. Sometimes units were not always as particular as they might have been in unoccupied houses and did not always leave them clean on their departure.

We went back to billets at Zelobes, beyond Vielle Chapelle, and, as usual, went on with a daily routine in drilling and practising necessary work.

CHAPTER VII.

The Battle of Neuve Chapelle, 10th to 13th March, 1915—Billets after the battle at Calonne.—Orders received for the two Battalions to be amalgamated and styled "The Garhwal Rifles.".

WE remained in billets at Zelobes for a week. Here Captain Burton, who had been acting as Brigade Major for Major Stewart, who had been sick and rejoined on 2nd March from hospital, came back to the Battalion, and Lieut. Clarke, Quartermaster, went sick. We soon got to know that in the near future an attack on a larger scale than we had hitherto delivered was in contemplation. On 7th March all British and Garhwali officers went up to the front line to reconnoitre the ground as far as possible over which the attack was to be delivered and the approaches up to the front line, and the particular route the Battalion would take in getting to its place in the position of assembly. The Garhwal Brigade was to attack in conjunction with the British 4th Corps on our left, from a portion of the front line held by the Bareilly Brigade, which portion ran along the main Estaires-La Bassée road to "Port Arthur," and thence in front of the Rue du Bois down the old front held by the Regiment in October, 1914, in its first occupation of the trenches. This preliminary reconnaissance by any commander, high or low, is of paramount importance and should never be neglected. As our Field Service Regulations say: "Time spent in reconnaisance is seldom wasted." It is applicable to the section and Platoon Commander up to the Battalion and higher commanders. Yet it is extraordinary how often this necessary and most obvious precaution is neglected. "Regrettable incidents" in warfare are generally, if not always, due to the neglect of the "A.B.C." of the profession. It is impossible to write and issue proper orders without a close first-hand knowledge, as far as you are able to obtain it, of the ground over which you are to operate. This reconnaisance well carried out, and good, clear orders issued, and a reserve kept in the commander's hands, you have done all that it is humanly possible to do and, if after that, anything happens, or your companies do not keep direction, then it is not your fault. You can thereafter only influence the fight by means of your reserve. The rest is in the hands of your subordinate commanders, and the initiative they display, strengthened by the good and sound training and instruction that you have given them in peace time. Again, it is most important that your companies, prior to an assault, should be *placed absolutely straight and parallel to the front they have to assault*. Men cannot, and will not, go straight to their objective under heavy fire if their noses are not first trained in the correct direction. It is easy enough to go off the line of direction, especially if the advance is a long one. In this case it was not a very long advance, or distance, to traverse to the first hostile trench. The idea was that ladders should be placed in the trenches for the men to climb out of the trench on when the time came for the assault to be started. Bridges were also placed in position over the further ditch alongside the La Bassée road at night for the men to pass more easily over. I did not altogether like this arrangement of ladders, though no doubt some contrivance to enable the men to get quickly out of the trench was necessary. Steps made of sandbags are best, as one knows how clumsy fully-accoutred men are when climbing up ladders, especially our hill men, who are unaccustomed to them.

When reconnoitring the ground the day before from the front-line trench and small salient at that part where the right of the Battalion was to rest, it was noticed that the ground of the field running down from the edge of the small orchard along which the German front line ran, sloped slightly down to the ditch on the edge of the main La Bassée road, and that if one lay down quite flat on the edge of this ditch one could not be seen from the German trench. This was lucky, as by getting out the assaulting companies during darkness to lie quietly there during the bombardment meant that they would have a much better "take off," get quicker into their stride and over the

AERIAL MAP

showing German Trenches covering the village of Neuve Chappelle to the N.W. and W. before the battle of 10th March, 1915, attacked by 25th Bde. and objective G–H attacked by 2nd Battalion.

ground, and so make surprise much more certain when the time came to start. Also by cutting away the edge of the ditch by night, and making a shallow trench along the edge, increased the available cover and aided concealment. This was done, and it turned out a success.

We had a conference at Brigade headquarters at Zelobes, at which the General personally explained his plans and orders so that all should thoroughly understand them, or ask questions if they did not. Everything being thus satisfactorily settled we left our billets at Zelobes on 8th March on a very cold and windy day at 6.45 p.m., and were billeted in the ruined houses of the village of Richebourg St. Vaast. The 9th was also a cold morning, with frost and snow during the day. We made final preparations for proceeding to the trench from which we were to attack, and took over bombs, extra ammunition, &c.

The Battalion left these billets at 1.30 a.m. on 10th March and marched down the Rue des Berceaux past Lansdowne Post or Fort A.1, as it was originally called, on to the communication trench near where the Rue des Berceaux joined the La Bassée road, and down which the Battalion had to file to get to the portion of the front trench it had to occupy prior to assaulting, and which the 6th Jats of the Bareilly Brigade were holding.

I arranged that the two assaulting Companies, Nos. 1 and 2 Companies, the whole under Captain Burton, should lead the march with their left in front, as on arrival in the trench at the small salient they had to wheel round to the left and file out through a small gap that I had had cut at night in the parapet of the side of this salient, and this would bring them correctly drawn up with their right nearest the salient. This saved a lot of time and probable confusion, and moreover it is very essential that companies should *at first* be drawn up for an assault in the way that they always fall in on any parade and to which they are most accustomed. The other two companies which formed my reserve marched with their right leading as they remained in the main trench straight in rear and would only be sent up in support as the attack developed. The machine guns, under Captain Lyell, attached to the Battalion from the Brigade Machine Gun Company, took up their position on the extreme right, where I had my temporary headquarters with the telephone near the above-mentioned small salient.

The Battalion was on the extreme left of the line, and the units next in order were the 2/3rd Gurkhas, then the Leicesters, and on the extreme right the 1st Battalion in the "Port Arthur" Salient and adjacent "Roome's" trench, with the 3rd Londons in rear of the centre in a breastwork in Brigade reserve. Both on the right and on the left the flanks were protected, that on the right by machine guns and the fire of the Bareilly Brigade, and that on the left, where there was a large gap between us and the 25th Brigade, by the Brigade machine guns of the Garhwal Brigade, under Captain Lodwick, 2/3rd Gurkhas.

The 4th British Corps, of which the 25th Brigade was the nearest unit to our Brigade, was attacking practically at right angles to our line of attack, so that we and their right met in the village of Neuve Chapelle and, finally, after clearing the houses, advanced a short distance towards the Bois de Biez and entrenched beyond the village. It was a specific duty given the 2nd Battalion after capturing the hostile trenches to join hands with the British troops of the 4th Corps on our left. The Battalion was in position by the time ordered, *i.e.*, 4.30 a.m., or a short time before, and this information was telephoned to the Brigade headquarters, which was established for the battle at Lansdowne Post. At 5.15 a.m. I directed the two first assaulting lines to file outside and line the edge of the ditch and await the hour of assault.

We had now to wait patiently till daylight and the time decided upon for the artillery bombardment to commence. The orders and reports to be read in conjunction with the map will be found in Appendix VII.

It was cold waiting in the trenches. I had arranged that each man should take his great coat, wrapped loosely round him, on account of this. Coats could be thrown off when the Companies rose to the assault and left in the trench, from whence they would be collected for me later by the regiment then holding the front-line trench. The men thus would be much lighter for the advance and be able to get across the muddy and sticky fields quicker. At last it began to get light. We anxiously looked at our watches from time to time. The bombardment was to begin at 7.30 a.m. The first ten minutes was to be an intensive bombardment to cut the German wire, and at 8.5 the guns would lengthen fuze and range, when the assaulting companies were to rise at once and deliver the assault. While waiting in the trench for 8.5 a.m. to arrive there was a terrible din going on with our own bombardment, and with the German one too, for they were shelling us hard at the same time. We had several men who were in the assaulting companies outside killed by shell fire while waiting to advance, but the risk was well worth it on account of the advantage gained by being able to get away quicker. With my adjutant, Captain Berryman, and my orderly, Rifleman Keshar Sing Rana, I was seated with my back against the parados. There was also a man of the 6th Jats who was seated alongside my orderly next to Captain Berryman, so that there were four of us close together in a line. Suddenly a shell came over and exploded in the trench just a couple of yards or less from where we were seated, with the result that my orderly and the man of the 6th Jats were killed instantly. Keshar Sing Rana, who had been awarded the Indian Distinguished Service Medal for gallantry at Festubert in November, 1914, had two pieces of shell blown right into his forehead, killing him instantly. I missed him greatly, poor fellow. The man of the 6th Jats, too, had a big piece of the back of his neck blown out. He was leaning a bit over, and behind Captain Berryman at the time, so it was a lucky escape for us both. The extraordinary thing was that we all four were seated touching each other, Berryman on one side and I on the other, with the two men in between us, and yet neither Berryman nor myself was touched or hurt beyond a bit of a shaking from the explosion. Such is war! You can never tell when it will be your turn, so it is no good worrying about it. They talk about dum-dum bullets and the wounds they make, but to my mind a piece of shell does a great deal more damage and makes a far greater mess.

The bombardment was an excellent one,

THE BATTLE OF NEUVE CHAPELLE,

10th March, 1915. The 2nd Battalion Garhwal Rifles charging over the La Bassée Road.

and the artillery made first-rate shooting. The wire in our front we found was splendidly cut, so that when we advanced it afforded no obstacle to us. As one leaned up against the parados the sound of the guns going off (and the sound was continuous) was just like the blows of a huge hammer. I mentioned this fact afterwards to a member of the Press when describing, at request, the part we took in the battle. Some of the field guns were only 1,000 yards or so behind us. We could see the howitzer shells coming over quite easily, and it was most interesting watching them while we had to wait seated during the bombardment. You could track them from the culminating point in their trajectory right down to the time they exploded on the enemy's trench. So good was the bombardment that the Boches' heads were well kept down and our men in the main trench were able to stand up during the latter part of the bombardment and enjoy the spectacle, which was like a grand pyrotechnic display.

When 8.5 a.m. arrived (we had all synchronised watches with the Brigade the day before), the two assaulting Companies were up and away without a moment's hesitation, which was splendid. Both these Companies were on a two-platoon front, the second platoon following the leading one at 30 yards' distance. Now was found the advantage of having the assaulting Companies ready outside the trench beyond the ditch. They got to the enemy's first trench before the Germans could get out of their dug-outs and man the parapet for firing on them. The attack was so complete a surprise that our men suffered little loss; in fact, none at all from the front-line trench. What casualties occurred were caused by machine guns to the flank and in rear. They did not stop at the first nor at the second trench, but went straight on to the objective G—H (see map), where a short halt was made to rally and collect and send back the prisoners captured. Patrols were sent on ahead to the village, and the companies followed on after and commenced clearing the houses in conjunction with the units of the 4th Corps which had, by now, also begun arriving in the village. Part of No. 2 Company, which was on the left of the assaulting line, also went on with Captain Burton's Company, and the other half remained on working up the trench towards their left to gain touch with the British regiment on the right. It was in one of these parties bombing up the trench to the left, whose commander had been killed, that one of the party, Rifleman Gobar Sing Negi, had the initiative to assume command and carry on bombing and rounding up prisoners and working up the trench. This action also drove others of the enemy into the hands of the British unit on our left. A machine gun detachment was thus captured. He, gallant, fellow, was unfortunately killed later on, but I am glad to say that he was awarded the Victoria Cross

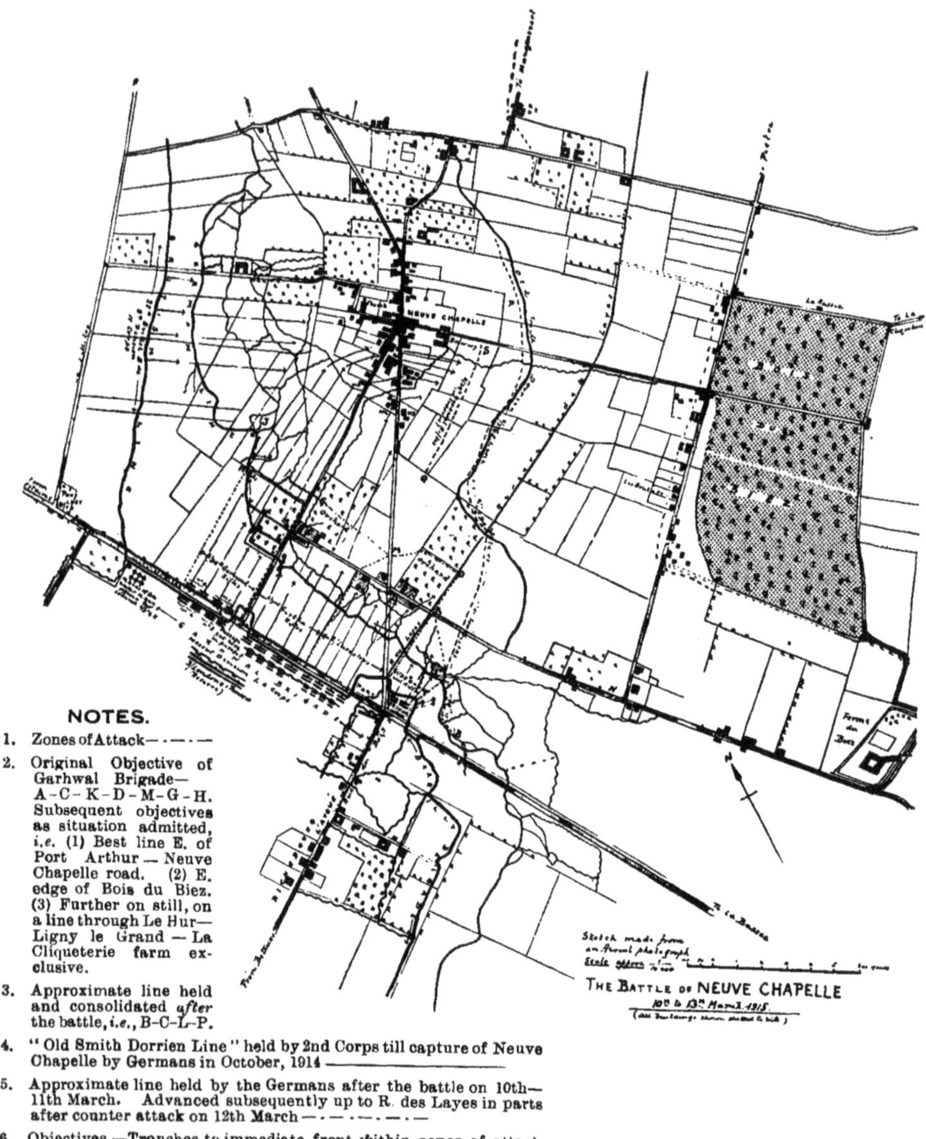

NOTES.

1. Zones of Attack— · —— · —
2. Original Objective of Garhwal Brigade—A-C-K-D-M-G-H. Subsequent objectives as situation admitted, *i.e.* (1) Best line E. of Port Arthur — Neuve Chapelle road. (2) E. edge of Bois du Biez. (3) Further on still, on a line through Le Hur—Ligny le Grand — La Cliqueterie farm exclusive.
3. Approximate line held and consolidated *after* the battle, *i.e.*, B-C-L-P.
4. "Old Smith Dorrien Line" held by 2nd Corps till capture of Neuve Chapelle by Germans in October, 1914 ————————
5. Approximate line held by the Germans after the battle on 10th–11th March. Advanced subsequently up to R. des Layes in parts after counter attack on 12th March — · — · — · — · —
6. Objectives.—Trenches to immediate front within zones of attack and in addition the following:—
   1/39th Garhwal Rifles—C, and eventually B by working down trench.
   2nd Leicesters—Group of houses round D.
   2/3rd (Q.A.O.) G.R.—Group of houses at F.
   } All shaded in.
   2/39th Garhwal Rifles—G-H, and to join hands with 8th Division on our left.

for his great gallantry that day. This made the second V.C. that the Regiment had gained since arrival in France—one in each Battalion.

The assaulting Companies under Captain Burton rightly did not remain at the first objective G—H, but went right into the village, after sending back the prisoners they had captured. The assault had succeeded so well and beyond expectations that by 9.30 a.m. the whole village was in our hands and those of the Brigade on our left.

The remainder of No. 2 Company had by now joined up in the village, and I had sent up No. 3, under Captain Wilcox, to support them, and the whole were now in the village, where, after helping to clear the houses, they swung round after rallying and reorganising, to the S.E., facing the Bois du Biez, and commenced entrenching a line in support a short distance behind the 2/3rd Gurkhas and Leicesters, who were practically on the line of the old "Smith Dorrien" trench which had been dug to cover the village before it was captured by the Germans in 1914.

Shortly after sending up No. 3 Company in support, I sent Major MacTier with half his Company to start digging on the line G—H in case a line in further support was temporarily needed, but on going up shortly after myself with the other half I saw that this was of no use, so took him on with his whole Company forming my reserve to join up with the rest of the Battalion to prolong the line which had been already begun in support. On the left of this line, which we were now digging away at hard, we linked up with the Rifle Brigade and the trench they were digging on our left.

On advancing myself to the village, I asked the O.C. 3rd Londons in Brigade reserve to send up and occupy the place I had vacated with one Company. So far the battle had gone extremely well all along the line except on the extreme right, where our 1st Battalion was. Here they had got into difficulties. Their assaulting Companies for some reason took a wrong initial direction and went too much to their right towards "C—B" instead of going straight for the trench to their front between the Rivière des Layes, on which their left was to rest and the point "C," which was with the trench to their front, their object first to take, and then to work down to "B" and consolidate the whole line. The result of the wrong direction was that these Companies ran up against uncut wire and had very heavy casualties in eventually capturing the trench, which they did with great gallantry. That portion between the R. des Layes and "C" was eventually captured in the afternoon by a fresh attack, in which the balance of the 1st Battalion, about one Company, reinforced by the 3rd Londons, attacked frontally, aided by a flank attack made from the direction of the cross-roads at "D" by two Companies of the Seaforths of the Dehra Dun Brigade.

This temporary check on the right, with the other check of 4th Corps on the extreme left, after the capture of the village, caused the delay that ensued, for instead of the Brigade in close support, the Dehra Dun Brigade, being pushed up at once to complete the work done and further the advantage gained by the Garhwal Brigade early in the day, and the Bois du Biez captured, nothing seems to have been done till late in the day, when about 4 p.m. they advanced to the attack of the wood. I remember well seeing the 9th and 2nd Gurkhas going through our line as they advanced towards the Bois du Biez, and when the day was fast closing in and it was already getting dusk.

The trench which we had dug in support was made strong by the evening. as we were fortunate enough to find a lot of sandbags and other revetting material in a ruined house close by which had evidently formed a small depôt for the Germans on that front.

Owing to the very heavy casualties that the 1st Battalion had suffered this day, their Commanding Officer, Colonel Swiney, being among the wounded, I received orders about 6 p.m., when it was dark, to go up to "Port Arthur" and arrange about consolidating the right flank there. My Battalion was to remain in readiness to move at a moment's notice. In trying to get there I tumbled into a shell hole and hurt my knee, and so sent up my second in command, Major MacTier, temporarily to arrange. and I followed later. When I got up it was so dark that I found it difficult to find the 1st Battalion headquarters. After tumbling into several trenches opposite "Port Arthur," which ran across the road, having been cut through it, and stumbling on dead Germans lying thickly in them, I found their headquarters, but Colonel Swiney had by then been evacuated to the field ambulance. I also received a note from Major MacTier saying that he had been ordered by the G.O.C. to take over command of the 1st Battalion. Captain Harbord was also sent over temporarily to complete their numbers. So I started to return to my Battalion at S—Q, which I had left with directions to come up under Captain Burton when the orders came for them to move. On my way back about 1 a.m., however, I met them coming up about the cross-roads at "D," so these other arrangements having been made, I brought the Battalion back and re-occupied our trench at S—Q.

At 5 a.m. that morning, 11th March, the Battalion received orders to be temporarily attached to the Dehra Dun Brigade in order to cover their right flank during their contemplated attack that morning on the Bois du Biez. It was a cold, damp, misty morning. We left our support trench at S—Q and went down the main road in the direction of "Port Arthur" and turned up the road "D—N" at the cross-roads at "D" and went through the front line held at that part by the Seaforths and the Leicesters on to the open ground beyond where the Battalion took up a position, lying down in the slight folds of the ground and the shell holes for cover, with three

Companies in the front line and support and one Company with machine guns in reserve. The Dehra Dun Brigade were in position along the Rivière des Layes on the left, to which position they had retired the night before. When it was light enough to see, the Germans opened a smart rifle fire from the Bois du Biez, and we had 30 odd casualties in a very few minutes while we lay out there in the open. The attack on the Bois du Biez was eventually postponed and the wood only was bombarded the whole day, so I withdrew the Battalion back to the line of the trenches held by the Leicesters and to an orchard behind, where the Companies entrenched themselves. We remained there the whole day while this bombardment continued, and we noticed that the German trenches were apparently full of men, as we saw a lot of movement going on and men in full marching order, *i.e.*, with knapsacks and pickelhaubes, kept getting out of and running along the top of the trenches to get cover in the wood. Nothing more transpired, and so darkness fell once more. Our rations, which we much needed, as we had had nothing to eat since leaving Richebourg St. Vaast, beyond the emergency ration which is kept for such occasions as this, when it is difficult or impossible to bring up rations as usual, were brought up by a party of the 8th Gurkhas about 4 p.m. From 4 to 5.30 p.m. the Germans opened a fairly heavy shell fire upon us without doing much damage. We remained in this trench till midnight, when orders came for us to proceed at once to La Couture, where we arrived at 3 a.m. On the Rue des Berceaux, along which we had to go, we met a lot of other troops coming up in support to take the place of the Dehra Dun Brigade going back. The Germans were shelling this road heavily. These troops suffered some number of casualties, as they were pretty thick on the road the whole way along, together with some transport, which added to the congestion. As I sent the Battalion back by Companies independently to rendezvous at La Couture we suffered only three casualties. Here at La Couture we settled down, having arrived at 3 a.m., but again at 7.30 a.m. further orders came ordering us back to billets near Croix Marmeuse, where we arrived at 9.30 a.m., and had a long wait for the officer responsible for apportioning off billets.

All this marching and lack of sleep are, of course, unavoidable in such operations. It was with a glad heart that the men settled down to cook a good meal. However, it was not to be of long duration, as the course of events necessitated our returning to Richebourg St. Vaast once more, for urgent orders came to return there forthwith at 4.30 p.m. So we packed up again. The food almost cooked was quickly gulped down, and we left at 5.45 p.m. for Richebourg St. Vaast, arriving there at 9.15 p.m. At the entrance to the village we were met by an orderly with a piece of paper with a rough sketch purporting to show us the portion of the village which had been given us for billets. It would have been much better if the responsible Staff Officer had taken the trouble himself to meet us and show us the billets he had selected for the Battalion, as he could have got his dinner quite as comfortably afterwards or even before we arrived—as he actually did—and it would not have taken him long, for all the houses into which we peered which were in that part of the village given us appeared already occupied, as heavy snores came from muffled forms. Some rooms here and there, one or two only, seemed empty, but when we scanned them closer we fled, as they were so dirty and appeared to contain the remains of some unit's meat ration. At length, after tramping along the whole village, we returned in disgust to find the missing Staff Officer of the Brigade, and eventually with his help we got some room and settled quickly down, after a hurried cup of tea, to sleep. It would have saved us a lot of trouble and time if he had personally come and done his job properly at first. I am afraid I must have shown my annoyance a bit. I was offered a glass of brandy, which I refused, as I never take spirits, especially on an empty stomach. The guilty Staff Officer sought to comfort us by saying "Tell your men the news that the Aubers Ridge has been captured and several heavy howitzers taken." This was incorrect, as we never captured the Aubers Ridge either then or during the whole time of the war. There is nothing so irritating to a regiment as the improper performance of duty by a Staff Officer. It is not so much the officers but the men who suffer.

Meanwhile, the Germans on the early morning of the next day, 12th March, delivered their great counter-attack, which was repulsed grandly at all points. Here the 1st Battalion got a bit of their own back for what they had lost on the 10th, their machine guns, under Lieut. Mankelow, as well as the others of the whole Brigade, under Captain Lodwick, the Brigade Machine Gun Officer, doing great execution.

The next day, 13th March, we received orders to relieve the 1st Battalion in the trenches, but this was cancelled later and we were ordered to march back to our former billets at Zelobes. We left Richebourg St. Vaast at 5 p.m. and reached

Zelobes at 7 p.m. Our 1st line transport did not get in till very late, owing to a great block on the road. Our mess cart got smashed up by some artillery ammunition wagons returning. As a rule these do not give you much room on the highway. It is a case of get into the ditch or get covered with mud or run over. On 14th March we all attended the funeral of Major MacTier, Captain Kenny and of Captain Owen, who had been attached to the 1st Battalion, and whose bodies had been recovered, and were now buried in the churchyard of L'Estrem Church. The Roman Catholic padre there most kindly allowed the burials to take place, and gave the necessary ground for the purpose. It showed a most liberal and Christianlike spirit, which is not as a rule met with among the clergy of that denomination in such matters.

After this, each unit was visited in its billets by the higher commanders as well as by the Brigadier. First, General Sir Charles Anderson came round and said some very kind words to us all, which were much appreciated. He said that "the Battalion had made a great name for itself which would last for ever, and that the regiment could not have done better than it had done." He congratulated all ranks on the way they had worked and added "that of all the regiments whose names had been sent in to higher authority as having done well, the names of the 1st and 2nd Battalions of the 39th Garhwal Rifles would head the list." (See Appendix III., Indian Army Order. Special dated Simla, 26th March, 1915). The Corps Commander came the next day and also said some appreciative words to the Battalion. As he finished and was turning away he was good enough to add, "You are a damned fine regiment." Brig.-General Blackader commanding the Garhwal Brigade, also issued a very complimentary order on the work of the Brigade.

Now that the events of the four days' battle were over, and one could in comfortable billets think quietly over all that had taken place, the first thing that one wondered at was why the Dehra Dun Brigade, which had not been engaged and was all along in close support, *was not immediately pushed up* to further the advantage won by the Garhwal Brigade. What was the reason for this paralysing inertia? The village of Neuve Chapelle was in our possession by 9.30 a.m. The Brigade in immediate support had in anticipation been moved up closer from La Couture to a short distance behind the Garhwal Brigade and by "11 a.m. was ready to issue from the trenches along the La Bassée road and to advance to the attack of the Bois du Biez." The foregoing were the actual words used by the Corps Commander. But the attack was postponed, and the whole day wasted in doing nothing. Why? The reason appears to have been that a small portion of the hostile trench on our right flank had not been completely captured; the attack on our left flank was held up also. One might just as well say that no attack at all should have been made, because the Brigades on our flanks were not attacking but were simply holding their trenches, for they were in an analogous position to those attacking units on our flanks, which were temporarily held up. This was recognised later as a great mistake, and directions were given that attacks were not to be held up for this reason, but such places were to be contained and the rest of the line must be pushed forward.

The Army Commander seems to have been urging energetic action to no avail. As late as 3.6 p.m. a final order was issued as follows: — "Information indicates that enemy in our front are much demoralised. Fourth Corps and Indian Corps must push forward at once regardless of the enemy's fire, using reserves as may be required. Fourth Cavalry Brigade has been ordered on Piètre. Second Cavalry Division has been ordered up."

If the enemy were demoralised at this hour how much more must he have been earlier in the day immediately after the success of the attack by the Garhwal Brigade? The assault of this Brigade should, without doubt, have been followed up immediately by pushing forward the supporting Brigade to make progress towards the further objectives laid down in orders. If the Commander had not received definite orders to push on, why did he not, after a personal reconnaissance, take the initiative himself and order his Brigade forward? He would have been supported by the Garhwal Brigade well entrenched immediately in their rear facing the Bois du Biez and only two or three hundred yards distance from its near edge. The further edge of the wood might, anyway, have been secured and entrenched. The Corps Commander, once he had received information that the village was captured, should have issued orders for the Brigade to push ahead at once, whereas the whole day was wasted in doing nothing, and then only when it was getting dark did the Brigade go forward to an impossible task about 4 p.m., the Germans having a whole day in which to bring up reinforcements.

It would appear that the policy of "hukum na mila" (no orders received) from the top to the bottom was the cause of this inertia. Oh, for a Crauford or a

Picton that day! What a different story there would have been to tell. The date, "Neuve Chapelle, 10th March, 1915," bright as it shines, would have shone indeed with far greater brilliance in the annals of the British and Indian Armies.

This policy, it seems, of "hukum na mila" has all along been inculcated by higher command in the British Army from the days of the Peninsular War.

There were some instances of this policy during this War, and as they make amusing reading I will quote two instances, taken from that interesting book, "Wellington's Army," by Professor Oman.

(1) "Sir James McGrigori*, whom I have quoted above, once moved some commissariat stores to Salamanca, where there was a great accumulation of sick and wounded. When I came to inform him, his lordship started up, and in a violent manner began to repudiate what I had done. I shall be glad to know, he asked, who commands this army—I or you? I establish one route, one line of communication—you establish another by ordering supplies by it. As long as you live, sir, never do that again. Never do *anything* without my orders. I pleaded that there had been no time to consult him, and that I had to save lives. He peremptorily desired me 'never again to act without his orders.'"

(2) "On September 25th, 1811, on the day of the combat of El Bodon, when Crauford, thrown forward into a hazardous position by his chief's orders, was twelve hours late in joining the main army. He had been told to make a night march, but waited till dawn, because he was moving in a difficult and broken country full of ravines and torrents, where he judged that movement in the dark was dangerous. By his delay the army was concentrated half-a-day later than Wellington intended. 'I am glad to see you safe,' observed the Commander-in-Chief with some asperity, as the Light Division filed into the scantily manned position at Fuente Guinaldó. 'Oh, I was in no danger, I assure you.' 'But I was, from your conduct,' answered Wellington. Whereupon Craufurd remarked to his staff, 'He's d—d crusty to-day.' In this case, it must be remarked, in justice to Crauford, that it was his chief who had placed him in the hazardous position, not himself, and that his judgement that the night march was impracticable was very probably correct. But he had disobeyed an order, and it was remembered against him by the inflexible Wellington."

I imagine, too, that Commanders are haunted by the feeling that if unsuccessful they will be "shelved," and by the fear of having many casualties, which, in the eyes of politicians and the public at home, is a serious fault, forgetting as they do that in these days of arms of deadly precision many casualties are bound to occur in any engagement, large or small, successful or the reverse. Some sacrifice must be made to attain the object.

It is, I know, very easy to criticise in the light of after events, and still easier for one who was not there to do so from a comfortable armchair, but as one who was in the firing line the whole of that day and the next, *I am convinced that if the initiative had been seized*, and this Brigade had been at once ordered to advance and seize the wood and consolidate a line beyond its further edge and, if necessary, the left flank refused and a defensive flank formed, that line could have been captured without any opposition and held. And I agree with the 1st Army Commander who said that having at any rate got up to the nearer edge of the wood, the Brigade should have held on to it and entrenched, as there was no object in retiring back such a short distance to the Rivière des Layes.

As it was, the Germans eventually consolidated a good portion of their line along this river. The best thing for us would have been to have got through and over to the further edge of the wood while there was no opposition to speak of and consolidated a line all along just beyond it. The Germans did make an unsuccessful effort to turn the left flank of the Brigade on the evening of the 10th, and if they did not succeed at that time much less would they have succeeded earlier in the day when they certainly must have had fewer men present. Opportunities, if not seized at the moment, vanish for ever!

The possession of the entire wood would have been a great advantage to us, as it would have formed a good screen from the enemy. As it was, this wood was never taken. The enemy made this portion of their line covering the wood strong with very wide wire entanglements in front, and several lines behind with many machine guns. Nor was their line down this front to La Bassée ever broken, so strong had it been made. In the spring of 1918, when the Germans made their final great effort, they broke our line here and penetrated as far back as Merville and Locon, for the line was then held by the Portuguese, who, I believe, gave way. The Germans got a good fright from this battle of Neuve Chapelle. They thought that their line was broken, and were preparing to evacuate Lille. If only more leadership had been shown and the supporting Brigade had been sent through

* Director-General Medical Department.

at once, as General Willcocks says in his book, page 216, "*on the heels of the first assault, great results might have been achieved.*"

I have mentioned how strange it is that one gets hit and another does not. While the bombardment on 10th March was going on, I had occasion to speak to the gunner at the telephone of the observing officer, who had his telephone close to mine, which was linked up to the Brigade. In order to make him hear I had to place my face close to his, almost touching it, owing to the din and noise of the bombardment. At the same moment a bullet whizzed past my head—it must have passed extremely close—and hit the gunner on his left cheek close to his nose and passed out behind his left ear. Strange to say, after he was bound up, he was able to walk back to the aid post without help. Naturally, there were many bullets flying about. The air was full of them! Two cut my putties without hurting or cutting the skin. Another, during the advance, hit the rifle Captain Burton was carrying, and another passed through the sleeve of Captain Harbord's coat, also without hurting either of them. When darkness fell, and we were still entrenching the line S—Q, feeling tired I took off my rucksack to get some chocolate. I always carried a rucksack as it was a great protection to the back, besides carrying one's small things and emergency ration. My wife had sent me a large piece as thick as one's wrist, sewn up in American cloth, and which I had not opened. When I looked at it to open it I picked out a shrapnel bullet which, having gone through everything I had in the rucksack, had finally embedded itself in the chocolate. So that time the rucksack saved me from a nasty wound in the back or spine. I have since treasured this piece of chocolate and bullet as a souvenir.

THE CHURCH, NEUVE CHAPELLE.

The casualties sustained by the two Battalions during this battle were as follows:—

1st Battalion.

7 British Officers killed (including Major MacTier, attached from the 2nd Battalion).
5 British Officers wounded.
6 Garhwali Officers killed.
2 Garhwali Officers wounded.
120 rank and file killed (including missing).
190 rank and file wounded.

330 Total casualties.

2nd Battalion.

3 Garhwali Officers killed.
3 Garhwali Officers wounded.
47 rank and file killed.
69 rank and file wounded.

122 Total casualties.

The captures of the 2nd Battalion were 3 officers, 187 rank and file, with three machine guns and any amount of equipment which was left for other units specially detailed to collect.

The German soldier must have had it impressed upon him that we always shot or made away with all prisoners, probably as part of their system of propaganda in order to get them to avoid capture as much as possible and fight on to the last, as these men asked me at once not to shoot them. I replied that we never killed our prisoners. They at once recognised me, and seemed much more at their ease, for they turned out to be the same men of the 16th Regiment who had come out and fraternised, as I mentioned in a previous chapter, at the informal armistice on Christmas Day.

I picked up at this battle a very nice brand new pair of fur-lined motor gloves and also a splendid pair of Goertz prism binoculars, both of which I found extremely useful. Captain Nixon, commanding the Dogras attached to the Battalion, also got a nice pair of binoculars similar to my pair.

The Battalion remained at Zelobes in billets till 28th March, carrying out the usual drill and work and furnishing working parties frequently to dig or improve communication trenches up near the front line. On 29th March the Brigade marched to Calonne *via* Paradis and Pacaut, and we arrived at our billets at 3.30 p.m. Orders also came this day for the two Battalions, owing to casualties, to be temporarily amalgamated into one regiment and to be styled "The Garhwal Rifles." So all the men of the 1st Battalion (231 in number) and the British Officers, with some 90 men of the Tihri Imperial Sappers and Miners, who had just arrived as reinforcements, came over to the 2nd Battalion and made one regiment for the rest of the time that we were in France and Egypt, till our return to India in the spring of 1916. All Dogras that had been attached to the two Battalions were transferred to the 41st Dogras of the Bareilly Brigade. The Dogras that were attached to the 2nd Battalion came from the 91st Punjabis, and were commanded by Captain Nixon. They did very well at Neuve Chapelle.

CHAPTER VIII.

Long spell of Billets—Short Leave again opened—Visit of the Lord Bishop of London while at Calonne—Arrival of reinforcements—Visit of Lord Curzon—War Correspondents visit the Trenches and make sketches of the men and front line—Trenches again—Preparation for another attack.

THE Regiment now enjoyed a good long rest in billets up to 26th April. Short leave was again opened and officers went off as before in batches. It was still cold in the mornings and there was slight frost occasionally. On 2nd April—Good Friday—we had a visit from the Lord Bishop of London. In the absence of our General, I received him as commanding temporarily. An open-air service for all troops in the area was held in some fields adjoining the village and was well attended, and also much appreciated by all. The same day a reinforcement, consisting of two British Officers and 62 men of the Burma Military Police (Garhwalis) arrived. The Tihri Sappers and Miners had come over with the 1st Battalion contingent, as they had just joined them a short time before. The strength of the combined battalions then came to 13 British Officers, 21 Garhwali Officers and 793 rank and file, after all the Dogras who had been attached to both battalions had been transferred to the 41st Dogras.

The usual work went on day by day. Large working parties were supplied daily to dig trenches, &c., near the front line. One of these I remember was sent a long way off so that it left at 8 p.m. and did only two hours' work, returning at 5.30 a.m., after 6½ hours' marching there and back.

Easter Sunday was a wet day, and it continued wet all the next day, though the weather was mild. The Divisional Commander inspected all the reinforcements that had joined us since 1st January, including those just arrived. He selected 22 men whose length of service and chronic ailments rendered them unfit for the campaign, and they were sent back to the base for return to India. On 8th April General Sir Douglas Haig, commanding the 1st Army, saw all Commanding Officers in the Brigade. He congratulated the regiments on their splendid achievements. The Commander-in-Chief, Sir John French, was also to have inspected the Brigade, but the parade was cancelled at the last moment owing to a violent snowstorm.

On the 10th we changed billets to Vielle Chapelle. The Brigade usually made their headquarters in a house, in fact, the chief house of the village. We once had our headquarters in the same house when the Brigade headquarters were elsewhere. The owner and his wife were most kind and obliging. They put themselves to an enormous amount of inconvenience, giving up practically the whole house to those billeted there and keeping only one room for themselves. We used to have many friendly chats with the family and visited them on other occasions when we were billeted elsewhere. I often wonder how English people would have acted in the same circumstances. Think of it! Year in and year out your house perpetually given up for billeting, orderlies and servants with muddy boots tramping up and down the stairs and your kitchen taken possession of to cook the meals for the mess, so that they had to snatch a fleeting opportunity to cook their own. No, English people have not yet in the very slightest experienced what the French people have in their way, and therefore they "may down on their knees and thank God fasting" that they have not had an invader to lay waste their home and cities. It is always very hard for those so far away from the strife, and even the sounds of strife, to realise the great discomfort of it all, with their male relations gone to the front and possibly all killed. I made a special visit to see these good people when I went over there in April, 1921, in order to see the owner and have a chat over past times, but he was absent from the village, for, poor man, his house had been utterly destroyed when the Germans advanced in the spring of 1918. There was not a vestige of it left, not even a bit of the large iron gates or trees at the entrance. Think of it, ye English people, whose hearths and homes have been kept inviolate! It is thus very easy for some of them to talk of letting the "poor Germans" down easy in regard to the terms of repayment to France and the Allies. It is easy for our rulers and representatives in Parliament to talk in the same way whether they sit in the House of Commons or the House of Lords. I often wonder what tune they would sing if their palatial residences had been razed to the ground so that not a stone of them was visible ? Quite a different tune, I am sure.

One could not help admiring these French people, especially the farmer class, with whom one came more in contact. Day after day up about 4 a.m., working hard the whole day and to bed at 10 p.m., or a little earlier, and yet always smiling and obliging and outwardly happy.

On the 13th we went back again to La Couture close by after a brief stay at Vielle Chapelle. At 2.45 p.m. Commanding Officers with two India Officers from each Regiment were called into Brigade headquarters, as Lord Curzon was paying a visit to France and wished to interview representatives of Indian regiments. Two Garhwali officers, Subadars Bishan Sing Rawat, 1st Battalion, and Sangram Sing Negi, 2nd Battalion, accompanied me.

While in billets the men had a good time at the Divisional baths, which had been established at Vielle Chapelle. They all went in turn by Companies and received changes of clean underclothing.

On the 14th some war correspondents came round to see the trenches. They visited our billets and made sketches of the men, and then went up to the front line, accompanied by Captain Burton, where they made more sketches. Mr. Frederick Villiers and Mr. Robert Cleaver were among them. Both these gentlemen made a fine sketch of the regiment, the former of the 2nd Battalion at Neuve Chapelle shown in this book, and the latter of the regiment in the trenches, near Neuve Chapelle.

We stayed at La Couture till 22nd April. Here we furnished one company to garrison Fort A.1, or Lansdowne Post, as it was called later. For two days only we went back to Calonne, and again returned to La Couture on the 24th, where we remained till we went into the front line once more on the evening of 27th April, relieving the 1st Battalion of the 4th Seaforths. The regiment marched at 7.30 p.m. *via* Croix Barbée to the Estaires-La Bassée road, where guides met the regiment. From this point Companies went at five-minute intervals to avoid losses in case of the enemy shelling the main road, as they often did. Two Companies were in the front line, two platoons in a small redoubt called the "church" redoubt just close to the little church, or what was left of it, and two platoons in support and one Company in reserve about 200 yards behind regimental headquarters. The relief was completed by 11 p.m. While in the trenches here we received news that Rifleman Gobar Sing Negi, of the 2nd Battalion, had been awarded the Victoria Cross by His Majesty the King for his bravery at the Battle of Neuve Chapelle. Some other awards were also notified. Two Indian Orders of Merit and three Indian Distinguished Service Medals to the 1st Battalion and three Indian Orders of Merit with two Indian Distinguished Service Medals to the 2nd Battalion. Lieut. Mankelow, 1st Battalion, was also awarded the Military Cross for his good work with the machine guns at the battle of Neuve Chapelle.

On 1st May the Germans opened a heavy shell fire on our front-line trenches and on regimental headquarters and the ground in rear which supports would have to traverse in coming up to reinforce the front line. It opened at 4.20 a.m. and ended at 5.25 a.m. It was found out after that they expected us to attack that day, which, I believe, was originally intended, but was postponed. Our guns replied to the bombardment. No other attack was made by the enemy. Their aeroplanes were busy during the morning, when they had expected our attack to come off.

On 5th May we received orders that the Manchesters and 59th Rifles would relieve us in our section of the line. Their officers came up as usual in daylight to arrange what could be done before the dark. Guides were to be sent to Pont Logy to meet their Companies at 8 p.m., the time fixed. The Manchesters arrived at 10.45 p.m., but the 59th did not arrive till 1 a.m., long after their time, owing, it was said, to blocks on the road. This was quite the latest relief we ever had, our last Company not getting away till 2.15 a.m. The regiment went into billets at Loretto Road, where the last Company to be relieved arrived at 3.30 a.m.

The next day was rather muggy. All British Officers with Garhwali Officers went up to the front line near our old original portion to reconnoitre the ground and trenches in the vicinity, for a large attack was being planned.

On 6th May H.R.H. the Prince of Wales paid the regiment an informal visit in its billets in a large farmhouse in Loretto Road. I brought him into our mess and introduced him to all British Officers and afterwards to the Garhwali Officers. He said some very nice, kind and appreciative words about the regiment and its work. He asked several questions about the men and regiment, and said how pleased he was to come and see us all and congratulate us on the splendid work the regiment had done. This visit "bucked" us all up very much, and the

Garhwali ranks were ever so pleased with it. H.R.H. has the knack of saying things which are so much appreciated, and more especially so at such a time of stress that we were going through.

We remained in these billets now till the contemplated operations, which were being arranged, commenced. On 7th May we heard sounds of a heavy bombardment which was being undertaken by the French in the vicinity of Arras, with 14 Divisions and 2,000 guns on a front of seven miles. We also received operations orders, which were subsequently cancelled. I went into Divisional headquarters with our General to attend a conference regarding the forthcoming operations. A special additional detachment was being arranged, which was to be under my command to attack the Bois du Biez after the attack on enemy's trenches by the Dehra Dun Brigade, if that were successful. I will leave the account of the operations for the next chapter.

CHAPTER IX.

The Battle of Aubers, 9th May, 1915—Battle of Festubert, 15th to 25th May, 1915.

JUST on the north side of the Rue du Bois from Port Arthur down to the village of Richebourg L'Avoué, a number of trenches had been dug which were called "assembly trenches." It was in these that the troops in support of those actually in the front line and executing the attack were assembled waiting their turn to advance. They were numbered G1, G2, G3 and B1, B2, &c. The detachment that I was to command consisted of the 2/8th Gurkhas and the Garhwal Rifles with details, and some guns detailed to cover our advance towards the Bois du Biez, which we were to attack and clear after the attack of the Dehra Dun Brigade, if it was successful. The detachment was to advance through our front line and make a wheel to the left and go straight for the western edge of the wood, and go right through it and clear it to the further or eastern edge, and capture the estaminet situated there called La Russie. Our orders were to be in position in G1 assembly trenches above mentioned by 1 a.m. on 9th May. We had issued to each Battalion some smoke bombs as well, so that we could indicate our position by using these during our advance through the wood. Thus if we advanced after the attack of the Dehra Dun Brigade we would get behind the opposing trenches covering the whole Bois du Biez, and which now were very strong indeed. The small ruined houses along its northern edge along the road were full of machine guns.

The detachment was in position by the time named in orders, marching by Pont Logy and up a long communication trench

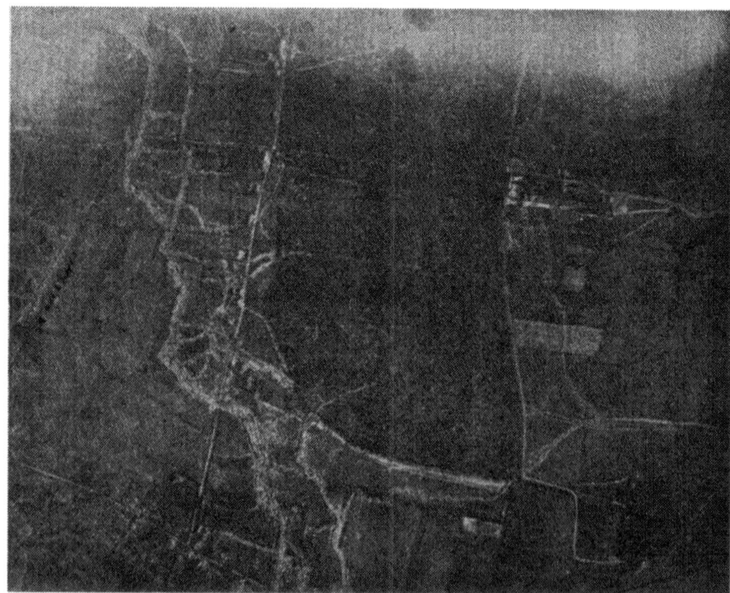

Ferme du Biez.

AERIAL MAP

showing German trenches covering the BOIS DU BIEZ with opposing British trenches after the battle of NEUVE CHAPELLE.

AERIAL MAP

showing British trenches (2nd Battalion Garhwal Rifles' old original section) with opposing German trenches, after the battle of NEUVE CHAPELLE. (Compare this photo with the one showing trenches *before* the battle and notice how the German trenches have been strengthened).

which ran into these assembly trenches. These assembly trenches were not very thick nor had they very strong cover as they were only intended for concealment and a short occupation till the advance took place. As it happened, it will be seen that the attack by the Dehra Dun Brigade was not successful, and we had to remain in these trenches the whole day and be subjected to a severe artillery fire for thirteen hours.

The bombardment started at 5 a.m., and the Dehra Dun Brigade commenced their attack. Our bombardment did not seem to have made much effect on the enemy or damaged their tenches much, for some of the Germans could be seen standing up, head and shoulders exposed, and firing into our advancing men. Some of our troops, though most gallantly advancing, did not get much further than 20 or less yards owing to the heavy machine gun fire, as the machine guns did not appear to have been knocked out at all. One specially designated object of our attack was a point styled V.6, a small redoubt, which was situated in rear of the enemy's front line in vicinity of their support trench. It was never captured, as our troops did not get anywhere near it. It was, as it happened, an exceptionally strong place, and would have to have been greatly damaged by artillery fire before our men would have had the slightest chance of taking it. I saw this in April, 1921, what was left of it, and, like the front trench, it was very strong, with concrete dug-outs for machine guns, &c.

The first attack having failed, a second attack was ordered for 7 a.m. by the same Brigade, which also failed. Another bombardment was then ordered from 3 p.m. till 3.40 p.m., and an attack was then delivered by the Bareilly Brigade, which was also repulsed. Meanwhile we had been in the assembly trenches all this time and subjected to a severe bombardment by the enemy for a total period of thirteen hours, the shelling only ceasing at 6 p.m., after

AERIAL MAP

showing British trenches (1st and 2nd Bn. original front) covering Rue du Bois, the Ferme du Bois and German trenches opposite, after bombardment.

which only intermittent fire supervened, which died down at dark.

The total casualties for the day amounted to a good number. Major Woods, our medical officer, was killed, Captain Berryman and Lieut. Saunders were wounded. Five Garhwali Officers were also wounded, and two rank and file killed and 94 wounded, and this without delivering any attack and being under some sort of cover. At dusk all available stretchers and bearers were sent up to the front trench to aid and bring in the wounded.

The day having been unsuccessful, there was no need of my special detachment, so the regiment remained in the assembly trenches that night. The next day, 10th, we were ordered to move up into the front line on the left of the Leicesters, in front of the orchard which was in our old original section of the winter, 1914, in front of Richebourg L'Avoué. This was with a view to making an attack at 3 p.m. on the redoubt V.6. The attack was to be preceded by a bombardment from 11 a.m till 3 p.m. However, these operations were cancelled, and a night attack arranged for. This order was also cancelled at 4 p.m., and the regiment was withdrawn from the front line and occupied the Orchard redoubt just behind the front line we had vacated. Here we were in support of the 3rd Londons. In this redoubt we were shelled a bit and had some casualties during the 11th and 12th.

In front of this portion of the line ran a ditch full of water. To enable the men to get over it quickly bridges were to be put out. On the night of 12th May the ground was reconnoitred for this purpose. During the day there was the usual shell fire, and Captain Wilcox was killed. During the day our guns also bombarded the enemy's trenches with high explosive, which we were now beginning to use. The General asked me to report on the damage done, so Captain Berryman and I observed the fire which it was hoped would breach his parapet. However, as far as we could see, very little damage was done. Some 9.2 howitzers were now being employed for the first time, and they were most effective. Owing to the force of the explosion it was not safe to bombard the enemy's front line, as it was too close to ours, so other points further off were taken, the result of which we could not see so well.

Meanwhile another attack on V.6 was ordered, to be preceded by a bombardment for 36 hours, for the night of 14th-15th May. On the 13th the regiment was withdrawn from the "Orchard" and went into assembly trenches in the rear of the R.E. depôt, just north of Rue du Bois in order to rest it a little after the continuous shelling that it had been subjected to for the last six days. Our guns were concentrated on V.6 in order to break the parapet and destroy obstacles.

The 14th broke fine and sunny. The proposed attack on V.6 was postponed for twenty-four hours, and orders came that it would be made at 11.30 p.m. on the night of 15th May. The artillery bombardment, which had been normal but continuous, was to cease at 11.25 p.m. At 2 p.m. on the 14th orders came for the regiment to go back to the Rue des Berceaux to some trenches near "Windy Corner" (so called because the enemy were always shelling round the cross-roads there) for a short rest for one day. To-day, unfortunately, Lieut. Mankelow, who had been placed in charge of the Brigade bomb guns, was killed by a shell. Captain Gatherer, attached, was also slightly wounded in the calf by shrapnel, and there were also one Garhwali Officer. and 40 riflemen wounded by shell fire. We remained at "Windy Corner" till 7.30 p.m. on 15th May. The enemy shelled us and our vicinity intermittently all day on 15th, hitting the ruined house serving as regimental headquarters. We also had several premature bursts of shrapnel from one of our own batteries 300 or 400 yards behind us, and they kept hitting the walls of the house, so that one had to be on the *qui vive* when moving out of it.

At 7.30 p.m. the Regiment left by Companies proceeding up the "Crescent" communication trench and took up its position in accordance with Brigade operation orders. The attack, which was being delivered by the Indian Corps, was to be in conjunction with that of the 1st Corps, of which one Division, the 2nd, was on the right of the Meerut Division and both assaults were to be simultaneous, the object being to establish a line from Festubert to La Quinque Rue to La Tourelle and Port Arthur cross-roads. On our left was the 7th Division, which was also to deliver an attack in the early morning of the 15th.

The regiment had a frontage of about 60 yards. On our right were the Leicesters with a frontage of 100 yards, and we were supported by the 3rd Londons and 2/3rd Gurkhas respectively.

No. 2 Company, under Lieutenant Rogers, was in the front line on a front of one platoon, and filed out through the holes or openings in the parapet that had been previously made by the Sappers and Miners. They crossed over the ditch, which was full of water and of an average width of 9 feet, by bridges which had been previously placed in position by Captain Etherton and a working party, and formed up beyond.

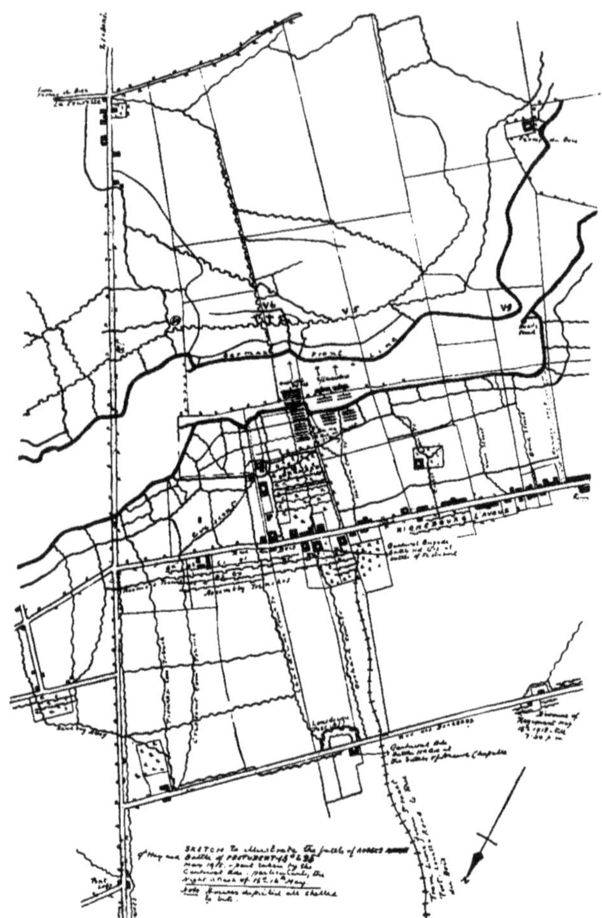

BATTLE OF AUBERS AND FESTUBERT.

No 3 Company, under Lieut. Fox, was formed into platoons and half filed out by the same exits, and took post between the parapet and the ditch. The other half of his Company remained in the fire trench ready to advance over the parapet. Nos. 4 and 1 Companies were formed up in the same manner on the open ground in rear of the fire trench, lying down till it was time to advance.

While the Regiment was moving up the communication through the "Orchard," a German shell exploded among the bombers of No. 1 Company who were carrying boxes of bombs, killing or wounding the whole party.

The O.C. Leicesters (Colonel Gordon) and I had established our headquarters next to each other in the fire trench, and while waiting for the time to launch the attack we were seated alongside each other on the fire step. Suddenly a German shell came over and fell outside the trench in the ditch and sent up a huge column of water, most of which fell inside our trench and on top of us. Luckily we had waterproofs on.

At 11.30 p.m. precisely the attack was launched, but owing to the heavy rifle and machine-gun fire it was unsuccessful. The leading Companies were reinforced by the remaining half of No. 3 and half No. 4 Companies. As it had not succeeded, no further reinforcements were sent up in the face of such heavy fire and a searchlight, which now began to play all over our front.

After this failure, orders were received for the 3rd Londons to relieve us, and for them to make another attack preceded by a bombardment at 3.15 a.m. The regiment was therefore accordingly withdrawn to the

"Orchard," close in rear in support. A certain amount of mixing up occurred here in the trenches owing to the heavy shelling of the "Orchard" by the enemy. Eventually we reorganised successfully.

The 3rd Londons were to deliver an attack in combination with the 2/3rd Gurkhas on their right, who had been sent up to replace the Leicesters. This was also unsuccessful, as the moment the men

CONCRETE MACHINE GUN EMPLACEMENT

in German trenches facing portion held by the 2nd Battalion covering Rue du Bois and Richebourg L'Avoué.

appeared a heavy fire was opened on them with rifles, machine guns and artillery. As it was now getting light nothing more could be done, and so orders came for the Regiment to withdraw to assembly trenches on the north side of the Rue du Bois, where it remained till 8.15 p.m. on the 16th, when it was withdrawn further back in reserve to bivouac trenches near Croix Barbée. Our casualties during the 15th-16th May were Lieut. Rogers wounded, Jemadar Padam Sing Rawat wounded, 15 rank and file killed and 136 wounded.

It is not surprising that we were not successful in this attack. As I saw this portion of the line during my visit in April, 1921, the whole German front at this part was very strong. Many deep and heavily constructed concrete dug-outs were at intervals all along the front, and here and there thick steel mantlets for observers to sit in and keep watch.

While in these bivouac trenches Captain Burton rejoined us from hospital. We moved into billets on the 17th close by the bivouac trenches, while the rest of the Brigade went into the front line trenches from the "Orchard" to the "Cinder Track," south of the Rue du Bois, while we acted as Divisional Reserve. Here Captain Kunhardt, 74th Punjabis, and Lieut. Lamb, I.A.R., joined the regiment as reinforcements on the 19th, and Lieut. Collins joined from the 9th Gurkhas on the 21st to complete our numbers.

Meanwhile the attacks continued by other Brigades, the other "Orchard," *i.e.*, "Leicester Orchard," lower down the line, being re-taken, though the Battalion immediately on the right of our Brigade had been unable to advance any more. So the two trenches, *i.e.*, the one on their left as far as they had advanced in their attack and ours on our right, were joined by a trench forming a sort of defensive flank. This ran up to the Boar's Head, as the particular point was called, opposite the German trench, which was marked V.1, and formed a right-angle bend at this part.

On 18th May the Indian Corps received orders to attack the Ferme du Bois in conjunction with attacks made by both the 7th Division and Guards Division further to the south. Attempts were made to advance with the progress made by the Guards Division, but all attempts failed, though a temporary success was gained by the 4th Gurkhas near the Ferme du Bois later on 21st May.

The Regiment remained as Divisional Reserve till the 25th, when it went up into the front line to relieve the Leicesters in what was now called "A" sub-section from the "Cinder Track" inclusive to "Copse" communication trench inclusive south of the Rue du Bois. Two attacks were made this night near Festubert by the 47th

GERMAN CONCRETE DUG-OUT

for Field Gun at corner of the Bois du Biez but with the concealing cover of grass and turf all washed off.

London and Canadian Divisions and some progress made. This date saw the end of the prolonged battle of Festubert, it having begun on 15th May.

While in Divisional Reserve the Regiment had furnished Companies to go up and clear the battle fields of Rue du Bois, where all this heavy fighting had taken place. A tremendous amount of debris, so to speak, is left after a battle. In addition to the dead, there are many wounded to be brought in, countless rifles and other equipment to be collected and returned, as it can all be done up and re-issued again, and the country thus saved expense.

Captain Burton was temporarily lent to the Highland Division to help on their staff, so Captain Harbord took over temporary command of No. 1 Company and Lieut. Fox joined headquarters to act as Adjutant vice Captain Etherton, who had gone to hospital with a slight attack of measles. Lieut. Tibbs, I.A.R., attached, was sent to act as Brigade bomb gun officer in place of Lieut. Mankelow.

The regiment remained in occupation of this portion of the front line till the end of May, when it was relieved and went into billets in Vielle Chapelle.

The original order was for the 57th Rifles to relieve us, but these were changed to the 4th London Regiment. These orders were again changed later, and our front ordered to be taken over by four different units—the 57th Rifles, 4th Londons, 129th Baluchis and the Connaught Rangers. The relief, therefore, took a long time, not being finished till 1.30 a.m. The last company got to billets at 2.30 a.m.

CHAPTER X.

Billets at Vielle Chapelle—Working Parties out Digging Trenches—Trenches again Rue du Bois—In support—and after in Front Line—Change of portion of Line to another less nice bit—Information received of certain Honours for Officers of the Regiment for Neuve Chapelle—Continued Shelling of our Line—Take over Temporary Command of Brigade during absence on leave of Brigadier—Billets again at Vielle Chapelle—Inspection of the Brigade by Lord Kitchener—Go back further to other billets at Heverskerque—Proceed on Short Leave—Captain Mainwaring rejoins—Visit of Sir John Hewett, late Lieut.-Governor of United Provinces India—Inspection of all Reinforcements by the Corps Commander—Bt.-Colonel Swiney rejoins Regiment—He is appointed to command all Convalescent Details and others from Marseilles as a Reserve Battalion—Command of the Garhwal Rifles remains with me—Go into the Front Line north of Neuve Chapelle.

AFTER the stirring times the Regiment had lately been through, we had a somewhat quieter time for a bit. We moved to some nicer billets at Vielle Chapelle, or a little beyond the village about one mile. We carried on the usual drilling and parades and furnishing large working parties whenever required. Practise was done with live bombs—the "jam pot" kind, "hair brush" and French pattern. We left our comfortable billets on 7th June to take over bivouac trenches in support of those in the front line, north of the Rue du Bois, near "Chocolate Menier Corner," so called because of a large advertisement of Chocolate Menier on the house at the corner of the cross-roads here on Rue du Bois. While here the whole Battalion formed working parties on a communication trench.

We were now in the middle of June. The weather was warm, the trees in full leaf and the orchards getting full of ripe fruits. As one went along a communication trench when such ran, as it did in parts, through an orchard, you could see the fruit over your head, and it could only be got either at night or by throwing something up at the branches. The birds, too, especially the skylark, were not, strange to say, at all deterred by the shelling. I suppose those that had not been killed must have got accustomed to it, as they soared up into the sky singing joyously as though no war was on. The flies, too, had now become rather bad. In some parts of the line, like near the part called the "Boar's Head," they were very bad. This was owing to so many men having been killed during the late attacks. You could easily track a man going down a communication trench by the cloud of blue bottles he disturbed. They swarmed and buzzed round him as he went along. At one part of the "Boar's Head," where the sandbags were white, as this had been a part of the German line and they used sandbags of any coloured cloth, they looked like black sandbags, but when you got up to them you saw that they were covered with big blue bottles, which swarmed up at your near approach, so saturated with human blood was this part of the line. The sanitation in the trenches had to be very carefully supervised. In billets the water supply was a difficulty, as in these parts, where there were only small villages and no big towns with a proper water supply, you had to rely, like the inhabitants, on either pumps in the farms, which were generally situated over the "midden," or get water from the roadside ditch. Therefore it had to be chlorinated. These "middens" were a great asset to the French farmer. He stored all his manure in it and kept it for his fields. But they produced flies in abundance, so orders were given to cover them all with earth after clearing them out and cleaning them. Notwithstanding all this the health of the Regiment, in fact, the whole Corps, all the time it was in France, had been excellent. In fact, it could not have been better, despite all the hardships and privations that had to be undergone. This speaks volumes for the care and supervision given by the medical officers and services.

The regiment left the support trenches on 18th June and relieved the 2/3rd Gurkhas in the front line, which ran along the part which had been captured in the battle of Festubert in front of the farm, Cour d'Avoué. While digging a new bit of front-line trench here to replace the old bit and a little nearer to the enemy's line, we found an orange-coloured insulated wire running under ground. We cut the same in case it might have been a mine or perhaps a telephone line, as it could easily be tapped if necessary by our Signalling Officer, but apparently it was unused and of no importance. Here we were very near to the German line and also to the Cour d'Avoué farm. The ground in front of our line was covered with long grass and was on a very slight rise, but yet enough to conceal us from each other. Consequently we had out, day and night, small patrols, which kept watch and remained hidden in the grass to our front. To our left was the Ferme du Bois. Both these farms were very strong posts of the enemy's and resisted all our attacks during the battle of Festubert. We had one or two small skirmishes with German patrols at this part, both during the day as well as at night. There were some old trenches and communication trenches which had formed part of their line before capture in the Festubert battle, and we both could take advantage of these as well as the folds in the ground and the long grass. It was a case of stalking each other. I know one time we got a few nice grenades of the "hair brush" pattern from them which a patrol dropped in their hurried retreat one day when ours fired on them. They were an excellent pattern, with an easy friction method of ignition and arrangement for hanging on to the belt.

Lieut. Clarke, our former Quartermaster, rejoined from hospital on 13th June, and joined No. 4 Company after an absence of nearly four months. Contrary to their usual practice, the Germans took to firing shrapnel and howitzer shells at intervals during the night. On the 22nd they did this every ten minutes, which interfered with working parties digging. On the 23rd we heard that we were to go into a different portion of the line, more to our left, from a point numbered R.5, along to the "Boar's Head," opposite point V.1, our line being continued by the 2/8th Gurkhas up to the "Hazara" communication trench and thence by the 3rd Londons on to the "Orchard." This meant our Corps line was somewhat lengthened out, which relieved other troops for another portion of the front.

While in occupation of this portion of the line the news was received of the awards of some decorations and rewards for the battle of Neuve Chapelle. A C.M.G. was given me; Captain Burton, 2nd Battalion, received the D.S.O.; Captain Blair, 2nd Battalion, a mention in despatches; while Jemadar Bishan Sing Rawat, 1st Battalion, and Jemadar Pancham Sing Mahar, 2nd Battalion, got the Military Cross. Major Stewart, 2nd Battalion, our Brigade Major, also was awarded the D.S.O.

There was a good deal of shelling by the enemy at parts of our line. There was a small projecting bit of trench which had been dug, and which was called the "Junior Duck's Bill," owing to its projecting so. The larger "Duck's Bill" was at another part opposite Mauquissart, north of Neuve Chapelle. This was eventually mined under by the enemy and blown up. This lesser "Duck's Bill" was frequently knocked in by heavy shells, or "crumps," or "Black Johnsons," or "Marias," as they were styled.

On 29th June our G.O.C. got short leave, so I had to go into Brigade headquarters to command temporarily in his absence, while Lieut.-Colonel Morris, of the 8th Gurkhas, commanded our section of the line. We did a lot of digging and revetting trenches while in this part, also making and finishing some small keeps which were called "Pall Mall" and "Ritz" and "Factory" posts.

The regiment was relieved by the 2/4th Gurkhas on 4th July and went to our old billets at Vielle Chapelle. Here the men had a good time at the baths and had clean kit issued to them. An inspection of all kits was made here, too, as was done frequently from time to time. It is very necessary on service to see that everything is in good order, that men are in possession of what they should be, and are not accumulating odds and ends of rubbish. I remember once at Richebourg St. Vaast we had to send some men off to our second line and, when inspecting them, I noticed that one man's haversack looked uncommonly large, so made him turn out the contents. This he did slowly and reluctantly, and this is what it contained in addition to what it should have:—Three Balaclava caps, four pairs of socks, 18 boxes of matches, and some other odds and ends, which included a bit of an old lace curtain. Men are very funny in this respect, and will keep all sorts of rubbish if not frequently inspected. I remember on one march a number of men of a certain unit fell out, and a similar state of affairs was revealed when their rucksacks were inspected. Here was the cause of so many falling out!

Besides the usual parades held daily the regiment furnished, as usual, large working parties for digging near the front line every night.

On 8th July the Brigade was inspected by Lord Kitchener. We marched at 9.45 a.m. to the rendezvous, and returned at 12.45 p.m. This was his first visit to us. He came again in September.

We now left Vielle Chapelle and were sent further back to other billets at Haverskerque, which place was reached at 5.30 a.m. on the early morning of 10th July, having been relieved at very short notice by the Royal Scots Fusiliers at 11.30 p.m. on the 9th.

This was a pleasant place and well in rear. Here short leave was again opened and officers proceeded in turn. Captain Mainwaring rejoined the regiment here and took over the duties of adjutant from Captain Etherton. Also Colonel Swiney came back to the regiment. Both these officers had been wounded at the battle of Neuve Chapelle. Colonel Swiney was appointed by the Corps Commander to command a battalion of convalescent details to form a reserve battalion, while the command of the combined Battalions remained with me.

We were also inspected by the Corps Commander at this time, and especially all the reinforcements that we had received.

Altogether we had been in these billets for twelve days and had had a most comfortable and quiet time. Now orders arrived on 21st July for us to take over the front line again to the north of Neuve Chapelle. On this date we all went over to Estaires and then down to the right sub-section to see and arrange what we could, remaining in Estaires, as the distance we had to go was about ten miles and too far to return that night. So the regiment came on next day with the 2/8th Gurkhas, under the senior officer, and reached our billets near Laventie at 9.30 p.m. The next day, 22nd July, we relieved the Black Watch in " D " sub-section, completing the relief at 12.30 a.m.

CHAPTER XI.

Occupation of the Line facing Mauquissart—Attached to Sirhind and Bareilly Brigades for a short time—Usual period of rest at Pont du Hem—Help French Farmers in Harvesting Crops—Relieved by the 1st Seaforths—Take over another portion of the Front by Fauquissart—Heavily shelled by Minenwerfers and Howitzers—Officers of Kitchener's Army attached for instruction for a few days—Departure of M. Brée, our Interpreter—The Indian Mule is changed for Limbered Waggons for Machine Guns—Receipt of Her Majesty Queen Alexandra's and late King Edward's Birthday Cards—Preparation for another Battle.

THE part of the line called "D" sub-section we were now in had never been occupied by us before. Our regimental headquarters were far back on the Rue du Bacquerot, which necessitated a long tramp over the open fields, which were frequently shelled, to get to the communication trench which would take us up to the front line. Half-way up was a small post, or strong point, one of a number in our second line, which we occupied with a platoon. One of these occupied by us called South Tilleloy post, had a 4.2 howitzer shell dropped clean into the middle of it, luckily without harming any of the garrison. One did not get to the communication trench leading to the front line till one reached the main road called Tilleloy Road. It led past what had once been a very fine farm, called on the map Ferme Vanbiesan, and which we called on our maps "The Moated Grange."

A trench for local reserves was required much nearer than where our regimental headquarters were situated. A line called Line "B" was being constructed a short distance back from the Rue Tilleloy which, when completed, was to be made use of.

Our regimental headquarters were situated in an orchard where there was a small pond. In this pond were a pair of moorhens which, somehow, had remained there notwithstanding that shells had fallen right into the pond, made huge holes and blown the mud all about.

Our local reserve was placed close to our headquarters in a garden just to the south of the main road where a farm, called Min Farm, had once been. This the enemy shelled one morning on 26th July. Our first line transport was also in a ruined farm on this Rue du Bacquerot, some distance down towards the La Bassée Road, and was shelled one day, three followers being wounded. Each day we were subjected to some shelling by the enemy at regimental headquarters and Min Farm.

All this time we had been attached to the Sirhind Brigade, under General Walker, V.C. When that Brigade went into billets we remained on and came under the Bareilly Brigade for a short time. General Walker, V.C., just before leaving the front line with his Brigade, came round and met me on my rounds. He was kind enough to say how pleased he had been to have had us attached to his Brigade.

We noticed some pipes lying on the enemy's parapet while in occupation of this line, which was reported, and our 9.2 howitzers were put on to them, which soon made them pull them in. It was thought at first that they might have been for use with gas. On 30th July the limits of our front were altered to "Sign Post Lane" (inclusive) on the right, to "Winchester" road (inclusive) on the left. On 1st August the enemy shelled our headquarters and the ruined house where we had our mess. They commenced at 8 a.m.—only a few minutes before we generally went in for breakfast. They made one direct hit on the part where we had breakfast laid out. It blew up and twisted all the aluminium utensils and coloured the bread man-of-war grey. Another minute or two and we would have been seated there, which would have been very unpleasant! In the afternoon we took over the part held by the Leicesters, and they took over our part. In the night we were relieved by the 2/8th Gurkhas. All being finished by 11 p.m., we got off to billets at Pont du Hem. Billets here were a bit tight, one Company, No. 3, having to remain out in the open all night on 3rd August till room could be found in the other houses by squashing men up a bit. Captain Kunhardt was taken to act as Brigade Grenadier Company Commander. Lieut. Clarke was also attached to the Company, and proceeded with one N.C.O. to a school of instruction near Estaires. Twenty men from each Battalion in the Brigade formed the Company. Here we were visited by the official photographer to the Government of India, Dr. Girdwood, who took some cinematograph photographs

GROUP OF OFFICERS THE GARHWAL RIFLES.

Taken at Pont du Hem, August, 1915.

Capt. D. Blair, Capt. G. W. Burton, D.S.O.,
Lt. R. Lamb, Lt. A. E. Clarke, Capt. F. N. Fox, Capt. P. T. Etherton, Capt. G. R. Mainwaring,
Lt.-Col. D. H. Drake-Brockman, C.M.G.,
Lt. R. T. Collins, Capt. G. L. Duncan, I.M.S., Lt. Rana Jodha Jang Bahadur, M.C.

of the Battalion marching and in the trenches and groups of British and Garhwali officers and some of the men. Besides the usual parading daily the men were employed in making wire balls to throw outside the parapet amongst the wire entanglements in order to make it more effective. These could easily be thrown out without one having to expose himself. Working parties were also furnished daily to dig or improve communication trenches, &c. On three occasions the whole Battalion was out digging near the front line.

On 8th August we went further back to billets at Riez Bailleul, and the 1st Seaforths took over those at Pont du Hem. Their C.O. was good enough to say they were the cleanest he had ever taken over. Here we were able to benefit by the baths at L'Estrem, which the men wanted very much. Men were also again inoculated, as well as the British officers.

The crops in the fields were well advanced in these parts and also up as far as Pont du Hem, so to aid the farmers we sent large batches of men under British officers to help cut their crops. This was work our men were very *au fait* with, as they are of the cultivator class in their villages.

While here we received the news that Subadar Major Nain Sing Chinvarh and Subadar Makar Sung Kawar, both 2nd Battalion, had been awarded the Order of British India, 2nd Class, with the title of Bahadur.

On 16th August we again went into the front line and took over a part still further north, extending from Bedford Road on the right to approximately the Rue Masselot on the left, by Fauquissart. This was certainly quite the nicest bit of the line that we had hitherto been in. Headquarters was in a dug-out behind a ruined house in a delightful orchard close to the front line, and a long communication trench ran back to the junction of the Rue Masselot with the Rue

THE GARHWAL RIFLES MARCHING DOWN THE LA BASSEE ROAD, August, 1915.

du Bacquerot, where we had a small detachment in a post in an orchard. This portion was the furthest north ever held by us.

On the 19th the enemy gave us a good dusting with minenwerfers. The larger size of this "delectable instrument of war" carries a large bottle-shaped missile which you can easily spot coming through the air as the velocity is not very great, its extreme range being, I believe, only 600 yards. This is a great convenience, as when they alight they burst with an appalling crash and the splinters of the shell make a frightful wound, so one can quickly withdraw to either side while that portion is being shelled.

We were treated to this from 4.45 p.m. to 7.15 p.m., and so our men were quietly withdrawn to one side while they harmlessly bombarded that portion of our trench. In order not to give away the position of the minenwerfers when fired, they fired a 5.9 howitzer almost at the same time as they discharged the former, so as to disguise by its explosion the discharge from the minenwerfers. They fired about 80 shells that evening. One of the minenwerfer shells blew a willow tree near our support line right into the air, making a huge hole. We suffered only six casualties and had six rifles damaged, which was due to the men having been slightly withdrawn to one side while it went on, and to our being able to spot the direction they came from. A portion of our parapet was damaged, but the majority of the shells fell just behind the front parapet, making huge holes. It was difficult repairing the damaged portion of the parapet at night, as the enemy kept up a rifle and machine-gun fire on it. However, we managed to repair it sufficiently so that by daylight we had good cover.

On 20th August we had attached to us for instruction for 48 hours four officers of the 6th Wilts Regiment of Kitchener's Army.

During this night, while our working parties were out, the enemy opened a heavy bombardment on our trenches at 10.30 p.m. with 5.9 howitzers and some field guns, but chiefly on our support and communication trenches, where we had our working parties. In the intervals they opened rifle and machine gun fire. Another extraordinary instance occurred of a shell exploding right in a dug-out where a man was sitting, but without killing him. He was only severely bruised.

Orders came on the 21st for Captain Harbord to join the 1/4th Gurkhas, who were going to the Dardanelles. I was sorry to lose him. The four officers of the 6th Wiltshire Regiment left the next day and four more from the Loyal North Lancashire Regiment joined for instruction for the same period of 48 hours. On the 23rd we received orders that the 6th Battalion Oxfordshire Light Infantry would relieve us on the night 27th-28th. We also heard the welcome news that the Russians had sunk in the Baltic one Super Dreadnought, two cruisers and seven destroyers of the German Fleet and had repulsed a landing at Pernau in the Gulf of Riga, in which the Germans lost all their boats. As the Leicesters had received orders on our right to send up, as an experiment, a white rocket, we took the opportunity of cheering when it went up, which was carried a long way down our line, in honour of this naval victory.

The officers of the relieving Regiment came round on the 24th to see the line and make preliminary arrangements. Also four more officers from the South Lancashire Regiment were attached for instruction.

As the Germans never got really true news, I wrote a short account in German of this Russian naval victory and our scouts at night stuck the letter, with a copy of "Life," an American paper, on a stick in front of their line for them to take in. The next morning when I looked it had gone! Some of the cartoons in the paper were very funny and not altogether complimentary to the German. It was in this part of the line that our scouts captured a German flag which was stuck up outside their parapet and which now adorns the Mess at Lansdowne.

On the 26th the Regiment was relieved by 9.15 p.m., and the Companies had a long march back to billets at La Gorgue, where we were billeted for one night in a large, fine, and most comfortable farmhouse, arriving at 1 a.m.

The next day our French interpreter, M. Brée, left us to go back to Madagascar to his business, as the French Government required his services there. We were very sorry to lose him; he was such a nice officer, and a very sound one, too.

On 28th August we relieved the 1st Gurkhas in the trenches just south of Neuve Chapelle, facing the Bois du Biez. Our regimental headquarters were in a dug-out in a small orchard which the 2nd Battalion attacked on 10th March. There was a good deal of confusion on the road with all the traffic of troops and rations to and from the trenches.

A deserter from the enemy said that the Germans were bringing up liquid fire and gas in their front opposite us. However, I am glad to say it was not used, if his statement was true. It gave the authorities, however, some anxiety, and a new pattern smoke helmet was issued, as another deserter of a Bavarian regiment also said that a lot of gas cylinders had been brought up on our front. On 1st September the 47th Sikhs relieved us, and the Regiment got back to billets at the same farmhouse at La Gorgue at 2 a.m.

Here we furnished fatigue parties as usual. One of 300 men went out on the night of the 3rd and had to march six miles before commencing work, and the men got wet through in the rain, and only got back to billets at 3.20 a.m.

We were at last supplied with limbered wagons for the machine guns, and so the faithful old Indian "khachar," or mule, with his pack saddle, was sent away.

A large number, 558, of birthday cards of H.M. Queen Alexandra and the late King Edward VII. were received for distribution to the men.

Arrangements were gradually being made now for another big attack in conjunction with other British Divisions on the German positions right down as far as Loos and Hulloch, and in conjunction with an attack made by the French.

On 10th September I went round the front line, accompanied by Captain Etherton, reconnoitring the whole of it and the communications. The same day all Garhwali officers, under Lieut. Rana Jodha Jang Bahadur, went to see an experiment with gas and its effect on men wearing gas helmets. The Garhwal Brigade relieved the Dehra Dun Brigade in the trenches facing Mauquissart on the night of 12th September, taking over the line from Sign Post Lane to Moated Grange Street. We, with the 3rd Londons, being in the front line and support with one campany each of the Leicesters, 2/3rd and 2/8th G.R. in local reserve, all under my command. The remainder of the 2/8th Gurkhas were in line B as Brigade reserve to be called upon by me if necessary. Work was continued hard upon the front line in view of the impending operations, making extra trenches or deepening those in rear of the fire trench. The Londons did good work on the "Duck's Bill," and the Leicesters worked away hard, doing good work, as they always did, on the trenches given them to improve. A gun emplacement for a field gun was also made near the entrance to the "Duck's

Bill " by Sign Post Lane, as it was proposed to use this gun in the fire trench at this close range in order to breach the ememy's parapet. A large new aid post was also made, and all communication trenches much improved to aid the traffic problem, having separate ones for up and down traffic.

On the 18th we were relieved by the 4th Seaforths and proceeded to the same billets at La Gorgue. Here we received a reinforcement of two British officers and 218 rank and file. Renewals of clothing and boots were issued and general preparations made for the coming operations.

It was while in occupation of that part of the line facing Mauquissart that our Chaplain asked me to put up a cross which he gave me over Major Becher's (2nd Gurkhas) grave, which was in the garden of the small house on " Sign Post " Lane, called Pump House. (See map of Battle of Piétre). He had been killed in the early days of the war in November, 1914, while gallantly defending that portion of our line against which the Germans had made a determined attack.

CHAPTER XII.

Brigade marches to Rendezvous at Pont Rouchon for Inspection by Lord Kitchener—Rehearsa by Brigade in getting into position for the intended Operations—Regiment goes into bivouac at Bout Deville—Heavy rain while in bivouac—Trenches full of mud and water—Regiment detailed at Brigade Reserve—Occupation of the Front Line preparatory to the Attack—Mine under the German Salient on " Winchester Road " sprung as the signal for the Attack to commence—Action at Piètre by the Indian Army Corps being part of the Battle of Loos—Withdrawn after the Battle to billets at Harrow Road and then Regnier L'Eclerq.

WHILE in billets at La Gorgue, general preparations went on for the forthcoming battle in having a general clean up and issuing new boots and clothing. All reinforcements were inspected by the Corps Commander. Orders also came for the inspection of the Brigade by Lord Kitchener at 10.30 a.m. on 20th September. The Regiment left at 9 a.m. for the appointed place of inspection at Pont Rouchon. His Lordship was due at 10.30 a.m., but did not arrive till 11.50 a.m., being delayed en route unavoidably. The Brigade was drawn up in line of battalions. each Battalion having its companies in line of quarter column of platoons. He inspected each unit minutely. On arrival at the Regiment he spoke only a few words, but what he did say was most complimentary. He said to me that the " Garhwalis have made a great name for themselves and done very well, better than the others." The Army Commander, General Sir Douglas Haig (afterwards Field Marshal Earl Haig) also added " Yes, and all through the campaign." This eulogy coming from such high officials was most gratifying. He spoke a few words to Lieut. Rana Jodha Jang Rahadur, a relation of the Rajah of Tihri Garhwal, and who was attached to the regiment. The death of this great man some time later by drowning in the " Hampshire " was an irreparable loss. What the country would have done without him goodness only knows. It is something to be thankful for that he was spared till he had started and got well under way that great army which bore his name and which saved the situation. At night a rehearsal of taking up our positions in front line took place.

All units were again practised getting into position on the night of 21st September. The 22nd and 23rd were fine, though cloudy days, but on the night of the 23rd, when the Regiment went into bivouac at Bout Deville, heavy rain fell, making it most miserable for the men in their bivouac with the cold and mud. Preparations had been made to use poisonous gas in this attack if the wind was favourable. Cylinders were placed in the parapet well down to be secure against premature bursting by shell fire by the special detachments trained for this purpose. We also sent up ready in the trenches Vermorel sprayers with jars of anti-gas solution. The 24th broke a dull, wet, miserable day, and it rained all day. The men, considering the miserable time spent in the mud and rain in their bivouac, were uncommonly cheerful. There was nothing to do now but to wait till the evening, when we were to march to take up our position for the attack the next day. The regiment left bivouac at 7 p.m. The route lay down the Rue du Bacquerot for a short way, and then a long communication trench was entered which brought us up into the front line. The regiment was detailed to act first as Brigade reserve and to take up its position in the " Home Counties Trench." (See map of battle of Piètre). It was in position by 10.30 p.m. The communication trenches were extremely sticky. The clayey soil very nearly took the heel of one's boot off at each step, and it was necessary to screw one's heel round to prevent this.

Messages by telephone had to be sent periodically through the night saying what the strength and direction of the wind was, in order to see if it was suitable for the use of gas. What wind there was blew very faintly, and was not quite in the right direction for its use. Preparations had been made in operation orders for the attack to be with gas and without gas, by the issue

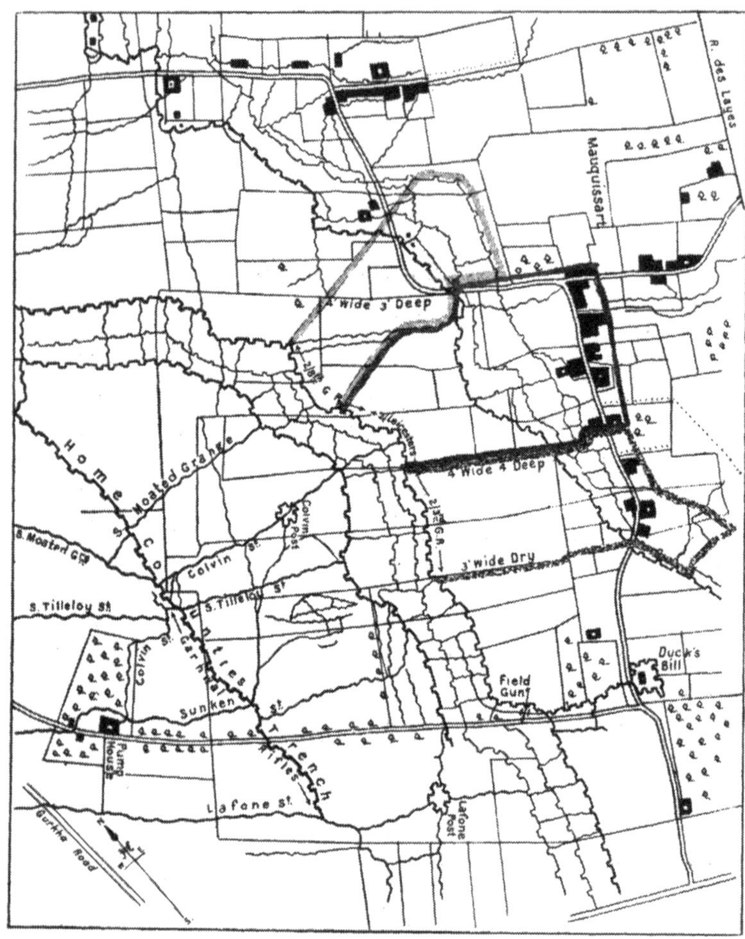

ACTION OF PIETRE.

Plan of the Battle of the 25th September, being a portion of the Battle of Loos, showing the part taken by the Garhwal Brigade of the Indian Army Corps. Sketch made from an Aerial Photograph.

of separate instructions, so it would have been quite easy for the attack to have taken place without the gas. In addition to the use of the poisonous gas, units on the flanks were detailed to light up smoke bombs in order to make out that it was real gas and to provide a good screen. This, as it happened, would have been best, and no gas at all used, as the wind for its successful use must be steady and of a certain gentle velocity so as to carry it forward to the hostile trenches. The net result of this, our first use of gas, was *nil*. Instead of going forward it hardly moved at all, but hung and came back a bit, with the result that our men fared worse from its use, I am afraid, than the enemy. During the bombardment that ensued an enemy shell burst one of our gas cylinders in the "Duck's Bill," where the 3rd Londons were, with the result that some of them were gassed.

The night passed without incident. Morning was beginning to dawn, and we made a hasty meal with a cup of tea and waited for the sound of the springing of the mine. Eventually this went off to time. One felt the earth tremble at the explosion. It was an excellent one, too. Those responsible for the mining had done it so well that the whole salient in the German line on Winchester Road had been mined right under, and it was blown clean up into the air. This lay opposite the Bareilly Brigade front. Away went the troops! The regiment, on the mine going off, immediately commenced filing out of the "Home Counties Trench" up the communication trenches allotted to it in order to get to our front line, which it was to hold from "Sunken Street" to the "South Moated Grange Street" communication trench. A rather long front for one battalion. I had not left the dug-out which my adjutant and I had occupied more than one minute when a 5.9 made a direct hit on it! The trenches were very narrow, and when other supporting troops began to arrive later, the congestion was something terrific. It made communication between me and my companies absolutely impossible. There was a check at the very commencement, as instead of finding the front trench clear of the attacking companies of the other units of the Brigade with the exception of the 2/8th Gurkhas who had all got off, there still remained some of the other two units, and this made it impossible for the Regiment to take up its allotted place. All this time the front line and support trench were being heavily shelled, which added to the confusion. Then wounded and half-gassed men of our attacking troops began to wander back, and augmented the congestion. Owing to the gas and smoke barrage the atmosphere was something like a November fog, one could not see very much at first. A few men of the Leicesters lost their way and took to an old trench in "No man's land" in the fog, thinking that it led on to the German trenches, but eventually found themselves coming out on our right at the "Duck's Bill." The 2/8th Gurkhas had done splendidly and got right into the German trenches. Their part of the front line being vacant, I was enabled to get one of my companies, No. 4, into position after some delay. The battalion reserve of the 2/3rd Gurkhas was still in hand, or some part of it, and these, with some of the Leicesters, made it difficult for the other companies to get into position, so they had to remain in the communication trenches and support line till the way was clear. I sent in a report to the Brigade by telephone. Owing to the regimental headquarters of the Leicesters still being in the front line and occupying the place where the telephone line was established with the Brigade, I had to get my message sent through their telephone, as I could not erect my own. A message came back some time later for me to organise two attacks of half a battalion each, with two bombing parties, to reinforce the 2/3rd Gurkhas on the right and the Leicesters on the left. Owing to the crowded state of the trenches it was impossible to get this done for a long time. It took a single man half-an-hour to get 50 yards. The two trenches were so narrow and so deep, and had been made so in anticipation of a heavy bombardment from the enemy, but it would have been better if they had been a bit wider to allow of men passing each other sideways at least. I remember a brawny Highlander trying to get along. He, with all his equipment, got stuck and he said to his pal behind, "Give us a shove, Jock!" This his pal did, with some result, for he gave him a hefty shove which fairly sent him along.

As the regiment was, I said above, spread out over a front of 600 yards about from Sunken Street to the South Moated Grange Street communication trench, it was a herculean task to get in touch with my company commanders, and as the two headquarters dug-outs of the two attacking units were still being occupied and which I had anticipated would have been empty and available for me and my telephone, added to the difficulty.

At this time now the Dehra Dun Brigade began to arrive and added still more to the congestion and confusion. They had been ordered to go forward and attack Haut Pommereau and La Cliquiterie. Fortunately I met the G.O.C. Dehra Dun Brigade coming up near my place by No. 4 Company, which was in position, and pointed out the congestion to him, and that I had received orders to organise an attack, but the arrival of his Brigade made it all the more difficult, as it increased the congestion in the already crowded state of the trenches, and that progress was impossible. The other unit of our Brigade also was asked to clear the front line in order to facilitate this. The G.O.C. Dehra Dun Brigade arranged to clear his troops off to the left and leave our area clear. In the meanwhile time had been going on. What had been happening on in front it was impossible to say. I had sent up to the 2/8th Gurkhas a platoon with extra ammunition. This had been kept there by the senior officer on the spot of a unit of the other Brigade, and so did not return, at least only one or two did eventually. It was from this platoon that the only prisoners of war of the Regiment were ever taken.

It began to get a bit clearer later on when the smoke and gas had cleared away somewhat, and one was then able to see the hostile trenches. I noticed on a portion of the German trench that a small red, white and black flag was flying on the parapet. So the line at that portion which would have been opposite the centre unit of the attacking troops of our Brigade, could not have been occupied by us, or, if it had been, those that had got in must have been killed or captured. Anyway, bullets now began to hit along our parapet from machine guns, which showed that the Germans must have got back to their original line, if they ever had been driven out of it at the commencement. Messages from the Brigade were sent to me, but owing to the frightful congestion, never reached me till very late, long after the fleeting opportunity had passed and which, if one had been able to seize at the commencement, might have been attended with successful results.

It was not till 2.30 p.m. that I had gathered my companies from the other part of the line and got them in readiness for an attack. The G.O.C. Dehra Dun Brigade also, it appeared, had been directed to organise an attack, too, so as we were ready at the same time I suggested that both should take place together. I am afraid that such an attack without any artillery preparation against a trench which was occupied by the enemy had not much chance of success. However, No. 4 Company, with another of the 2nd Gurkhas of the Dehra Dun Brigade, went over the top. Immediately a strong fire broke out from the hostile trench, men falling in the act of climbing over the parapet. I saw, and the G.O.C. Dehra Dun Brigade concurred, that it was a useless sacrifice of life to send any more over, so the attack was stopped. Our men got about 40 yards off, and then those who were not hit crawled in the longish grass and some light folds of the ground for cover. These leading platoons that attacked were under the command of Lieut. Rana Jodha Jang Bahadar, and right well he led them. I am glad to say that this officer was awarded the Military Cross later for gallantry again at Givenchy in October.

It was now beginning to get dark, and those that were still out and alive were withdrawn under cover of darkness. To make matters worse and more uncomfortable it began to rain very heavily about 6 p.m., and fairly made a climax to our discomfort, for the trenches were like rivers, over knee-deep in running water and mud, and made any progress along them a great labour. I shall never forget the great discomfort of that day and night. I got the Regiment eventually re-organised, and we held the same length of front of the fire trench, *i.e.*, from Sunken Street to South Moated Grange Street, for the night, the other three units of the Brigade, or what remained of them, going back into support. A miserable night was spent and our rations came up with difficulty. The total casualties of the regiment came to one British officer wounded (Captain Kunhardt attached and commanding the Brigade Grenadier Company) and 77 rank and file, and this with only a portion having taken part in any forward movement. The heavy shelling was responsible for the majority of casualties. This part taken by the Indian Corps was styled the "Action of Piètre," being a portion of the battle of Loos. Captain Kunhardt, who was wounded while in the front trench, had a narrow squeak. He was taking a look over the top and I warned him that there was a sniper paying a good deal of attention to that particular spot. However, he had his look, and almost at the same moment he got a bullet in his chin which knocked him clean over as if Jack Johnson had given him one under the jaw! Poor Captain Romilly also was killed about the same spot while looking through a machine gun loophole. He was then acting as Adjutant of the Leicesters.

The other Brigade on our left had made greater progress on its front, some getting very nearly up to the Moulin du Piètre, the objective, but unfortunately they were eventually forced to retire owing to the Germans being heavily reinforced, and who then managed to regain all their lost trenches. But they had done magnificently.

Morning broke at last, but there was still the same lowering overcast sky and another miserable day was spent. The enemy started in the morning to send over some 45 big minenwerfer shells. A few of them fell unpleasantly close to where I had my headquarters, which was in a miserably damp dug-out just off the fire trench. I was much relieved when they ceased, for there was nothing that I disliked more than this big "Minnie," more even that the big howitzer shells!

Orders came along later in the day for our relief by the 2nd Gurkhas. This was carried out by 4.30 p.m., and the last Company reached billets in Harrow Road by 6.30 p.m.

The men now got a good rest and clean up after their very damp and muddy experiences of the past few days. Good news was heard of the French success down in Champagne, many guns and some 20,000 prisoners having been taken, which helped to cheer us up. The weather still continued wet and stormy. Brigade headquarters went back to Calonne on the afternoon of 29th September. A platoon under a British officer which had been sent to garrison "Min" Post on the Rue du Bacquerot, rejoined on the evening of the 28th on relief by men of the King's Own Shropshire Light Infantry.

It rained again heavily during the night of the 29th, but the 30th broke fine and clear, with a cold north wind blowing. During the morning orders came for the regiment to march at 2 p.m. to new billets at Regnier L'Eclerq between Merville and Calonne. We arrived after a cold march of nine miles at 5.15 p.m. Here the billets were very nice and comfortable, and in the particular farmhouse where I had my quarters the lady of the house was a most kind and motherly soul. Nice hot coffee was made at once for me on arrival, and the French *do* know how to make good coffee, and I was most comfortable. On our leaving she was good enough to tell me that the men had been so good in her barns, &c., so different from some units, which she said differed a lot.

CHAPTER XIII.

Lieut. Clarke taken to command the Brigade Grenadier Company, vice Captain Kunhardt, wounded —Extra Regimental Appointments like these deplete a unit—Billets changed to other at Mesplaux—Another Reinforcement of two British Officers and 72 rank and file join the Regiment—Receipt of Rucksacks—Regiment goes into other billets at Essars—Major Lumb rejoins the Regiment—Regiment takes over Trenches covering Givenchy on 11th October—Captain Burton killed by a shell—Demonstration by Indian Corps to aid attack by Forces south of La Bassée Canal—A Persistent Sniper near edge of Canal spotted—Regiment is relieved and takes over Trenches in its old spot, the Rue du Bois, on 20th October—Final relief after nine days and billets in King's Road.

OUR stay at the comfortable billets at Regnier L'Eclerq was of short duration, being only three days. While here, owing to Captain Kunhardt having been wounded, I had to supply another officer on 1st October to command the Grenadier Company, so Lieut. Clarke was sent. This taking of officers from a unit, though perhaps in some instances is unavoidable, as officers have to be found somehow, depletes a unit of its more experienced officers, as one only got new hands in their places. Second-Lieut. Rana Jodha Jang had now to command a company. The Regiment now only had myself with three Captains, one of whom was Adjutant. All the others were junior Second-Lieuts. The last reinforcements received last month, too, were quite lads, whose training in India had to be rather more hurried through than would have been the case in peace time. It took quite nine months in peace time before one could attest a recruit, and then he was only beginning to learn his more serious work when he joined his company. However, they did very well, though naturally their stamina, being so young, was not as good as that of older men. On 1st October the Divisional General came round to see us all in billets. General Sir Charles Anderson had taken over the command of the Corps as Sir James Willcocks had been relieved in September, and General Jacob (now Field-Marshal Sir Claude Jacob) took over the Division.

On 3rd October the Regiment marched to other billets at a place called Mesplaux, between Locon and Rue du Bois, leaving at 12 noon, and took its place with other units in line of march of the Brigade. The route lay *via* Paradis and Locon. Here we did some parade work. Another detachment of 72 young soldiers joined us, with two more British officers, Second-Lieuts. Gore and Banon, the latter being an I.A reserve officer. We stayed here for five days and then moved to billets at Essars, near Gorre, preparatory to going into the trenches again, this time covering Givenchy. Men continued to go in batches for training to the Brigade Grenadier Company. Sounds of heavy firing were heard daily, showing a big battle to be in progress. In fact, it was practically a continuation of the battle of Loos-Hulloch. News was received that the German attack, which was made south of the La Bassée canal, had been repulsed with heavy loss. Rucksacks were received here. These I consider preferable to haversacks, especially for our hill men, who are accustomed to carry loads on the back.

On 10th October I was glad to get Major Lumb back. He had been away a long time, having been invalided some time in February. One had not too many experienced senior officers. The next day we took over trenches covering Givenchy, with our right resting on the canal bank. The German line here was some distance off, except on the left, where it drew gradually nearer till just beyond our left their line and ours almost touched each other and mining and counter mining were in progress. (See aerial map of trenches covering Givenchy). It was possible in this part to make the relief in daylight, owing to the rising ground on which Givenchy was built giving the necessary screen. The Regiment marched at 9.45 a.m., and the relief was completed by 1.30 p.m. Sounds of heavy bombardment went on all day. Regimental headquarters were situated behind a large slag heap some 300 yards distant behind the front line here, and we had our mess in a cellar of a ruined house close to the bank of the canal, and one of the main communication trenches up to the front line ran past the cellar. It was most amusing to see individuals going by.

AERIAL MAP SHEWING TRENCHES COVERING GIVENCHY, with Mine Craters, British and German, October, 1915, held by Garhwal Brigade.

They invariably peered into the somewhat dark interior, expecting to see some weird kind of troglodyte, or something, and owing to a stone exactly opposite the entrance slightly sticking up a little unevenly, they all tripped as they passed, nearly coming on their noses!

Near headquarters was a small, strong point garrisoned by a detachment of the 3rd Londons. Down on the banks of the canal anyone washing at the water, which was very low, and, owing to the curve the canal took at that point, was quite invisible. One day some men of the Londons were washing some clothes there. We had found an old German rifle grenade about the place, and I said to the Adjutant that he had better throw it into the canal. This he did, little expecting anything to happen. It fell into the water, but whether it hit anything hard I cannot say, but it went off properly and, owing to the confined space in which it exploded, with the high banks of the canal above, it sounded more like a field gun. Goodness, didn't those men take cover! They must have thought a German shell had come over.

The total strength of the Regiment was, at this time, only 589 rifles in the trenches.

We were occasionally treated to a little of the big "Minnie" here. One day one of its shells fell into the canal close to the right flank of our line. It blew a large stone right into the air some distance. It came hurtling down and fell into our trench without doing any harm. But the black mud which was blown up painted that portion of our trench man-of-war grey.

There was also a most persistent sniper at this part who was hard to spot. However one morning, looking with a periscope and powerful binoculars, he was spotted, and we got the field battery on to him, which put a stop to his sniping. Major Samuel, of the 3rd Londons, also got on to him with his telescopic rifle.

On 12th October, seeing, I suppose, some of our men carrying up corrugated iron sheets and revetting material which showed a bit above the top of the trench, the enemy commenced shelling with howitzers and, unfortunately, Captain Burton, who commanded the reserve Company, and who was superintending the work on the communication trenches at that place, was struck by one which came over and hit the edge of the top of the trench, blowing it in and killing him, I am sorry to say, and wounding others. He had done so well all along, and was one of the very few experienced officers I had left and had gained the D.S.O. for his good work and gallantry at the battle of Neuve Chapelle. He was a great loss. He was buried in a cemetery near Gorre.

Meanwhile, daily heavy shelling went on, our batteries behind us co-operating. From the top of the large slag heap in front of my headquarters I had a grand view. We had machine guns well concealed in this place, and by lying low one could see well from under cover for a long distance in the direction of Loos. The country over there looked so scarred and burnt up by the tremendous heavy shelling. It was as if a fiery furnace had passed over it. On 13th October we took a minor part to aid this attack by "make believe" in sending over phosphorus bombs which looked like a gas attack, and as if we were going to attack after it. At any rate it induced the enemy to open rifle and machine-gun fire all along his line in our front, and he also lit up fires along his parapet in order to disperse what he thought was gas. Heavy bombardments went on all day in the direction of the Hohenzollern redoubt and beyond, in which we heard that the enemy had suffered heavily. A letter taken from a German staff officer killed a short time before is of interest and runs: "An Army Corps Commander writes—'Please give instructions for a large number of proclamations to be issued to the Prussian soldier. I rely upon the secret order of the Emperor William on this subject being executed. It is necessary to do everything possible to weaken the Russian Army, which is escaping from our grasp and withdrawing to an unknown destination. Time is not far distant when our situation will become intolerable, and it is possible that we may be compelled to sign a Peace Treaty, of which the terms may be dictated by our enemies. Men who formerly had dreamed of conquering the world no longer think to-day of taking London, Paris, Petrograd: this task will be reserved for our grandsons and not for the heroic German warriors who are now sacrificing their lives on the endless fields of Russia.'"

This shows that even at this period the Germans were beginning to lose faith in their invincibility and in any chance of winning the war.

In this part of the line they were very fond of sending over several of that very nasty little thing, the rifle grenade. You could hardly spot them coming over like you could the minenwerfers. One day there was a meeting of the machine gun officers of the units of the Brigade towards the left of the Regiment's line and suddenly, out of the blue, came one of these nasty little things, hitting the parapet just where they were standing and talking, and killing two of them in its explosion. We retaliated with ours, but it was difficult to make very accurate shooting, at any rate with those which we had at that period of the war.

On 18th October we received orders to leave this part and go back to our old bit which we knew so well, covering Richebourg L'Avoué. Poor old shattered Rue du Bois, along which we had had many a weary trudge in the dark when relieving and being relieved by other units. We were relieved by one of the Battalions of the Buffs, whose officers came round to make the usual arrangements for taking over. We went into billets for the night of the 19th at Locon, and the next day took over the line extending from near the Cinder Track up past V.1, or "Boar's Head," and as it was now sometimes called, the "Glory Hole," on some distance towards the Ferme du Bois, relieving the 8th Gloucesters of the 19th Division. The line from near the Cinder Track made a right-angled bend, which was owing to the line having been advanced to the right of it during the battle of Festubert, while the other portion did not get on. The ground over which the attack was successful was saturated with human blood, as so many attacks, minor and major ones, had been made over it. When one went down the communication trench and up to the "Glory Hole" one could tell when anyone was coming or going by the cloud of bluebottles which, being disturbed, buzzed around the head. While on the "Glory Hole" itself, what one thought were black sandbags were only a mass of green bluebottles covering the white cloth!

The time spent here was quiet on the whole, beyond, of course, the usual daily shelling and sniping, and the usual casualties therefrom. The weather was not good—damp and misty and rainy—and the ground waterlogged.

At this time names to be submitted were called for from the Division for two Garhwali officers, as it was intended to send some Indian officers over to England in parties to see the country. However, before ours could go, as they did later, we had been all relieved and the Indian Army Corps left France for good, leaving only the Indian cavalry behind.

Our little dug-out which we used for our mess, notwithstanding being built up nearly all above the ground level, was six inches deep in water and was most uncomfortable. The C.R.E. who came round said he could do nothing, as it would require an officer to do necessary levelling, and he could spare none, being short-handed, so we did the best we could. We were much occupied all this period in the trenches in doing many repairs and finishing the small strong posts made in the support line. We were relieved by the Leicesters on 28th October on a dull, wet, and miserable day. The trenches fell in many places and needed constant attention day and night. The Regiment went into billets in King's Road, close to Le Touret and Rue du Bois, which did not hold them all, so some bivouacked in dug-outs and trenches dug in rear as a second line. Men from here went out nightly working on the communication trenches, which were full of mud and water.

On 1st November intimation was received that the Meerut Division would embark shortly at Marseilles for "an unknown destination." Rain continued almost daily, so that no parades or work could be done, though at night, whatever the weather was, working parties had to be sent out revetting communication trenches or acting as carrying parties for the sappers.

Short leave was opened, and so we started to go in batches. I went off on ten days this time as special concession, as I had been out the whole time and not absent for any period. Others went off, too. Unfortunately, after my third day at home I got a telegram ordering me to return at once, so my special ten days did not come off. I only got the telegram just in time to enable me to catch the only train and boat that would have enabled me to rejoin in time, getting it while in my bath just before breakfast. However, I managed to catch it all right, and I arrived back in France at a small station just before you get to Aire, and walked the two miles to Pecqueur, where I arrived at 2 a.m., finding the regiment in good billets there, and where it had marched to on 3rd November. By the night of 6th November all officers had rejoined from leave, and orders came for us to entrain at Thiennes railway station on 7th November, at 6.25 p.m. We were seen off by the Corps Commander, General Sir Charles Anderson, who had relieved Sir James Willcocks, and our Brigadier, General Blackader. We took with us 100 men of the Leicestershire Regiment. Just before we left we received a most complimentary message addressed to the whole Brigade from the Field Marshal Commanding-in-Chief Sir John French (afterwards Lord French), complimenting us all on the excellent work done and wishing us success. (Appendix III.).

We were very sorry to say farewell to Sir Charles Anderson, who was now our Corps Commander. I especially was sorry to leave his command, as I appreciated his qualities as a commander and soldier, which gave us all such confidence in him. The Meerut Division was indeed fortunate in having had him so long as its commander, and the Corps, too, for the remainder of the time that we were in France.

The railway journey was not very comfortable, though the French railway authorities did all they could and the arrangements for the men left nothing to be desired. But the British Officers had to get their food as best they could by rushing out to some inn or estaminet for it, as there were no arrangements made for them, and there was not always too much time after one had seen one's men properly fixed up. This is a matter that should not be overlooked, as they require food, &c., just as much as the men, but in Indian regiments where all that is necessary is done for the men's comfort, the British Officer is often quite forgotten.

We arrived at Marseilles on 10th November at the Gare d'Arenc at the very inconvenient hour of 2 a.m., being some hours late. We marched at once to the docks close by and embarked on two ships, headquarters and half on the "Aronda," on which General Blackader with his staff also came, and the other half embarked with the 2nd Gurkhas, on our old friend the "Coconada."

The voyage was uneventful, no submarines being sighted, though a vessel employed as a cruiser came close to us and informed us that one had been sighted off Cape Ras-el-Tin on the coast of Africa, about 80 miles distant.

We touched at Alexandria on the 15th for orders, as no one seemed to know what our destination was, and we were told that we had better have gone on to Port Said. An A.P.M. came on board to arrest any civilians, and it appeared there were two newspaper boys on board, who were taken off. Orders came eventually, and we left at 4.30 p.m. the same day for Port Said, where we arrived the next morning at 5 a.m. The "Coconada" was behind us, as she was a much slower ship, and, as she had all our mess kit on board, we were rather out of it, but owing to the kindness of the 56th Rifles stationed there, and whom we relieved, we were allowed to use their mess till ours arrived, but unfortunately it had all been put with the 1st Line Transport on some other boat, the "Urlana," so we had to hire the essential things. The Regiment camped temporarily on the sand near Port Said railway station.

CHAPTER XIV.

Regiment takes over Detachments held by the 56th Rifles—General Blackader hands over command of the Brigade to Major-General Sir Vaughan Cox, K.C.M.G.—Brigade Headquarters is stationed at Kantara—Usual routine of parades daily—Entrenchments at each place held by the Regiment strengthened and improved—Redoubt at Salt Works partly washed away by the Sea—Visit Camp of Armenian Refugees—Troops of Indian Army Corps pass through on their way to Mesopotamia—Orders come for the Regiment to proceed to Ismailia—Entrains on 23rd December—News of the torpedoing of the "Persia," which had several of our officers on board—Colonel Swiney and Captain Lodwick drowned in "Persia"—Captains Lyell and Berryman saved and ordered to rejoin the Regiment—Regiment leaves Ismailia for Suez—Marches to El Shatt and thence to Aiyun Musa or Moses Well to garrison the defences there of No. 1 Section Canal defences.

NO time was lost now in getting out the detachments to relieve those of the 56th Rifles. First one under Captain Etherton took over the defences at the Salt Works. Another, under Lieut. Clarke, went to Ras el Aish, down the railway on the borders of the canal, and another to Tineh. That at the Salt Works consisted of a company, while the other two consisted of two platoons each. The rest of the Regiment remained in camp in the huts near the railway station and carried out usual routine work of parades, &c. Here we were in civilisation, being quite close to the town of Port Said, with its amenities. Tennis could be got if one wished, and so time passed quite quickly.

On 17th November General Blackader got his orders to return to France for a command there, so he handed the command of the Brigade over to Major-General Sir Vaughan Cox, but did not leave till 23rd November. The whole Brigade was very sorry to lose him. We all had great confidence in him as a man of decision and who knew his own mind. On wishing me "Good-bye," he said how sorry he was not to be able to see us all, but owing to the many detachments it was not possible. He also said that he could not sufficiently thank me and the Regiment for all that we had done for him.

Meanwhile there was plenty of work for the men to do who were on detachment, as all the defences needed improving and doing up very much. Part of the redoubt at the Salt Works got washed away owing to the high wind which drove the sea up against the north side, completely destroying it. Also the water was driven across the sandy spot behind the fort and cut off the detachment for a time. After getting material we repaired most of the damage done, but portion on the north, or sea front, required more skilled labour and heavy material. All along the front of these Salt Works was a great sheet of water which quite precluded any attack being made from that quarter, but lower down the defences were all actually situated on the canal bank, which could not, of course, properly defend the canal. Why the proper line some miles well ahead was not taken up originally one cannot say, but to try and defend any position, much less such a vital artery like the canal, by sitting on its banks, was impossible. What was eventually done, viz., a line taken up well ahead, should have been done at first, but perhaps it was more comfortable sitting on its banks! No wonder the Turks could get right up to it without any losses. Why they did not bring up some heavy howitzers and sit some nine miles off and perpetually shell the canal I can't conceive, as that alone would have made it impassable for traffic. It would have been very easy for them with aeroplanes to spot when any traffic was going down and shell them.

Opportunity was taken while here to visit the Armenian refugee camp. There were about 4,000 of them in it, men, women and children, and all were well looked after, even down to Red Cross nurses, some of whom, I think, were Armenians trained by the French. They had all been brought by a French man-of-war to save them from the oppression of the Turk.

There were now six commands in Egypt. They were Cairo District, Alexandria District, Western Frontier Force, Canal District, Fayum and Inspector General Canal District. This last-named one was taken over by General Sir V. Cox and our Brigade by Lieut.-Colonel Smith, of the 2nd Rajputs.

Orders were received to send two platoons

ARMENIAN REFUGEES AT PORT SAID.

with ten days' rations further down the line to a place called El Ferdan, to increase the garrison there, but when all preparations had been made, and the detachment was on the point of embarking, a message was received countermanding its move. They were just caught in time before they got off.

All this time, units of the Indian Army Corps kept arriving and passing through on their way to Mesopotamia. The Meerut Divisional Staff, with Bareilly and Dehra Dun Brigade Staffs, also came through on 14th December.

On 20th December advanced parties of a British Division arrived, and we had to move our men into other huts to make room for them. This undoubtedly looked like being relieved soon. On 21st December the Jullunder Brigade passed through on its way to Mesopotamia, and also the 31st British Division arrived and commenced disembarking and putting up their camp here. Orders came at the same time for our relief by a unit of the 93rd Brigade of this Division, and for the regiment to proceed to Ismailia. All our detachments were now relieved except the one at the Salt Works, which was relieved later and joined us on 27th December. Our train was very late, only arriving at 8 p.m. We got into camp at 9.30 p.m. All guards held by the Indian Base Depôt stationed here were taken over, and they came to a good lot, some 93 men daily. The camp was in a delightful spot under the tamarisk trees on the borders of the lake. There were tennis courts close by, which the club most kindly allowed us to use when we liked. Owing to the tall tamarisk trees very little of the town of Ismailia is visible from a ship, but it is quite a decent-sized place, and, like all French places, well laid out.

While here the balance of the Tihri Sappers and Miners, who were still with us, was sent off. They went on to Mesopotamia for their legitimate duty as Sappers. We were not to be left long here, for on 1st January we heard that the Regiment would proceed to Suez on the 3rd, and all the duties would be taken over by the Australian and New Zealand Corps stationed here.

We received the bad news while here that the " Persia " had been torpedoed in the Mediterranean, and, as she had on board several officers from our station of Lansdowne, we were very anxious for more news. Colonel Swiney and Captains Lyell and Berryman of our regiment were on board, and also Captains Lodwick and Fisher, of the 2/3rd Gurkhas.

We left Ismailia on 3rd January. It was a fine morning with a strong wind. The Regiment entrained at Moascar at 7 a.m., and the train left at 8 a.m., arriving at Suez at 1.30 p.m. On arrival the 2/3rd kindly gave us lunch and tea, and our camp was pitched next to theirs. It was here that we heard from them that a wire had been received from Fisher saying that both Lyell and Berryman and he were safe, but little hope for the others. This was most sad. Poor Colonel Swiney and Lodwick, after all they had been through, to get knocked out like this through such an act on the part of the enemy was bad luck. The transport was sent to Kubri, and thence it marched to El Shatt, where we picked it up on arrival. The 2/3rd left us here for Kubri. We gave 100 men to help load up their train as a friendly act to our old friends. We were sorry to lose them, as we had been associated together for so long. Originally we were to have gone over to Aiyun Musa by lighters to the quarantine station landing there, but the wind was too strong, so this was abandoned, and we went over to El Shatt on 8th January and stayed one night. The Brigade to which we now belonged was still the 20th (Garhwal Brigade) of the 10th Indian Division, under the command of Brigadier-General Watson, C.M.G., C.I.E., M.V.O.

A draft of reinforcements was received here under Lieut. Rogerson and 113 rank and file.

At El Shatt we had to wait till the camel transport came in from Aiyun Musa. It arrived at 10 a.m., but was not quite sufficient, so a little had to be left behind to come on the next day.

CAMP OF THE GARHWAL RIFLES AT SUEZ.

CHAPTER XV.

Arrival at Aiyun Musa, or Moses Well—Relieve the 69th Punjabis—2/3rd return and join the Brigade—Inspection by the C.R.A. and C.R.E.—Front is patrolled by Cavalry and Infantry Scouts—Entrenchment of the position commenced—Captains Lyell and Berryman rejoin—Reconnaissance under G.O.C. towards Bir Mabeuk—Inspection of the line by Major-General the Hon. Sir Julian Byng (now Lord Byng), with Divisional and Brigade Commanders—Usual Musketry and training continues concurrently with the entrenching of the position—Post at Point 198 commenced—Regiment takes over part commenced by the 2/3rd to finish—Exchange our Mark VII. Rifles and Machine Guns with the 14th Sikhs for their Mark VI. Rifles—Second Inspection by General Sir Julian Byng—Go for a short cruise with the G.O.C. in H.M.S. "Jupiter" —General Sir Julian Byng returns to France, and General Sir F. J. Davies takes over command —Rumours that we are to be relieved and return to India—Visit of His Excellency the Commander-in-Chief General Sir Archibald Murray, K.C.B.—Complimentary remarks by him—Orders for our relief and to march to El Shatt for embarkation in S.S. "Muttra"—Arrival at Bombay—Receipt of Telegram welcoming the Regiment back from the Commander-in-Chief in India—Intimation received from the Adjutant-General in India that the Second Battalion had been selected as His Excellency the Viceroy's personal escort at Simla—Address by the G.O.C., Bombay District—Leave in two trains for Lansdowne—Halt at Agra—Official Reception by the Commissioner representing the United Provinces Government and residents of Agra—Entertainment of the Regiment—Journey continued—Arrival at Kotdwara—Reception by Asst. Commissioner and the Garhwal Sabha—Arrival at Lansdowne—Reception by the Deputy-Commissioner, Garrison and Residents—Regiment divided up again into the two Battalions and settles down to re-organise and train for further service.

THE Regiment left El Shatt on 9th January and marched to Aiyun Musa, reaching camp about 2.30 p.m. Aiyun Musa, or Moses Well, consists of low-lying sandy ridges, or undulations, covered with palm trees, forming an oasis. About a mile distant on the sea shore is the quarantine station. This grove of palm trees can be seen from the ship as you arrive at Suez. There are about twelve wells all together, formed in a rather curious way. The water seems to well up very gently. You can see it coming up, and it pushes up a little sand each time, which, I suppose, has, after so long a period, helped to form the small mounds where the so-called wells are situated. Most are in the grove of palm trees, and one or two are outside the grove.

C.O. Mainwaring, Actg. Adjt.

THE GARHWAL RIFLES ON THE MARCH

from El Shatt to Moses Wells.

AYUN MUSA OR MOSES' WELL.

Gore. Collins.

REGIMENTAL HEADQUARTERS CAMP, MOSES' WELL.

CAMP AT AYUN MUSA OR MOSES' WELLS, SUEZ.

The water is very brackish and unpalatable. It is only fit for washing and only just bearable when boiled for tea. The palm trees formed welcome shelter. There were some Sheik's houses situated in the biggest grove, which were used as mess houses. Under cover of the rising sandhill on which the groves were situated the camp of the Brigade was pitched, and so was under cover and hid from sight. In front there was absolutely no cover at all, and the dreary sand plain stretched away to the red-looking bare hills some ten miles distant, the plain being broken from about a mile off by sand hills, giving cover from view and also by some "Wadis," which ran out of the hills. It was very uninteresting country, and often hazy in sand storms. On our arrival a small portion of the front line had been commenced. However, the line chosen did not appear to all the C.O.s as the best line, so we asked to be allowed to entrench the front line further forward just on the crest of the low ridge, but just far enough back to be quite invisible without spoiling the extensive field of view and fire that was obtainable by entrenching at this place. This was agreed to, and we commenced in right earnest the work. We held this front line while it was under preparation also with a thin line of half a platoon from each company, the other half-platoon remaining in camp in a state of constant readiness, while scouts patrolled the front all night, only withdrawing at daylight.

The 2/3rd Gurkhas after all rejoined us here, at which we were glad, and remained in the Brigade. Each Regiment was on duty for a week and had to hold a post some two miles north by east of the camp, called Point 198 on the map. The Regiment also had to furnish a detachment of 100 men over at the quarantine station, where Brigade headquarters were situated.

During the day the unit on duty for the week sent out three covering parties some five miles to the front as supports for the cavalry patrols, who were out all day, to occupied points 250, 270 and 310 on the map. It was also decided to hold the whole Brigade front with one-and-a-half Battalions, with half-a-battalion garrisoning Point 198, the rest being Brigade reserve.

On 15th January Captains Lyell and Berryman rejoined. Glad they must have been after their very harrowing experiences in the torpedoing of the "Persia." The latter, I am glad to say, was awarded the Bronze Medal of the Royal Humane Society for his gallantry in being instrumental in saving the life of a French lady who was going out to join her husband at Calcutta. Berryman, now being the senior of the

CAMP OF THE GARHWAL BRIGADE AT AIYUN MUSA, OR MOSES WELL, NEAR SUEZ,

showing the portion of the position entrenched by the Garhwal Rifles and 2/3rd Gurkhas.

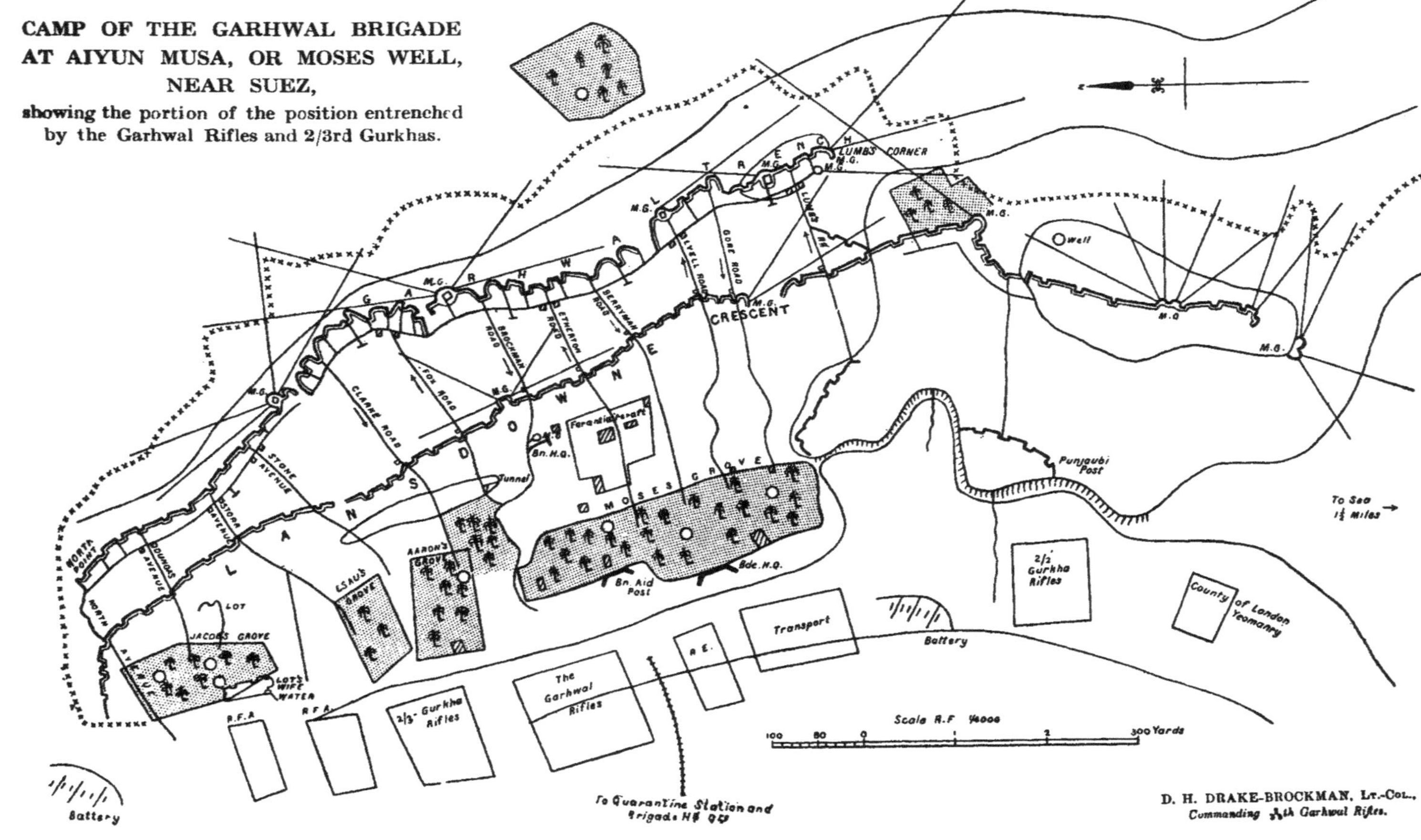

D. H. DRAKE-BROCKMAN, Lt.-Col.,
Commanding 1/39th Garhwal Rifles.

ENTRENCHMENTS AT MOSES' WELLS.

two Adjutants, took over the duties of Adjutant, and Lyell the command of No. 3 Company.

On the 17th the G.O.C., accompanied by the Brigade Major and two officers from each unit, made a reconnaissance escorted by a squadron of cavalry, towards Bir Mabeuk, about eleven miles distant. It was here that a strong party of Turks came down in their march towards and attack on the Canal some time before. Their entrenchments could still be seen. The ground was well reconnoitred to the west, so that in case of need all would be acquainted with the lie of it.

Work meanwhile had gone well on the entrenching of the position. We received two visits from Major-General the Hon. Sir Julian Byng—one on 19th January and again on 4th February. At the latter inspection he expressed himself as very pleased with the work done. By now the work on the entrenchments had proceeded so well that only three companies worked on them daily, while the fourth did drill and manoeuvre parades. One day we set apart also for Battalion training. The line was very well entrenched indeed, little or nothing being visible at all from the front. The front, too, was well wired. A place for Battalion and Brigade headquarters was dug and well revetted, also an emplacement for machine guns to be used for anti-aircraft purposes. An aid post was also established in rear and under cover of the palm grove. The 2/3rd now got orders to leave their portion of the line and to entrench with the Gwaliors, Point 198, so we took over their portion as well as our own to finish. The front was now divided into two sections, a battalion to each. One battalion to garrison Point 198 and the fourth held in reserve. Orders came later for rifles to be exchanged, so that all should have rifles of the same mark, that is for the same mark of ammunition. Ours were therefore handed over to the 14th Sikhs with machine guns, and we took their Mark VI. ones over in lieu. The balance required to complete us was received from the Ordnance Department. On 6th February, in order to settle with the senior naval officer the best point for H.M.S. "Jupiter" to remain in any attack, so that she could best cover our right flank by her fire, the G.O.C. and myself went for a short cruise in her down the coast. A spot near a point called on the map Ras Mesalla, was determined upon, and from here she could move up and down or anchor, whichever was thought best, and so cover effectually by fire our right flank from any enemy advancing from the direction of Nekhl.

General the Hon. Sir Julian Byng left the command of our corps, the 9th Corps, on 11th February, handing over command to Major-General Sir F. Davies, K.C.B. The latter inspected our line on the 12th,

REGIMENT MARCHING IN DESERT
beyond Ayun Musa or Moses' Wells, Egypt.

Berryman, Adjt. C.O. Mainwaring, M.G.O.

BUILDING REGIMENTAL HEADQUARTERS
in entrenchments at Moses' Wells.

MACHINE GUN EMPLACEMENT FOR ANTI-AIRCRAFT PURPOSES,
Moses' Wells.

and expressed himself highly pleased with what he saw. He considered everyone should come round and view our trenches to see what trenches should be like. He had lately received intimation that we, with others, would be shortly leaving Egypt for India. He would be sorry to lose us, having a great affection for the Garhwal Brigade, which had stood by him so often in France.

Several units had by now left, including the 2/8th Gurkhas. On 17th February we were asked for our numbers for embarkation, which looked more like moving soon. The weather all this time had been ideal. Only latterly had it been a bit cloudy with wind and some rain. It was an extremely healthy climate, and one felt very fit all the time.

On 22nd February we received a visit from His Excellency the Commander-in-Chief, General Sir Archibald Murray. He was accompanied by General Sir F. Davies, and on parting at the conclusion of his inspection was most complimentary, and said to me, "Excellent! I can say no better and no more! Excellent!" This was a welcome and gratifying reward for all the keenness displayed by all ranks in the good and hard work done on the entrenchments. On 24th February the transport arrived to take us over to El Shatt for embarkation at Suez. We were relieved by the Ulwar Imperial Service Infantry at 9 a.m., and we left at 11 a.m. The G.O.C., Brigadier-General H. D. Watson (now Major-General Sir Harry Watson) came to see us off, and wrote me a very nice letter of farewell, thanking us all for the good work done while under his command. (See Appendix III.). The 2/3rd Gurkhas gave us a grand send-off, lining the route out of camp and giving us three cheers, which was very nice and kind of them and more appreciated as they were our old friends.

It was a dusty march. We reached El Shatt at 2 p.m., camping to the north of the Brigade already there. Here we remained four days, embarking eventually in S.S. "Muttra." Kit was loaded up in lighters and sent off to the docks and loaded on board. The Regiment was on board by 3 p.m. After taking on board some 600 tons of high explosive ammunition for India, and when coaling was finished by 3 p.m. on 28th February, the vessel left for Bombay at 4.15 p.m. We were somewhat crowded on board, but this was due to a draft of reinforcements which had arrived for us rather too late and so had to return with us to India, and convalescents and other details. The strength of the regiment was now 16 British Officers, 20 Garhwali Officers and 1,310 rank and file.

The voyage was slow and uneventful; the weather delightful. Bombay was reached at 10.30 p.m. on 11th March. The ship went into the new Alexandria Dock the next morning at 6 a.m. A telegram was given to me immediately on tying up from His Excellency the Commander-in-Chief in India, which congratulated the Regiment on its deeds and welcomed us back to India. (Appendix III.). Also a letter from the Adjutant-General in India, informing me that His Excellency the Viceroy, Lord Chelmsford, had specially selected the 2nd Battalion to be his personal escort during the coming summer and following winter. All this was most gratifying. The G.O.C., Bombay District, Brigadier-General Knight, C.B., D.S.O., came on board to welcome us and addressed us all and the Garhwali Officers. Fruit and sweetmeats were handed round to all the men. In the meantime the two troop trains which were ready were loaded up, and finally both left, the first at 12.29 p.m. and the second at 2.30 p.m. for Kotdwara, our railhead for Lansdowne, *via* Agra. The trains were, unfortunately, very late, losing time all along the route. It was a great pity, as at Agra a grand reception on behalf of the Government of the United Provinces was to be given us, and it kept the officials and all residents who attended to give us the welcome rather a long time waiting. We waited at Agra cantonment for the second train to catch up a bit when the first train steamed slowly into Agra Fort station, where all European and Indian residents were assembled to welcome us. The station was crowded, and the Commissioner, Mr. Molony, welcomed us on the platform, where we all gathered. After the empty trains had cleared out the whole regiment was formed up on the line facing the platform and Mr. Molony gave us his address of welcome. (See Appendix III.). I replied in a very few words, thanking him. Mr. Pundit Deen Dyal then addressed the men in the vernacular. After this a move was made to the club in motors, which were kindly provided for us, and where we all had lunch, while the men were regaled with refreshments to their liking by the Indian residents of Agra. I think I am correct in saying that my Regiment was the only one in the Indian Army that was accorded such official reception by the Government. The welcome was most hearty and spontaneous, and was greatly appreciated by us all. Bands played as the trains entered the station "See the conquering hero comes," &c.

ENTRENCHMENTS AT MOSES' WELLS.

The festivities concluded, we all returned to the station, and the Regiment entrained once more for the onward journey. The first train left at 5.30 p.m. and the second at 6.15 p.m., each being heartily cheered as it steamed out.

The next morning we arrived at Najibabad, the junction for Kotdwara. As the gradient is rather steep, the trains had to proceed in four portions. The last portion reached Kotdwara at 12.30 p.m. Here the Assistant Commissioner, Mr. Barker, and Mrs. Barker, met us. The whole place was gaily decorated. The President, Mr. Govind Prasad, and the members of the Garhwal Sabha also met us and scattered rose leaves over us all and garlanded some of us. In the evening the Regiment fell in at 4 p.m. to receive an address of welcome from the members of the Garhwal Sabha, it being read out by the President and replied to by me. (Appendix III.). Later, when dark, fireworks were sent up in our honour.

The two marches up to the station of Lansdowne, 6,000 feet up, were done in two days. The second day, 17th March, was our final entry into our little station which we had left just eighteen months previously. We now returned sadly reduced in numbers, especially in our old comrades, both British and Garhwali Officers. The Regiment was met two miles out at the top of the steep climb at Dura, where we made a prolonged halt. Here tea and refreshments had most kindly been sent down by the 2/3rd Gurkhas for our men, and they themselves (of the depôt) turned up in force to welcome us. Also all the Garhwali Officers of our depôts were there. Colonel Sweet, commanding the 2/8th Gurkhas and at Lansdowne, had refreshments for British Officers sent down, which was most thoughtful of him. He also met us, the road was lined by men of the 2/8th and 2/10th Gurkhas, and cheers raised as we passed. The remaining distance to our barracks was soon passed, and we emerged on to the small parade ground near the Sadar Bazaar, being met by Mr. Clay, the Deputy Commissioner of Garhwal. He gave us a cordial welcome and marched the short way back with us to our big parade ground, the whole of which was lined by men from our own depôts. Here a short address was given us by the members of King George's School Committee.

The two battalions were now, after forming up, separated up into their original units once more, and I handed over the 1st Battalion to the senior officer, Major Lumb, while I retained the command of my own, the 2nd Battalion. Both then marched to their respective lines, and the British Officers all adjourned to the regimental mess, where lunch was partaken of with the Deputy Commissioner and others, after which the proceedings terminated.

Thus ended our first spell of service in this great war, and now we settled down to peace routine and training hard for further activities and for whatever might be in store for the Regiment.

CHAPTER XVI.

Regiment continues hard training and recruiting—Re-organising and squaring up accounts—Dispatch of Escort to Simla—Visit of the Lieut.-Governor of the United Provinces, Sir James Meston—Distribution of Medals to the Garrison—Leave for Delhi—Camped at Kingsway—No Camp pitched ready on arrival owing to tent poles not arriving with tents—Occupy pavilions on Polo Ground temporarily—Training continued—Inspection by the Northern Army Commander, General Sir Arthur Barrett—Inspection by the Quartermaster-General in India, also by His Excellency the Commander-in-Chief—Leave for Mesopotamia—Camped at Margil on arrival—Dusty Camp—No E.P. Tents available for the Battalion—Very hot for the men in single fly tents and Officers in 40lb. Tents—Am Invalided with Dysentery—Sent to Beit Nama General Hospital—Hand over Command of Battalion to Captain Berryman—Battalion proceeds to Amara—Finally to Baghdad—Joins the Force and takes part in the Battle of Ramadieh—Captures the Turkish Divisional Commander and Staff with guns and 2,100 prisoners—Gallantry and initiative of Captain Rodgerson, who is rewarded with an immediate award of the D.S.O.—Battalion finally leaves for another Theatre of the War—Salonika—Am relieved in command of my Battalion on completion of five years' tenure of Command—Battalion, after occupying Dardanelles Forts, Constantinople, and taking part in operations in Asia Minor, finally returns to India in the winter of 1920.

BOTH Battalions now settled down to re-organising and training hard. Recruiting parties were sent out, and recruits came in well. The War was yet, so to speak, only in its infancy, and it could not be long before one or both Battalions were sent off again to some other theatre of the war. Opportunity was taken now to get our accounts square, which owing to the original muddle made by the Accounts Department, required elucidating somewhat. This was, I am glad to say, practically done before we finally left for Mesopotamia, though one or two items could not be adjusted for some time. However, we were on the right side, fortunately, and had a surplus, and every one was settled up correctly, and the Depôt Commander, when we left, had a straight task to carry on.

The routine now differed little from that in peace time except that we had to recruit a greater number of men and train them. The number was laid down by the Adjutant-General's Department at Army headquarters from time to time. This meant much harder work in training so many men. The great difficulty was in getting a sufficient number of really efficient instructors. An experiment was tried by attaching two or three non-commissioned officers from some British regiment, which was a step in the right direction. It was first suggested that our men should go down to their regiment to be trained by them, but this was not nearly so good an expedient as attaching the N.C.O.s themselves to each Indian unit, as, though they might return well trained, this was bound to wear off after a bit, but with the presence of the British N.C.O.s this did not happen, as their presence acted as a stimulus to the men to keep up their efficiency. The Indian, as a rule, is a rather conceited fellow, and likes to think that you are looking on and, he hopes, admiring him. A bit of human nature, no doubt, but with him it is more accentuated. We had three very good men from a Territorial Regiment stationed at Delhi, the Duke of Cornwall's Light Infantry, who did excellent work. With their help the recruits' parade was supervised and classes held for the instruction of other likely men to help in the training of the large number of recruits we had on the parade ground. By the time we had to proceed again on service we had quite a number of well-trained men to complete our strength, though, of course, they were very juvenile compared with our pre-war standard, but with the healthy life they led on joining the Battalion and, above all, the good and ample rations that they received, they soon filled out.

During the rainy season we received a visit from the Lieutenant-Governor of the United Provinces, Sir (now Lord) James Meston. It was very nice receiving a visit from the head of the Province, both for us and for the little station as well. During his visit he did us the honour of distributing some decorations that we had received.

GROUP OF GARHWALI OFFICERS,
2nd Battalion.

Unfortunately, it rained very hard just as he was coming down to the parade, but nothing daunted, he took off his mackintosh and went through the whole of the inspection and gave away the medals after, though he (like us) got soaked to the skin. I don't think many " big wigs " would have done that. In the evening he was our guest at mess. His Excellency the Viceroy also distributed medals to the escort at Simla.

The summer soon sped by, and the winter, or, as we call it in India, the cold weather, was drawing nearer and nearer, when we were to go into camp at Delhi. Though this camp is a regular event every year, and must continue to be so till New Delhi is finished and the Viceroy can take up his quarters in the new Viceregal House there, it is extraordinary how difficult it is for units who have been selected to get definite orders well in time for their move. This especially is necessary for regiments like ours situated up in hill stations some miles off the railhead, and where there is no government transport available to transport the kit to the station. In our particular case we could not get definite orders, though I repeatedly asked for them, and therefore we were not able to indent on the civil authorities for the necessary carts. They required three weeks' notice to collect the number necessary for our move, and these must not be ordered too soon and kept waiting, else demurrage is payable to the cartmen. Then comes the usual haggle with the Accounts Department, which objects to the charge, though it is not your fault. A wearisome haggle which the Indian Babu usually delights in, but is very trying to the British Officer. However, we eventually got our orders at the eleventh hour. " Be in Delhi before the Viceroy arrives there on 29th October " was what I received about one week at most before we had to arrive there ! The result of this was that carts in sufficient number could not in any case be procured, for there are none in these hilly districts, but all have to be commandeered from the plains. However, the few that were procured could only arrive in time as far as Dogadda, the first stage from railhead, and so in order to comply with orders there was nothing else to do but to " hump " all the kit down on the backs of the men and recruits of both battalions to this stage, where it was loaded up and despatched. But this should not be, as men, though they must do all sorts of fatigue work, especially in war time, do not think, as a rule, that they should have to perform this sort of work, especially when it could so easily be avoided by just a little common sense and foresight on the part of the responsible branch at Army Headquarters. We got off at last and arrived at Delhi. On receipt of orders I had despatched an advance party to get ready what they could in the camp site and to pitch the big E.P. and other tents with which we units are generally supplied when in standing camp for any length of time. But these, of course, did not come in time. The usual delays with the Indian Department occurred. Tents had to come from one arsenal and the poles from another, so very characteristic of Indian "bandobast." The inevitable happened. When the tents did arrive, a large number, some 100 odd, came without any poles to pitch them. The men had to get under cover somehow. Fortunately, the Superintending Engineer of the Delhi Province was on the platform, and he very kindly came to the rescue and gave me permission to use the two empty pavilions on the polo ground which had been built in the 1911 Delhi Durbar, adding, however, a caution for the men not to lean too much against the supporting pillars else they might give way, owing to being eaten by white ants. The caution being duly given, the men squeezed into them both, while the balance shared with the advance party and others some empty cookhouses. The poles arrived eventually in two or three days, after a lot of wiring for them, and we got our camp pitched and straight. I often wonder what the language of the British soldier, of a Territorial regiment especially, would have been had they had to do as we did. These latter would have grumbled a lot.

However, when we got settled we were very comfortable. The necessary guards were taken over and the special orders for them learnt. Again, another point with these guards was the lack of accommodation as a guard room for the guard on his Excellency the Viceroy's House. Only a tent was supplied, which in itself is quite comfortable, but nothing on the ground. No boards or tarpaulins. How can men be expected to keep spick and span for such a guard if the floor of their tent is inches deep in dust, as it very soon was owing to the heavy boots of the men? Further, no bedsteads were supplied for them. Though they had a guard room at His Excellency the Commander-in-Chief's house, there were no bedsteads there either. Why such things cannot be supplied by Government one cannot imagine, expecially as this was a standing guard every cold weather, and had been for some years, and was likely to remain so for a number of years more while the Viceroy had to live in the circuit house behind the Ridge in the cold seasons and until his new residence at New Delhi was complete. So the Battalion had to buy these out of Battalion funds; but this should not be the case. Such petty economy, too, on the part of the Government.

Training continued here, too, and the more important half of collective training was carried out, companies being struck off duty in turn to carry out their Company training, and eventually to go into camp to fire their field practices. We had now come under the Dehra Dun Brigade commanded by Brigadier-General the Earl of Radnor.

As I had anticipated the Battalion being sent off again very soon on active service, I had taken the precaution to bring down all the necessary field service documents and books and get them written up as much as possible for each man, well knowing from experience that this was the only way (whether one had actually got orders or not) to avoid an awful rush at the last moment. So when the orders came we had everything ready, except the few entries, as advance of pay, &c., which could not be done till we were actually going and the advance was made.

The Northern Army Commander, General (later Field-Marshal) Sir Arthur Barret, inspected the Battalion and was, I think, well pleased with it and its work. The cold weather was now rapidly drawing to a close. In March the Government of India and army headquarters began to flit back to Simla. We eventually got orders that we were to proceed to Mesopotamia. This I had received a hint of a short time before, and so we were all prepared. The Quartermaster-General in India also inspected us. Then finally His Excellency the Commander-in-Chief inspected both us and the Wiltshire Regiment, which was the British Regiment furnishing the rest of the infantry part of the escort, and which was going to Palestine. We fell in on the parade ground outside the Delhi Fort. He addressed both units and gave us some words of encouragement and praise, and bade us both farewell.

General Sir Charles Monro took over supreme command in India during the war. He had a most difficult task, as such always is where a lot of re-organising and clearing up, &c., is necessary. The muddle in the early days of Mesopotamia is well known, but things at once altered when he took over the reins of the military machine. Chaos departed, rations improved, and there was little or nothing to grumble at, I know, when we arrived in Mesopotamia. A charming, kind and hospitable man with a most charming wife, who made you feel at home at once whenever you went to their house. Military matters, too, in India, greatly improved, and the machine worked smoothly and without any hitch at all during his command. I had the pleasure of serving under him during this period, first as a Regimental, and, later, as a Brigade Commander. It is a great thing having a man in such a position, who has himself been a thoroughly good regimental officer, as he is better able to appreciate the difficulties that such have to go through and he can see things from their point of view better than one who has done little regimental work and spent most of his time on the staff or on extra regimental jobs. The Indian Army has good cause to be grateful to these officials, Lord Chelmsford and General Sir Charles Monro, for many of the benefits that the Indian Army has received during the past few years.

The Battalion left Delhi on 18th March, embarked at Karachi and arrived at Basra at the end of March, and went into camp at Margil two or three miles up stream from Basra. It was a dusty camp, which was unavoidable, but much of the discomfort could have been avoided if the responsible staff there had only recognised a first principle, *i.e.*, that infantry should always be camped to windward of any camp allotted to mounted troops. The prevailing wind blew steadily from the same quarter daily. They, however, marked out camps for the infantry close to the railway and to leeward of those marked out for mounted corps. The result was that when the troops of the Division from Nasarieh began to arrive, the mounted corps and any units with transport were all placed to windward of us, and when they went to water their animals, which they did three times a day, the dust they raised was terrific, so that you could hardly see a tent 20 yards off. To add to this the latrines also had been placed to windward. So we got all the dust and flies right into our tents, mess tent and food. Otherwise, the camp was more or less all right, and the best ground available, though only a mud flat. There was no shelter of any sort, and the heat began to get pretty high in the day-time in our single fly tents, which the men had, and the 40lb. officers' tents. Larger E.P. tents were all required up the line at Baghdad and elsewhere for the time, and so we could not then get any.

The rations were very good. The men even got a good ration of expensive tinned fruits as an anti-scorbutic. This, I understand, was done by the Commander-in-Chief in his care for us all. In fact, everything was quite good and plentiful. This shows what can be done when there is an able man at the head of affairs. After some time in this camp, I regret to say that I had to succumb to a bad attack of amoebic dysentery, and had, most reluctantly, to go to hospital. I was sent to the Officers' General Hospital at Beit Nama, and handed over command of the battalion to Captain Berryman, the next senior officer. This hospital was managed and commanded most excellently by Major Munro, C.I.E., I.M.S., and I was well looked after in every way, and especially by the kind Sister deputed to look after me, and whose name, I regret to say, has slipped my memory. While in this hospital a telegram came appointing me to the command of a brigade at the front, which, of course, the medical authorities could not permit me to accept.

Later on I went to Bombay to another hospital situated in the Gaekwar of Baroda's palace, also a well-run establishment. Then on two months leave and, finally, to the depôt, where my tenure of command being completed, I was relieved, and got soon after another appointment, first as Inspector of Depôts and, later, as General Officer commanding the Delhi Brigade.

The Battalion shortly after went up to Amara, which it eventually left, and arrived at Baghdad in September, where it remained only a very short time and then joined the 15th Division and came in for the battle of Ramadieh. Captain (Acting Lieut.-Colonel) Berryman ably commanded the Battalion in this battle, which resulted in the Battalion capturing the Turkish Divisional Commander, his staff, some field guns, and 2,100 prisoners. Captain Rodgerson specially distinguished himself in this action by his initiative and gallantry in pushing forward with his company and out-flanking the Turkish position and putting their field battery out of action with his Lewis guns, which was the primary cause of the surrender of the Turkish commander with his force. He was rewarded with an immediate award of the D.S.O., which was a well-earned one, and the Battalion was specially mentioned in the Commander-in-Chief's despatch.

The Battalion also took part in the subsequent minor operations in rounding up the remainder of the Turks of that force.

Some time after, in 1918, the 2nd Battalion was sent to Salonika, and from thence to the Dardanelles to garrison the forts there. Next to Constantinople, and, later, it took part in operations in the Ismid Peninsula in Asia Minor against the Turks, finally returning to India and Lansdowne at the end of November, 1920. Thus the Battalion had been continually on active service on four different fronts, *i.e.*, France, Egypt, Mesopotamia and Salonika and neighbourhood, from 1914 to 1916 and 1917 to 1920—five years, with one year's interval only to re-organise in 1916.

Meanwhile the 1st Battalion remained at Lansdowne on our departure to Delhi, finally going to Quetta. After a spell of cantonment life there it was sent to Mesopotamia, where it remained till its return to India in 1920. It was all through the fighting against the Kurds in the mountainous country beyond Mosul. Before this it took a good part in the final rounding up of the Turks left in Mesopotamia. Except for some time longer in cantonment in India, it had also been absent the same period as the 2nd Battalion, having likewise fought on three fronts in France, Egypt and Mesopotamia.

There remains nothing more to relate. The details in full of the period that the two Battalions spent after leaving India for Mesopotamia and elsewhere I leave to be told by someone who took part in, and so is more acquainted with, these operations. I conclude my narrative with this brief summary only of those doings in other parts where I was not present.

CHAPTER XVII.

RETROSPECT.

APART from the official despatches and records which are published after every campaign, there are generally a great number of memoirs and autobiographies written by private individuals which possess a considerable interest, especially those written by the rank and file, as well as by commissioned officers. This was very noticeable after the Peninsular War, and they formed most interesting reading, as giving the spirit of the regiment and the ideas and impressions gained at the time. Those written immediately after the events they record possess naturally a peculiar interest. It was in recognising this fact that made me so careful to make and preserve all sketches and plans and record most carefully in my own private diary, as well as in the official diary, all events of interest as they happened, as, if such notes are not made or entered up at the time when everything is fresh in the memory, it is most difficult to remember accurately afterwards all events with dates and times, &c. It is hoped, therefore, that this book will prove of interest and value as a record to those interested in the doings of the Regiment, and maybe to others, for I was fortunate enough to command my own Battalion, the 2nd Battalion, and after the battle of Neuve Chapelle the combined Battalions, 1st and 2nd, of the Regiment for the whole time that the Indian Army Corps was in France, and I was not absent for a day during that period, being so fortunate, through the mercy of Providence, in not being incapacitated either through wounds or sickness.

The war left a tremendous aftermath of unrest behind it at home and abroad. Signs of civil unrest appeared, disputes between capital and labour, and strikes and threats of strikes, which threatened to do away with all that we had fought for and all that those who had paid the supreme sacrifice had laid down their lives for.

I took the opportunity in the spring of 1921, when retired, of visiting the battlefields and front on which the Indian Army Corps had served during 1914-15. I thought that I knew all that ground well, but I was surprised to see how altered the country looked. At Givenchy it took me quite ten minutes to get my bearings. Of course the subsequent years of daily shelling and the last tremendous effort made by the Germans in 1918 accounted for what I saw. When we left France in November, 1915, for Egypt, there were remains of walls, some few shattered roofs and foundations still standing and visible, to show where villages had once been, such as Givenchy, Richebourg L'Avoué, Festubert and Richebourg St. Vaast, but now there was not one stone left upon another to indicate where these villages stood. If there had been a church in a village such as at Neuve Chapelle and Richebourg St. Vaast, only a ragged bit of one wall remained, the rest all being shelled to bits. Every single house in these villages had disappeared, and the sites overgrown with grass. Strange to say, in the churchyard at Neuve Chapelle the large crucifix still stood silhouetted against the sky. Where shells had fallen in any great number in an attack, as in the great German attack at Givenchy, in their effort in the spring of 1918, and where they had mined under the British trenches, which they blew up, I believe, with a whole British battalion, the ground all round that village, or where it once stood on slightly rising ground, looked more like a sea in stormy weather, covered as it was with long, rank grass. Notwithstanding the grass, the form of the trenches was still visible here and there where they had not been blown to atoms by the heavy shelling.

At Richebourg L'Avoué, in front of which the Regiment held the trenches in the winter of 1914, it was very interesting, especially viewed from the German side. Here their line was studded with thick concrete dug-outs for their machine guns at frequent intervals, and here and there was a thick bullet-proof steel mantlet embedded in the parapet, which was just big enough for a man to sit down in to observe from, as it had two small slits, one on each side of the two front faces which were shaped like a broad, obtuse angle.

As I stood on that ground it brought back a flood of memories, of the battles the regiment had been present at, of the frequent weary treks up to and from the muddy trenches, and the trench warfare of that period, with the bigger battles from time to time, both of which exacted a remorseless toll, and of the dead and dying for their country's sake. This war seemed a very inhuman one. One reads in other wars of short truces for both sides to collect their wounded and bury their dead, but in this war, waged between so-called Christian countries, there was never such a thing. The dead just lay out in front rotting. Many a man's life could, I feel sure, have been saved, if one had been able to collect the wounded after a battle that had been unsuccessful and no advance made, but instead they lay out and died in the mud and cold. If the battle was successful and an advance made, of course one could succour the wounded, but if an attack failed, there they just lay because, except at night, one could do nothing. If you did venture out the enemy shot you. Even at night it was a difficult and dangerous job. After seeing so many killed and dead lying about in all sorts of attitudes one is apt to get callous at such sights after a time. But one could not help thinking how unnecessary all this frightful waste of life should be with all its cruelty, just to satisfy a nation's or individual's ambition! When one recalls the wounded, the pain they must have suffered (and some of the wounds, especially shell wounds, were frightful), one gets a lasting impression of the uselessness and calamities of war, and though the profession is outwardly attractive with its uniform, field days and other gaieties, it has other and more painful features. However, as war is, it would appear a condition of this world, and is not likely to be abolished yet awhile, notwithstanding pacifists and conscientious objectors and others of that ilk, unless the League of Nations and League of Nations Union, backed up by strong public opinion, is able to affect and abolish war by having differences submitted for arbitration, which it is to be hoped it will eventually be able to do. But until there is a change of heart, less jealousy and mistrust in each other, I am afraid this much desired object is at present far from attainment. It behoves everyone who takes up this profession of a soldier to remember what a serious one it is, and to fit himself by every means in his power, and especially by study in peace time, to gain the necessary proficiency and also the confidence of those under him and so not find himself compromised on service from want of knowledge, and thus throw away unnecessarily the valuable lives of his men.

I also recalled the short periods of rest in billets when we were billeted among the French people—all their kindness and hospitality—and how they put up with every inconvenience for our sakes. How cheerful and jolly they were under it all! Up to work about 4 a.m., smiling all day, and to bed at 10 p.m., or earlier, and the same day after day, with all their men folk, except the old, away at the war and, in many instances, killed and their property ruined! One could not help admiring them.

And, lastly, I recalled the memory of those gallant comrades who had fought alongside me and who had made the supreme sacrifice. Gallant gentlemen and comrades whom I knew so well in peace time in our little station. Yet they are not forgotten, and never will be! Their names will be enshrined in the hearts of their dear ones and in our memory: they will live in the history of the regiment, and of their country. Indeed, they will survive as long as the English language is spoken!

APPENDIX I.

List of British Officers, Garhwali Officers and Rank and File of the 1st and 2nd Battalions 39th Garhwal Rifles who received Honours and Rewards for services in France and Egypt in the Great War, 1914-1917.

BRITISH OFFICERS.

Brevet of Colonel.

Lieut.-Colonel ...	E. R. R. Swiney	1st Battalion ...	L.G. of 17.2.1915

Companion of St. Michael and St. George.

Lieut.-Colonel ...	D. H. Drake-Brockman	2nd Battalion ...	L.G. of 23.6.1915

Distinguished Service Order.

Major	J. H. K. Stewart	2nd Battalion ...	L.G. of 23.6.1915
Major	K. Henderson	1st Battalion ...	L.G. of 3.6.1916
Captain	G. W. Burton	2nd Battalion ...	L.G. of 23.6.1915
Captain	J. Taylor, I.M.S. (attached) ...	1st Battalion ...	L.G. of 23.6.1915

Military Cross.

Captain	F. E. G. Lumb	1st Battalion ...	L.G. of 18.2.1915
Captain	J. T. Lane	1st Battalion ...	L.G. of 18.2.1915
Captain	H. R. B. Reed	2nd Battalion ...	L.G. of 1.1.1916
Lieutenant... ...	A. H. Mankelow	1st Battalion ...	L.G. of 8.5.1915
Lieutenant... ...	Rana Jodha Jang Bahadur, Tihri Sappers and Miners,	The Garhwal Rifles (attached)	L.G. of 4.11.1915

Mention in Despatches.

Lieut.-Colonel ...	E. R. R. Swiney	1st Battalion ...	L.G. of 17.2.1915
Lieut.-Colonel ...	D. H. Drake-Brockman	2nd Battalion (twice)	L.G.s of 17.2.1915 and 22.6.1915
Major	J. H. K. Stewart	2nd Battalion ...	L.G. of 22.6.1915
Major	K. Henderson	1st Battalion ...	L.G. of 1.1.1916
Major	G. H. Taylor	2nd Battalion ...	L.G. of 17.2.1915
Captain	F. E. G. Lumb	1st Battalion ...	L.G. of 17.2.1915
Captain	G. W. Burton	2nd Battalion ...	L.G. of 22.6.1915
Captain	D. Blair	2nd Battalion ...	L.G. of 22.6.1915
Captain	J. T. Lane	1st Battalion ...	L.G. of 17.2.1915
Captain	H. R. B. Reed	2nd Battalion ...	L.G. of 1.1.1916
Captain	P. T. Etherton	1st Battalion ...	L.G. of 1.1.1916
Lieutenant... ...	A. H. Mankelow	1st Battalion ...	L.G. of 22.6.1915
Lieutenant... ...	Rana Jodha Jang Bahadur, Tihri Sappers and Miners	The Garhwal Rifles (attached)	L.G. of 1.1.1916
Captain	J. Taylor, I.M.S. (attached) ...	1st Battalion ...	L.G. of 22.6.1915

GARHWALI OFFICERS.

Order of British India, Second Class.

Subadar	Nain Sing Chinwarh	2nd Battalion ...	G. of Ind., 725 of 1915
Subadar	Makhar Sing Kawar	2nd Battalion ...	G. of Ind., 725 of 1915
Subadar	Baij Sing Rawat	1st Battalion ...	G. of India of 7.7.1915
Subadar	Jagat Sing Rawat, I.O.M. ...	1st Battalion ...	G. of India of 1.1.1915
Subadar	Bije Sing Kandari	1st Battalion ...	G. of India of 7.7.1915

Military Cross.

Suba ar	Nain Sing Chinwarh	2nd Battalion ...	L.G. of 1.1.1915
Subadar	Dhan Sing Negi	1st Battalion ...	L.G. of 18.2.1915
Subadar	Bishan Sing Rawat	1st Battalion ...	L.G. of 23.6.1915
Jemadar	Sangram Sing Negi	2nd Battalion ...	L.G. of 23.6.1915
Jemadar	Pancham Sing Mahar	2nd Battalion ...	L.G. of 8.5.1915
2nd Class Sub. Asst. Surgeon	Ramkrishna Ganpat Shinde, I.M.S.D. (attached)	1st Battalion ...	L.G. of 23.6.1915

Indian Order of Merit.

Jemadar	Prem Sing Negi	1st Battalion ...	L.G. of 4.5.1915

Indian Distinguished Service Medal.

Subadar	Kedar Sing Rawat	1st Battalion ...	L.G. of 4.5.1915
Subadar	Dhan Sing Negi	1st Battalion ...	L.G. of 18.2.1915
Jemadar	Lachman Sing Rawat	2nd Battalion ...	L.G. of 18.2.1915
Jemadar	Guman Sing Negi	1st Battalion ...	L.G. of 4.5.1915

MENTION IN DESPATCHES.

Subadar	Dhan Sing Negi	1st Battalion ...	L.G. of 17.2.1915
Subadar	Bishan Sing Bisht	1st Battalion ...	L.G. of 22.6.1915
Jemadar	Sangram Sing Negi	2nd Battalion ...	L.G. of 22.6.1915
Jemadar	Pancham Sing Mahar	2nd Battalion ...	L.G. of 22.6.1915
Jemadar	Lachman Sing Rawat	2nd Battalion ...	L.G. of 17.2.1915
Jemadar	Ghantu Sing Bisht	2nd Battalion ...	L.G. of 22.6.1915
2nd Class Sub. Asst. Surgeon	Ramkrishna Ganpat Shinde, I.M.S.D. (attached)	1st Battalion ...	L.G. of 22.6.1915

RANK AND FILE.

VICTORIA CROSS.

No. 1909, Naik ...	Darwan Sing Negi	1st Battalion ...	L.G. of 7.12.1914
No. 1685, Rifleman	Gobar Sing Negi	2nd Battalion ...	L.G. of 28.4.1915

INDIAN ORDER OF MERIT, SECOND CLASS.

No. 762, Havaldar	Butha Sing Negi	2nd Battalion ...	L.G. of 4.5.1915
No. 1810, Havaldar	Alam Sing Negi	1st Battalion ...	L.G. of 1.1.1915
No. 463, Naik ...	Bakhtawar Sing Bisht	2nd Battalion ...	L.G. of 4.5.1915
No. 1283, Naik ...	Jaman Sing Bisht	2nd Battalion ...	L.G. of 4.5.1915
No. 2498, L/Naik ...	Shankar Sing Gusain	1st Battalion ...	L.G. of 1.1.1915
No. 2605, L/Naik ...	Khiyali Sing Gusain	1st Battalion ...	L.G. of 18 2 1915
No. 1342, Rifleman	Ganesh Sing Sajwan	2nd Battalion ...	L.G. of 1.1.1915.
No. 1541, Rifleman	Madan Sing Rawat	2nd Battalion ...	L.G. of 18.2.1915
No. 1674, Rifleman	Kalam Sing Bisht	1st Battalion ...	L.G. of 1.1.1915
No. 1715, Rifleman	Dhan Sing Negi	1st Battalion ...	L.G. of 18.2.1915
No. 2172, Rifleman	Ghantu Sing Rawat	1st Battalion ...	L.G. of 18.2.1915
No. 2285, Rifleman	Jawahir Sing Negi	1st Battalion ...	L.G. of 4.5.1915
No. 2417, Rifleman	Pertab Sing Rana	1st Battalion ...	L.G. of 18.2.1915
No. 2480, Rifleman	Banchu Sing Negi	1st Battalion ...	L.G. of 4.5.1915
No. 4423, Sepoy	Beli Ram, 30th Punjabis (attached)	1st Battalion ...	L.G. of 4.5.1915

INDIAN DISTINGUISHED SERVICE MEDAL.

No. 189 Havaldar	Diwan Sing Padhiyar	2nd Battalion ...	L.G. of 18.2.1915
No. 195 Havaldar	Mohan Sing Negi	2nd Battalion ...	L.G. of 23.6.1915
No. 617 Havaldar	Bir Sing Danu	2nd Battalion ...	L.G. of 18.2.1915
No. 939 Havaldar	Ranjor Sing Pundir	2nd Battalion ...	L.G. of 18.2.1915
No. 1489 Naik	Kedar Sing Mahar	2nd Battalion ...	L.G. of 18.2.1915
No. 324 L/Naik	Deb Sing Aswal	2nd Battalion ...	L.G. of 23.6.1915
No. 1321 L/Naik	Dangwa Sing Ramola	1st Battalion ...	L.G. of 4.5.1915
No. 2697 Bugler	Bhola Sing Bisht	1st Battalion ...	L.G. of 18.2.1915
No. 289, Rifleman	Kesar Sing Rana	2nd Battalion ...	L.G. of 18.2.1915
No. 870, Rifleman	Nain Sing Rawat	2nd Battalion ...	L.G. of 18.2.1915
No. 1085, Rifleman	Raichand Sing Negi	1st Battalion ...	L.G. of 18.2.1915
No. 1465, Rifleman	Gopal Sing Pharswan	2nd Battalion ...	L.G. of 4.5.1915
No. 1598, Rifleman	Chandar Sing Negi	2nd Battalion ...	L.G. of 4.5.1915
No. 1760, Rifleman	Kutal Sing Bisht	1st Battalion ...	L.G. of 18.2.1915
No. 2855, Rifleman	Keshi Sing Bisht	1st Battalion ...	L.G. of 18.2.1915

MENTION IN DESPATCHES.

No. 189, Havaldar	Diwan Sing Padhiyar	2nd Battalion ...	L.G. of 17.2.1915
No. 617, Havaldar	Bir Sing Danu	2nd Battalion ...	L.G. of 17.2.1915
No. 939, Havaldar	Ranjor Sing Pundir	2nd Battalion ...	L.G. of 17.2.1915
No. 1489, Naik	Kedar Sing Mahar	2nd Battalion ...	L.G. of 17.2.1915
No. 2605, L/Naik	Khiyali Sing Gusain	1st Battalion ...	L.G. of 17.2.1915
No. 2697 Bugler	Bhola Sing Bisht	1st Battalion ...	L.G. of 17.2.1915
No. 289, Rifleman	Kesar Sing Rana	2nd Battalion ...	L.G. of 17.2.1915
No. 870, Rifleman	Nain Sing Rawat	2nd Battalion ...	L.G. of 17.2.1915
No. 1085, Rifleman	Raichand Sing Negi	1st Battalion ...	L.G. of 17.2.1915
No. 1541, Rifleman	Madan Sing Rawat	2nd Battalion ...	L.G. of 17.2.1915
No. 1715, Rifleman	Dhan Sing Negi	1st Battalion ...	L.G. of 17.2.1915
No. 1760, Rifleman	Kutal Sing Bisht	1st Battalion ...	L.G. of 17.2.1915
No. 2172, Rifleman	Ghantu Sing Bisht	1st Battalion ...	L.G. of 17.2.1915
No. 2417, Rifleman	Pertab Sing Rana	1st Battalion ...	L.G. of 17.2.1915
No. 2854, Rifleman	Keshi Sing Bisht	1st Battalion ...	L.G. of 17.2.1915

RUSSIAN CROSS OF THE ORDER OF ST. GEORGE—FOURTH CLASS.

No. 1729, Havaldar	Padam Sing Rawat	1st Battalion ...	L.G. of 25.8.1915

RUSSIAN MEDAL OF ST. GEORGE—THIRD CLASS.

No. 1211, Rifleman	Man Sing Bisht	2nd Battalion ...	L.G. of 25.9.1915

RUSSIAN MEDAL OF ST. GEORGE—FOURTH CLASS.

No. 2103, L/Naik	Jit Sing Negi	1st Battalion ...	L.G. of 25.8.1915
No. 1448, Rifleman	Karam Sing Rithal	2nd Battalion ...	L.G. of 25.8.1915

APPENDIX II.

LIST OF BRITISH OFFICERS AND TH

	Rank.	Name.	Battalion.	LA BASSEE, 10th Oct. to 2nd Nov., 1914.	NEUVE CHAPELLE, 10th to 13th March, 1915.
1.	Bt.-Colonel	E. R. R. Swiney	1st	P.	P.
2.	Lieut.-Colonel	D. H. Drake-Brockman, C.M.G.	2nd	P.	P.
3.	Major	W. H. Wardell	1st	P.	—
4.	Major	H. M. MacTier	2nd	P.	P.
5.	Major	P. M. Home	1st	P.	—
6.	Major	J. H. K. Stewart, D.S.O.	2nd	P.	P.*
7.	Major	G. H. Taylor	2nd	P.	—
8.	Captain	K. Henderson, D.S.O.	1st	P.	P.*
9.	Captain	F. E. G. Lumb, M.C.	1st	P.	—
10.	Captain	G. W. Burton, D.S.O.	2nd	P.	P.
11.	Captain	A. W. Robertson-Glasgow	2nd	P.	—
12.	Captain	D. Blair	2nd	P.	P.
13.	Captain	J. T. H. Lane, M.C.	1st	P.	—*
14.	Captain	H. R. B. Reed, M.C.	2nd	P.	P.*
15.	Captain	W. G. S. Kenny	1st	P.	P.
16.	Captain	S. B. Orton	1st	P.	—
17.	Captain	A. G. Lyell	2nd	P.	P.
18.	Captain	B. C. Sparrow	1st	P.	P.
19.	Captain	P. T. Etherton	1st	—	—
20.	Captain	E. R. P. Berryman	2nd	P.	P.
21.	Captain	J. C. T. Wilcox	2nd	P.	P.
22.	Captain	G. R. Mainwaring	1st	P.	P.
23.	Lieutenant	A. H. Mankelow, M.C.	1st	P.	P.
24.	Lieutenant	F. N. Fox	2nd	—	P.
25.	Lieutenant	G. S. Rogers	1st	P.	P.
26.	Lieutenant	J. C. St. Welchman	1st	P.	P.
27.	Lieutenant	A. E. Clarke	2nd	P.	—*
28.	Lieutenant	C. H. C. Gore	2nd	—	—
29.	Lieutenant	J. F. Parkin, 113th Infantry (attached)	2nd	—	P.
30.	Lieutenant	L. B. Harbord, 44th Infantry (attached)	2nd	—	P.
31.	Lieutenant	R. T. Gatherer, 2/10th G.R. (attached)	Garh. Rifles	—	—
32.	Lieutenant	F. G. Kunhardt, 74th Punjabis (attached)	Garh. Rifles	—	—
33.	Lieutenant	R. T. Collins, 13th Battalion Sherwood Foresters (attached)	Garh. Rifles	—	—
34.	Lieutenant	Rana Jodha Jang Bahadur, Tihri Sappers and Miners (attached)	1st	—	—
35.	Lieutenant	R. Lamb, I.A.R. (attached)	Garh. Rifles	—	—
36.	Lieutenant	A. E. Courthope, I.A.R. (attached)	Garh. Rifles	—	—
37.	Lieutenant	A. Saunders, I.A.R. (attached)	Garh. Rifles	—	—
38.	Lieutenant	R. D. Tibbs, I.A.R. (attached)	Garh. Rifles	—	—
39.	2/Lieutenant	C. W. Hayne, I.A.R. (attached)	Garh. Rifles	—	—
40.	2/Lieutenant	S. Angelo, I.A.R. (attached)	Garh. Rifles	—	—
41.	2/Lieutenant	H. M. Banon, I.A.R. (attached)	Garh. Rifles	—	—
42.	Major	J. Woods, I.M.S. (attached)	2nd	P.	Sick
43.	Major	N. W. Mackworth, I.M.S. (attached)	1st	P.	—
44.	Captain	J. Taylor, I.M.S. (attached)	1st	—	P.
45.	Captain	G. L. Duncan, I.M.S. (attached)	Garh. Rifles	—	—

BATTLES THEY WERE PRESENT AT.

AUBERS, 9th May, 1915.	FESTUBERT, 15th to 25th May, 1915.	Action of PIETRE, in conjunction with Battle of LOOS, 25th September, 1915.	Remarks.
—	—	—	Wounded 10th March, 1915.
P.*	P.*	P.*	*In command of "The Garhwal Rifles."
—	—	—	Killed 23rd November, 1914.
—	—	—	Killed 11th March, 1915.
—	—	—	Sick. Returned to India.
P.*	P.*	P.*	*On the Staff.
—	—	—	Killed 13th November, 1914.
P.*	P.*	P.*	*On the Staff.
—	—	—	Sick, February, 1915. Rejoined on 10th October, 1915.
—*	—*	P.	*Sick. Killed 12th October, 1915.
—	—	—	Killed 13th November, 1915.
P.	P.	—*	*Transferred to Salvage Corps.
—*	—*	—*	*Sick.
P.*	P.*	P.*	*On the Staff.
—	—	—	Killed 10th March, 1915.
—	—	—	Wounded 23rd November, 1914.
P.	P.	—*	*Sick.
—	—	—	Killed 10th March, 1915.
P.	P.	P.	Joined during March, 1915.
P.	—	—	Wounded 9th May, 1915.
P.	—	—	Killed 12th May, 1915.
—	—	P.	Wounded 10th March, 1915. Rejoined during July, 1915
P.	—	—	Killed 14th May, 1915.
P.	P.	P.	Joined during January, 1915.
P.	P.	—	Wounded 15th May, 1915.
—	—	—	Killed 10th March, 1915.
—*	—*	P.	*Sick. Rejoined during June, 1915.
—	—	—	Joined on 4th October, 1915.
—	—	—	Joined 9th December, 1914. Wounded 10th March, 1915, as Brigade Bomb Gun Officer.
P.	P.	—	Joined 9th December, 1914. Transferred to 1st G.R. for Dardanelles during August, 1915.
P.	—	—	Wounded 14th May, 1915. Joined during March, 1915.
—	—	P.	Wounded 25th September, 1915. Joined 19th May, 1915.
P.*	P.*	P.	Joined 21st May, 1915, from 9th G.R. *With 9th G.R.
P.	P.	P.	Joined during March, 1915.
—	—	P.	Joined during May, 1915.
—	—	—	Joined during September, 1915. Taken for Forest Work in rear.
P.	—	—	Wounded 9th May, 1915. Joined 9th April, 1915.
P.	P.	P.*	*In charge of Brigade Bomb Guns. Joined 11th May, 1915.
—	—	—	Joined during September, 1915.
—	—	P.	Joined 18th September, 1915. Went sick 26th September, 1915.
—	—	—	Joined 4th October, 1915.
P.	—	—	Killed 9th May, 1915.
—	—	—	Transferred to Base Hospital.
—	—	—	Wounded 10th March, 1915.
P.	P.	P.	Joined during May, 1915.

APPENDIX III.

COMPLIMENTARY ORDERS AND LETTERS SENT TO THE 2ND BATTALION THE GARHWAL RIFLES AND BRIGADE OF WHICH THEY FORMED PART.

(A.) Copy of a Message from the Brigade Major Garhwal Brigade to Officers Commanding Battalions of the Garhwal Brigade.

B.M. No. 82, *dated* 2.11.1914.

Indian Army Corps Commander sends congratulations to the Brigade on the way they have worked and held their trenches.

(B). Copy of a message from the Brigade Major Garhwal Brigade to the Officer Commanding 2nd Battalion 39th Garhwal Rifles.

B.M. No. 186, *dated* 8.11.1914.

The G.O.C. Brigade asks me to thank you for the excellent report and the work done by the Battalion.

(C.) Copy of a Message from the Brigade Major Garhwal Brigade to the Officer Commanding 2nd Battalion 39th Garhwal Rifles.

B.M. No. 219, *dated* 9.11.1914.

Well done 2/39th G.

(D.) From Lieut.-General C. A. Anderson, K.C.B., commanding Meerut Div.

To the O.C. 2/39th Garhwalis.

10*th November*, 1914.

Through G.O.C. 20th Infy. Brigade.

I wish you to express to the Battalion under your command my commendation and congratulations on the excellent and satisfying manner in which the Battalion has been working and beg you to accept my personal approval of the manner in which the Battalion has been commanded by you and worked by the officers under you.

C. A. ANDERSON,
Lieut.-General.

(E.) Copy of a Message from the Brigade Major Garhwal Brigade to the Officer Commanding 2nd Battalion 39th Garhwal Rifles.

B.M. No. Nil, dated 14.11.1914.

Excellently done 2/39th G.

(F). Major-General Keary, C.B., D.S.O., Commanding Garhwal Brigade.

18.11.1914.

I am glad to forward to you the attached note by the Corps Commander conveying his appreciation of the good work of the 2/39th Garhwalis on which I have already congratulated the Battalion. Please forward this correspondence to the O.C. 2/39th Garhwalis with my congratulations.

Yours,
ANDERSON.

(G.) O.C. 2/39th Garhwalis. Headquarters I.A. Corps.

18.11.1914.

I am very pleased to hear from General Anderson how well the Battalion is doing. I am sure you will continue to do so throughout the war.

JAMES WILLCOCKS,
Lieut.-General I.A. Corps.

Through Major-General Keary, C.B., D.S.O.

INDIAN ARMY CORPS.

ORDER OF THE DAY

BY

LIEUT.-GENERAL SIR JAMES WILLCOCKS, K.C.B., K.C.S.I., K.C.M.G., D.S.O., COMMANDING.

Dated 7th December, 1914.

Now that the reports of the action on 23rd and 24th November east of Festubert are all to hand, the Corps Commander has learnt with great satisfaction of the conduct of the troops engaged under Brig.-General Egerton, C.B. Many signal instances of gallantry have come to light, and His Majesty the King has been pleased to confer a Victoria Cross on No. 1909, Naik Darwan Sing Negi, 1st Battalion 39th Garhwal Rifles.

A considerable number of the troops of both Divisions were engaged, and under the circumstances it is difficult to single out Corps, but the steadiness of the Black Watch and the portion of the 58th Rifles next to them, and especially the flank attack by the 1st Battalion 39th Garhwal Rifles, which helped to regain the lost trenches, merit special notice.

The artillery, under Lieut.-Colonel Duffus, is acknowledged by all concerned to have rendered most timely and necessary assistance.

The Corps Commander will have great pleasure in bringing the names of units and individual officers and other ranks specially deserving to the notice of the Field Marshal Commanding in Chief.

W. E. O'Leary, Brig.-General,
Deputy Adjutant and Quartermaster General.

Copy of a letter from the 21st French Corps Commander forwarded to the Lieut.-General Commanding the Division by the Indian Corps Commander :—

I have heard with the greatest satisfaction of the brilliant success of the Meerut Division on the night of the 23rd and 24th November. This satisfaction is shared by all the units under my command who have complete confidence in the solid assistance on their left. Allow me to congratulate most sincerely the Meerut Division on the bravery and tenacity which it has shewn and which are sure signs of a definite success for the Allied Armies.

Indian Army Corps.

ORDER OF THE DAY

BY

Lieut.-General Sir JAMES WILLCOCKS, K.C.B., K.C.S.I., K.C.M.G., D.S.O., Commanding.

Dated 5th January, 1915.

The G.O.C. Indian Army Corps has much pleasure in publishing for information of all ranks of the Corps the following telegram received from H.E. the Viceroy of India :—

"The Indian National Congress has asked that the following resolution may be conveyed to the Indian troops fighting in Europe. This Congress rejoices to place on record its deep sense of gratitude and pride in the heroic conduct of the Indian troops, whose deeds of valour and conspicuous humanity and chivalry in the great war are winning the respect of civilized mankind for the Mother Country, and resolves to send a message of hearty and affectionate greetings to them and their comrades in arms, with fervent prayers for their well-being and success."

SPECIAL ORDER OF THE DAY

BY

Brigadier-General C. G. BLACKADER, D.S.O., Commanding Garhwal Brigade.

14th March, 1915.

216. The following has been received by the Brigadier-General Commanding Garhwal Brigade from Lieut.-General Sir James Willcocks, K.C.B., K.C.S.I., K.C.M.G., D.S.O., Commanding Indian Army Corps, and is to be communicated to all ranks of the Garhwal Brigade :—

Begins. "Please convey to all ranks of your gallant Brigade my hearty thanks and congratulations on their splendid work at Neuve Chapelle. I am indeed fortunate and proud to have such fine soldiers in my command. I feel sure that, notwithstanding their great efforts, they are prepared for still greater in the immediate future." Ends.

In more than endorsing the above, the Brigadier-General wishes to congratulate every unit in the Brigade on the splendid example they have shown of gallantry, dash, endeavour and discipline in the operations of the last few days. He feels sure that every member of the Brigade is not only proud of the success they have achieved, but also of having added fresh honour to the past traditions of their units.

C. G. Blackader, Brig.-General,
Commanding Garhwal Brigade.

SPECIAL.

INDIA ARMY ORDER

BY

His Excellency The COMMANDER-IN-CHIEF IN INDIA.

Army Headquarters, Simla.

26th March, 1915.

Complimentary. — His Excellency the Commander-in-Chief has great pleasure in publishing the following message from Field-Marshal Sir John D. P. French, G.C.B., O.M., G.C.V.O., K.C.M.G., and directs that it should be made known to all Indian Units.

The following report has been received from Lieutenant-General Sir James Willcocks K.C.B., K.C.S.I., K.C.M.G., D.S.O. :—

All units of Indian Corps engaged in the recent fighting at Neuve Chapelle did well, and the Indian Units which specially distinguished themselves were :—

7TH (MEERUT) DIVISION.
Garhwal Brigade.

1st Battalion, 39th Garhwal Rifles.

2nd Battalion, 39th Garhwal Rifles.

N.B.—This includes Tihri (Garhwal) Sappers, Imperial Service Troops.

2nd Battalion, 3rd Queen Alexandra's Own Gurkha Rifles.

GARHWAL BRIGADE.

Will you please convey to the Battalion of your Brigade which carried out recently the work of burying men of this Battalion near RUE DU BOIS our best thanks for and appreciation of their gallant conduct ?

Sd., E. W. B. GREEN, Lieut.-Col.
Commanding 2nd Battalion,
The Royal Sussex Regt.

In the Field.
9/5/15.

II. S.C.1717.

O.C. GARHWAL RIFLES.

Forwarded.

Sd., H. R. B. REED, Captain.
Staff Captain, Garhwal Brigade.

10/5/15.

Copy of congratulatory Message from Sir John French, Field Marshal Commanding-in-Chief, France, to the Garhwal Brigade.

GENERAL HEADQUARTERS,
BRITISH ARMY IN THE FIELD.

7th November, 1915.

As the Garhwal Brigade is now leaving my command to take part in operations elsewhere, I wish to send it my personal thanks for the services it has rendered to the King-Emperor since reaching France more than a year ago.

The behaviour of the Brigade in action and its discipline have been excellent throughout, and it has always maintained its fighting spirit in spite of heavy losses and under the most trying weather conditions.

I wish the Garhwal Brigade all good fortune wherever its duty may take it, and feel sure it will everywhere maintain the excellent reputation it has earned in France.

(Sgd) J. D. P. FRENCH.
Field-Marshal,
Commanding-in-Chief,
British Army in France.

Letter of farewell and congratulations from Brig.-General H. D. Watson, C.M.G., C.I.E., M.V.O., Commanding No. 1 Section Canal Defences, Aiyun, Musa, Egypt.

23rd February, 1916.

My Dear Brockman,

The orders received to-night for the despatch of your gallant Regiment elsewhere is sad to me, though, of course, not unexpected. I am more than sorry that you are leaving us, and I wish to thank you and all ranks of the Regiment for the exceptionally good work done by them during the short time the Regiment has been under my command.

The work has been hard and uninteresting, but has been so cheerfully carried out and so well done that I cannot help saying "Thank you."

It has been an honour indeed to me to have commanded even for a very short time the Brigade in which the Regiment formed part.

Bon voyage and the best of good luck to you all.

Yours sincerely,
H. D. WATSON.

Telegram of congratulation from His Excellency the Commander-in-Chief in India.

INDIAN TELEGRAPHS.

Delhi,
Date—*10th March*, 1916. 15.30 *p.m.*
Bombay, *11th March*, 1916.
State—52 words.
Received here at 11.40 a.m.

Comdg. 39th Garhwal Rifles.
c/o Embarkation Commandant,
Bombay, R.

32947 over three. A.G. Ten. My heartiest welcome to you and all ranks under your command on your return to India from Field Service where all have so gallantly and devotedly maintained best traditions of the Indian Army.—COMDR.-IN-CHIEF.

PROGRAMME FOR THE RECEPTION OF THE 39TH GARHWALIS On the 14th March, 1916.

The first special train bringing the 39th Garhwalis is expected to arrive at the Agra Fort Station at 11.15 a.m. on the 14th instant, the second train being due shortly afterwards.

The trains will be received by the principal Civil and Military officers of the station, and by representative Indian gentlemen. Both Military bands will be on the platform and Guards of Honour from the 74th Punjabis Depot and the Agra Volunteer Rifles. As the trains come in the band of the 24th Battalion The Rifle Brigade will play " See the conquering hero comes," or some other similar piece, and the Guards of Honour will present arms. When the Regiment has detrained, and been formed up, speeches of welcome will be made both in English and Urdu. The Regiment will then be garlanded, and afterwards refreshments will be offered to all ranks :—To the British Officers at the Club, where they will be taken in motor cars ; to the Indian Officers by the Indian Officers of the Depots ; and to the rank and file by the Indian gentlemen on the platform. The two bands will play alternately during the whole time, and will play the train out of the Station when it leaves.

The first train is expected to leave Agra Fort Station punctually at 3.30 p.m., the second following immediately afterwards. The departure of the Regiment will also be a public one, and it is hoped that, in addition to the Official representatives mentioned above, a number of other European and Indian gentlemen and also ladies will be present to give a welcome back to India to this gallant Regiment, and to bid them farewell on their onward journey.

Special seats are being reserved on the platform for ladies.

The Guards of Honour and bands will fall in punctually at 11 a.m., at places selected for them on the platform, and all others attending the Reception are requested to arrive in good time before the first train is due.

Station Staff Office,
Agra.

Address by the Commissioner of Agra, J. Moloney, Esq., C.S., to the Regiment on its return from France and Egypt to India, on 14th March, 1916.

COLONEL DRAKE-BROCKMAN, OFFICERS AND MEN OF THE 39TH GARHWAL RIFLES.

On behalf of the Government of this Province I welcome this famous Regiment back to India from the war. I am speaking in English on behalf of the Government and also of the English-speaking community, and I leave it to my friend Pandit Din Diyal to speak in Hindi on behalf of the general Indian community.

2. The deeds of this Regiment have made it famous in every corner of the British Empire, but it requires an enumeration of the honours won by its officers and men to bring to our minds a full realisation of its extraordinary services.

3. Two men of the Regiment, namely, Naik Darwan Sing Negi and Rifleman Gobar Sing Negi, have won that famous and well-coveted decoration for valour, namely, the Victoria Cross, never before this war won by an Indian soldier.

4. British Officers have won one Brevet Colonelcy, one Companionship of the most distinguished order of St. Michael and St. George, four D.S.O.s and five Military Crosses.

Indian Officers have won four Distinguished Service Medals, six Military Crosses, five Orders of British India with the title of Bahadur, and one Indian Order of Merit.

5. The Indian rank and file have won fifteen Distinguished Service Medals, fifteen Indian Orders of Merit, one Cross and three Medals of the Russian Order of St. George, given by the Tsar of Russia.

6. With such a record it is not surprising that the Regiment has been often mentioned in despatches. I will just quote one instance only. Sir James Willcocks reported with reference to the famous battle of Neuve Chapelle that all units of the Indian Corps there engaged did well and that the Indian units which specially distinguished themselves were the 1st and 2nd Battalions 39th Garhwal Rifles, including the Tihri Garhwal Sappers of the Imperial Service Troops.

7. This wonderful record leads us to enquire why the troops, European and Indian alike, have fought heroically for the British Empire. The reason is that one and all believe in the ideals of liberty, justice and sympathy and wish to uphold these against the tyranny, injustice, cruelty and oppression with which the world is threatened.

8. Our pleasure in welcoming back to India this splendid Regiment is marred by the thought of the many gallant men who have fallen. Though we mourn their loss, the war has brought home to us the truth of the old Roman saying " Dulce et decorum est pro patria mori," that is to say, it is sweet and right to lay down one's life for one's country.

9. Very few of us in Agra have had the privilege of entering the field of battle, but we must all feel that a soldier's glorious death on the field of battle is the best of all possible deaths.

10. We feel that the gallant men who have fallen have in dying laid on us the sacred obligation of upholding the cause of liberty, justice and sympathy by prosecuting the war to the bitter end till the would-be tyrants of the world have realised that treaties are not waste paper, that national honour is a precious thing, that the small nations have a right to their own national existence, that might is not right, and that no nation, however powerful, may attempt to destroy liberty and justice throughout the world.

11. We feel that the destiny of the whole of the British Empire and indeed of the world depends on the maintenance of those principles of liberty and justice. We feel that these sacred principles will form a sure foundation for the world settlement that will be made after the war, and we feel that it is the bounden duty of every citizen of the Empire who is prevented from fighting for his country to place at its service his whole energies, his whole wealth and all his abilities.

12. It now remains only to wish you all good fortune, happiness and many peaceful years in your glorious Himalayan home country.

To Lieut.-Col. Drake-Brockman, c.m.g., other Officers and Soldiers, 39th Garhwal Rifles.

We, the members of the "Garhwal Sabha," on behalf of the residents of Garhwal, beg to accord you a hearty welcome on the occasion of your return from the front. Ever since the outbreak of the European war in August, 1914, when you left us, we have been delighted to hear, from time to time, of your valiant deeds in the battlefields of Flanders. Though the war has not come to an end yet, you have played your part splendidly. We pray for the success of the British arms, and we are confident that the Army and Navy of our King Emperor will soon bring the war to a victorious conclusion, by overthrowing the enemies of civilisation. There is hardly any other Regiment in India who has returned with a more brilliant record of bravery. You have won two V.C.s, and so many other much coveted honours: we heartily congratulate you all for these distinctions and for the excellent work done by you in the battlefield. We are legitimately proud of your being considered as one of the brightest luminaries in the firmament of Indian Regiments. By your illustrious deeds you have achieved for us, in a short time, the great glory which could not be won in centuries—you have made the Garhwalis famous throughout the length and breadth of the British Empire and the wide world.

We heartily welcome you back from the front and present this humble address as a mark of our true love and esteem for you.

We beg to ascribe ourselves,

Your most obedient servants,

The Members of the Garhwal Sabha.

Kotdwara, Garhwal.
15*th March*, 1916.

Letter of Welcome from the O.C. 1st King George's Sappers and Miners, Rurki.

Rurki,

17*th March*, 1916.

Dear Drake-Brockman,

We have heard through various channels that your Regiment has returned to Lansdowne, and on behalf of the First Sappers and Miners I write to welcome the 39th Garhwal Rifles back to India.

Our close connection with your Regiment dates from 1898, when No. 2 Company 1st S. & M. was in Chitral with you, and the formation of the Garhwal Brigade brought us closer together.

In France two of our Companies have been with you in the Meerut Division, where you suffered such losses and your Regiment did such brilliant work.

The sadness of the loss of so many officers and men in France may perhaps be lessened by the thought of their splendid gallantry, and of the undying fame which they have brought to your Regiment.

With all good wishes for the future,

I am,

Yours very sincerely,

E. C. Tylden-Patterson,
Commanding 1st K.G.O. Sappers and Miners.

APPENDIX IV.

NOTES ON TRENCHES.

Protection from artillery fire is more important than an extensive field of fire. In the fighting about Ypres one trench with a field of fire of 80 yards only was never located by the German artillery. Its occupants lost only a few men and inflicted heavy losses on the German infantry.

When entrenching at night, a German company advances in open order to the place where the trench is to be dug. Each man then digs a hole. When these holes are about 32 inches deep, they are joined together in sections between traverses. so as to form an irregular line for the whole company. The number of traverses varies according to the ideas of the company commander. In one prisoner's company there were only two men between adjoining traverses. In a neighbouring company, with six men between traverses, the losses were much heavier. The digging is then continued, and loopholes are made. Pyramid-shaped boxes are used, but " the narrow end is placed towards the enemy, on account of the accuracy of the Indians' fire aimed at the opening of the loophole." Loopholes are also arranged so that men can fire at an angle and be safe from sharpshooters directly to their front. The trench is steadily deepened and improved. Each man sees to his own step, so that he may be able to stand at just the height from which he can make the best use of his rifle. Each man also sees to the provision of undercut shelter. If the soil is not sufficiently stiff, door panels, or any other available supports, are used. Great attention is paid to the safeguarding of trenches from enfilade fire. This can be insured by providing a sort of hammer-head at either end of a trench. This hammer-head may take the form of a long traverse, with a fire trench all round it; or of an advanced or refused barricaded curve.

Flank groups are responsible for the construction of passages communicating with the trenches of neighbouring companies.

Communications to the rear consist of zig-zag connecting trenches, depth a man's height. Whenever possible, existing ditches, whether boundaries between fields, or alongside roads, are utilized and deepened. These communications lead to a second line of trenches, of the same nature as the front trenches.

The following description has been prepared from information supplied by German prisoners, and may be taken as giving good examples of the extent and thoroughness of German digging, which enabled one prisoner's regiment of three battalions, only 720 strong, instead of 3,000, to hold a front of 550-600 yards. All three battalions were up in the front line, each with three companies in the fire trenches, and one in reserve. The companies in reserve went into billets and made themselves as comfortable as possible.

Of the companies in the fire trenches, about a quarter of each company went at a time to rest and sleep in the support trenches. Reliefs thus worked out at six hours.

Normally, a battalion of pioneers forms part of every German army corps. Prisoners have stated that each of the four companies of the pioneer battalion of the XIV. Corps opposite to us had a short-range bomb-gun, probably locally made, calibre about four inches. Two of these have been captured by us. The term *minenwerfer*, or mine thrower, has been applied to these bomb-guns, both by ourselves and by German prisoners. The regular *minenwerfer* is, however, a " store " 9.8in. siege howitzer.

The pioneers alone are allowed by the Germans to work the bomb-guns, to fire pistols with illuminating balls, and to throw and fire grenades.

The method of advancing the entrenched line is always the same, namely, the pushing of saps, which are linked up by lateral trenches until a continuous advanced line is opened up.

German pioneers do all the sapping, covered by one or two groups, each of one N.C.O. and about six men. Against such parties bombs are most effective.

When the Germans capture a trench, they start immediately to push out saps at either end of the captured length. These saps are provided with head cover against frontal fire, and are generally strengthened by machine guns, which not only enfilade any remaining hostile trenches on the flanks, but also the whole length of the captured trench, so that men delivering a counter attack are caught by enfilade machine-gun fire just as they are reaching the edge of the trench. The only antidote is to outflank the whole length of trench, with its machine guns, by employing flanking parties.

The following diagram illustrates the result which may be expected if such flanking parties are not employed. A party from a certain unit attacked a length of German trench along the line indicated by the arrow. Owing to the absence of flanking parties, it passed between the two sap heads A and B, under fire from both, reached the length of trench C D, which was empty, and pushed on to E F, where it bayoneted some of the enemy, and drove out the remainder. In the meantime, however, the men in the saps and sap heads ran back and occupied C D, so that, when our attacking party started to return to its own trench, it was met by fire and lost heavily.

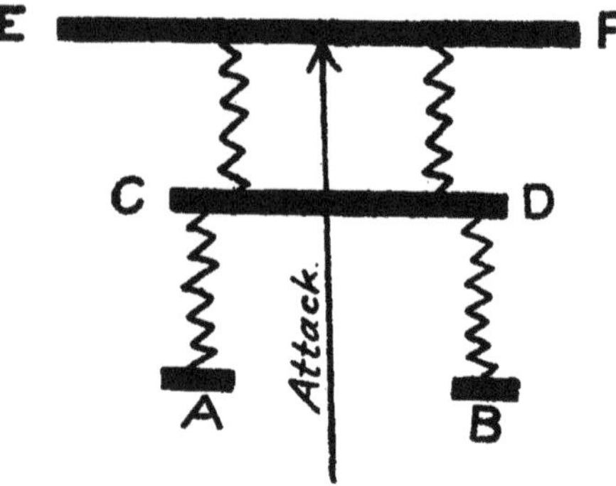

The German method of meeting the danger presented by a sap is to construct barricades in their threatened trench, so that, if it is blown in, the enemy's rush may be met, stopped and annihilated.

In attacking an enemy's trench through a breach made from a sap it would be necessary, therefore, to throw a large number of bombs to fall behind the barricades before attempting to storm the breach.

Experience has shown that German trenches are vulnerable to the following method of attack, namely, a heavy covering fire to enable a small party, provided with a plentiful supply of bombs, to get a footing in a part, preferably the end, of a trench. Men with fixed bayonets then precede the bomb thrower, who lights and throws bombs into the spaces between traverses, which are rushed in turn and cleared of any survivors. This process has been found in actual practice to be most successful.

To protect one's own trenches against a similar method of advance, loopholes should be constructed on the top of traverses, with steps for two men, so that fire may be opened on any length of trench between traverses which may fall into the enemy's hands.

Against occupied German trenches section volleys, at an angle to the enemy trenches, switched on suddenly and kept going rapidly, have been found very effective by one of the British divisions.

Attached is a plan of a section of trench made and occupied by a company of our gallant allies. It is interesting, both as an illustration of a system of entrenching, and of the gay spirit animating its defenders.

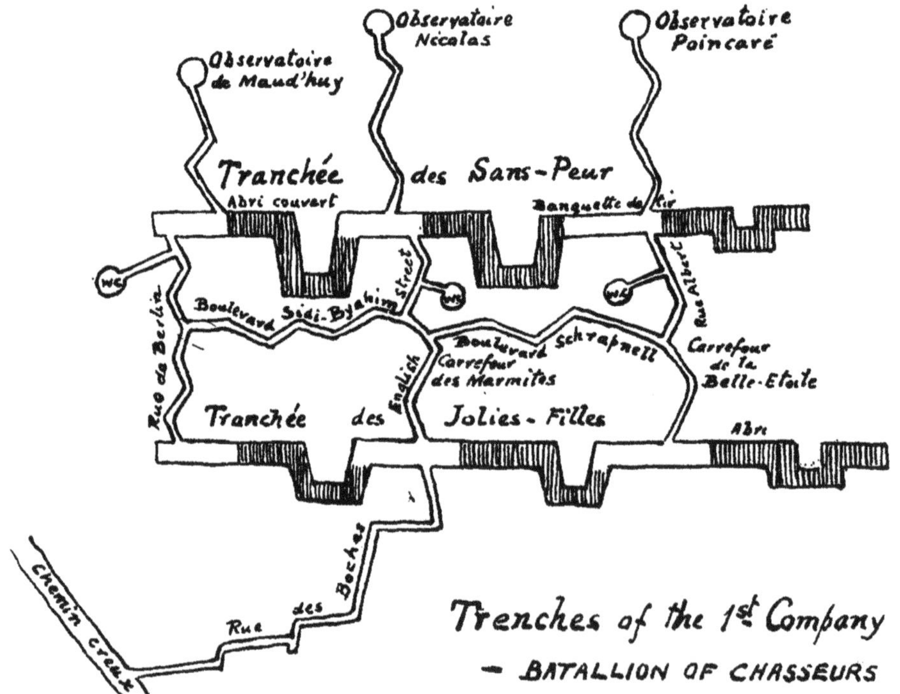

The latest German development in trench tactics is a perfection of the principle always adopted by them in all their tactics, namely, the provision of opportunities for their machine guns.

It is the construction of a V-shaped trench. Along the lines in prolongation of the arms of the V, machine guns, possibly concealed from frontal view, are so placed that they can sweep both arms. A sap is driven from the point of the V, to act as a bait. If the sap and V are attacked, the Germans vacate the latter, after a show of resistance, and retire to the real trench in the rear, in the hope that the attackers will crowd into the V. If they do so, they are wiped out by the machine guns.

The antidote is the capture of the sap, and the location of the machine guns by the aid of the pointers provided by the arms of the V. Arrangements can then be made to deal with the situation, as actually revealed, the main point being to avoid crowding into V, and to employ flanking parties.

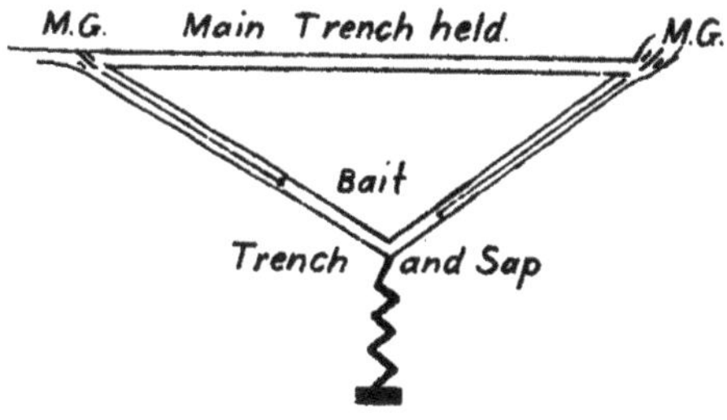

TRANSLATION OF A GERMAN COMPANY ORDER.

VERMELLES.

7th November, 1914.

1. Platoon commanders are personally responsible for the observance of the greatest cleanliness in shelters and trenches. For the remains of food, &c., holes must be dug which will be filled in every day. There should be a latrine near each shelter and trench were the men will go to relieve nature, spade in hand, so as to be able to cover their excreta at once with earth.

2. Before handing over shelters and trenches to another platoon, the platoon commander must ascertain that his sector is in good order. The platoon commander who is taking over the sector must also inspect it and report any defects to the company commander in writing.

3. All platoon commanders must improve their shelters and trenches without a company order for each particular case being necessary. The trenches should gradually be widened so that one can easily move past men firing, even during an engagement. Every two paces there should be a firing step on the front wall of the trench. These firing steps must be strong and horizontal to ensure steady fire.

The following sketch shows the profile of the trench :—

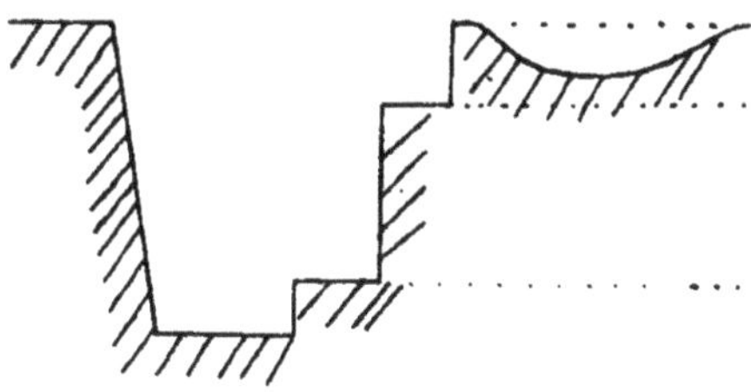

All communication trenches must be wide enough for a man to pass along with his knapsack on without touching the sides ; these must be cleaned and all projecting stones removed.

4. For observing and "sniping," lookouts and loopholes of wood will be constructed. Platoon commanders will detail as they think fit men who will be regularly relieved and whose duty will be to observe the enemy's trenches and to fire on any visible target. The rest of the men will be entirely under cover either at work or resting.

5. The platoon which is in the shelters should be employed, under detailed instructions from its commander, in repairing and cleaning clothing, boots, rifles, articles of equipment, &c. The ammunition will be counted and divided up equally The reserve rations will be checked. Every man must carry a tin of meat, one of vegetables and a bag of biscuits. The greatest care should be taken that none of the men consume these rations.

THE GERMAN TRENCHES.

The attached sketch illustrates the section of a German trench according to the information given by the prisoner, and the obstacles in front of, and between the German first and second line trenches.

The sectional drawing showing these obstacles between the first and second lines refers to those lines held by the Germans near Mauquissart.

Such information as has been extracted from the prisoner regarding the German trenches is chiefly a description of those held by the 13th Regiment, *i.e.*, between points 268 (M.24.d.3.2) and (M.36.a.4.4.), *i.e.*, between Fauquissart and Mauquissart, and thus cannot be taken as a criterion of the German line in front of the Indian Corps as a whole.

(a). *The Parapet* consists of two layers of sandbags on a layer of earth, the top being about three feet above ground level.

The front of the parapet slopes gently down to ground level, and is about 12ft. 6in. thick.

Parapets are mostly revetted with timber, sometimes with rabbit wire or fascines, at a steep slope.

The top of the parapet is about 4ft. 6in. from the firing step.

(b). *The firing step and floor of the trench.*—The firing step is about 1ft. 6in. wide and 4ft. 6in. from the top of the parapet, and is covered with planks. The floor of the trench is about 3ft. wide and about 7ft. 6in. from the top of the parapet, and 4ft. 6in. below ground level. The floor is not boarded or bricked, but is floored with wooden ladderwork.

(c). *The Parados* is about 15ft. thick and the top is about 3ft. above ground level. It is revetted with rabbit wire and fascines.

(d). *Dug-outs.*—There are dug-outs on both sides of the parados, but in no case is one dug-out directly behind the other.

Corrugated sheeting, covered in some cases with a layer of cement, constitutes the roof of the dug-out, which is supported by wooden beams.

The dug-outs are dug up to about 6ft. into the parados and are about 3ft. high.

Dug-outs are not constructed under the parapets as formerly, because it was found that :—

(1). Dug-outs under the parapet were more dangerous with heavy howitzer fire, and were often not bullet proof.

(2). In the event of a night attack troops were more liable to be trapped, with their backs towards the hostile position.

An inspection trench about 3ft. wide and 4ft. 6in. below ground level runs behind and alongside the parados.

(e). *Traverses.*—The distance between traverses is from 10 to 15 yards, and there are usually four men between traverses.

(f). *Loopholes.*—There are three or four loopholes for each " Gruppe " (Group), *i.e.*, eight men, but they are not often used.

(g). *Periscopes and periscopic rifles.*—One periscope is allotted to each Group, *i.e.*, eight men ; there are no magnifying periscopes.

There are a few periscopic rifles, used by specially selected snipers.

(h). *Hand grenades, bombs.*—Recesses are built in the parapet and parados for hand grenades, bombs, &c. Each Group has generally a stock of about 15 to 20 hand grenades in the first line, but there is always a larger supply in the second line.

(k.) *Rifle grenades.*—Rifle grenades are not stored in the trenches and are not fired by the infantry. Pioneers are told off for firing rifle grenades, and bring special rifles with them for this purpose.

(l). *Notice boards, lanterns, flags, &c.*—There are notice boards at the heads of communication trenches such as :—

" Verkehrs Graben " (Inspection or passage trench).

" Laufgraben nach der Ersten Linie " (Communication trench to the front line).

" Ausgang nach der Zweiten Linie " (Way out to the support trenches).

The object of these is to prevent congestion in communication trenches during an attack.

The length of trench held by the 13th Regiment is at present divided into three sections, which are marked by notice boards. There are no lanterns used in the trenches for marking flanks of Companies or Regiments. There are, however, red lanterns put up occasionally behind the lines to mark ditches, &c., for men moving about at night. No flags have been issued for demarcation of trenches captured *by* or *from* the enemy. There are no flags in the trenches for marking sections, or giving alignment for artillery. Such flags as appear now and again on the parapet have no significance and are merely examples of German humour. Each company has to send in a report, known as " Tagesbericht," every evening to battalion headquarters. This report contains a list of casualties during the past 24 hours.

About once every three days the Corporal in each Group has to send in a report showing the stock of S.A.A., hand grenades, &c., in his possession.

OBSTACLES.

(a). *In front of parapet.*—The line of the 13th Regiment is only protected by three rows of chevaux-de-frise, which are put out about 24 feet in front of the parapet. The rows are about three yards apart.

On the other hand the system of wire in front of the 15th regiment is more formidable and consists of wire entanglements on iron stakes as well as chevaux-de-frise. In other places rolls of loose wire are thrown out, which the prisoner says could be easily hauled in by us.

(b) *Between the first and second lines.*—The ground for about 80 to 90 yards from the parados of the front line is free of obstacles, but the system of wire entanglements on iron stakes 3ft. high is erected here, and continues for about five yards, after which the ground is open again until within about three yards of the second line.

Here there is a "Wolfsgrube" (lit. wolf pit) which consists of a ditch 5ft. broad and 3ft. deep full of wire entanglement and pointed stakes.

This ditch is about 3ft. from the parapet of the second line trench.

NOTES ON THE GERMAN DEFENCES ABOUT MAUQUISSART,

FROM THE OBSERVATION OF OFFICERS WHO TOOK PART IN THE ATTACK ON SEPTEMBER 25TH, 1915.

The attached sketches are from captured photos and from reports, and show the German trenches as accurately as possible.

FIRE TRENCHES.

It was generally agreed that the German trenches were much deeper and narrower than ours: at least a foot deeper. All estimates put the depth at not less than 8ft., and some at 9ft. This is clearly shown in the attached sketches.

SKETCH SHOWING GERMAN TRENCH (FROM PHOTO) NORTH OF NEUVE CHAPELLE in front of Mauquissart, and attacked by the Garhwal Brigade on September 25th, 1915, at action of Piètre—Battle of Loos.

Revetting is strong and well executed, with boards, brushwood and rabbit wire.

All firing steps are made of wood, on wooden legs, and are very narrow.

The parapet is higher than ours and about 12ft. thick. Sandbags are of every imaginable material and colour ; a lot look like ladies' dresses cut up.

Trenches seemed to be traversed rather less than ours, the same end being gained by making the trench very winding, this also having the advantage of giving good opportunities for flanking fire. This may also be due to the fact that the German position here is at an angle and has several salients. It must not, however, be supposed that there are no traverses : only rather less than in our trenches.

COMMUNICATION TRENCHES.

Communication trenches are very deep, apparently 9ft. to 10ft., and slightly wider than our own. They were mostly revetted with planks, *i.e.*, a sort of palisade revetment, sometimes with brushwood. The bottom was floored with wooden planks, carefully joined. These trenches were quite dry on the morning of the attack. A section of a communication trench is shown in the accompanying sketch.

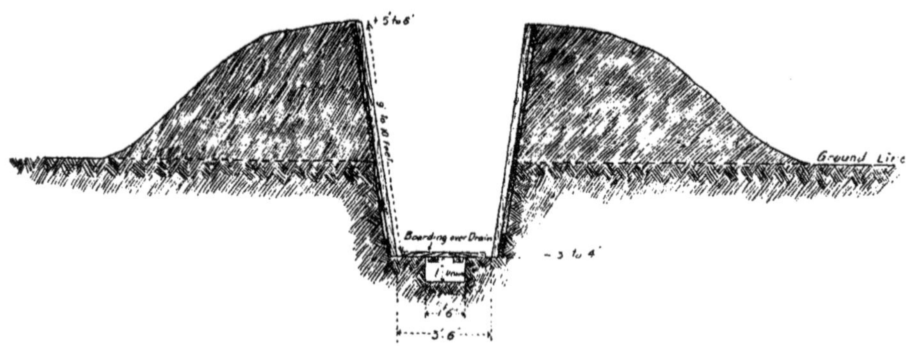

Section of a German Communication Trench near Mauquissart.

Communication trenches were mostly of the curved type, the curves generally being longer and more irregular than ours. Square traverses were uncommon ; where traverses occurred, they were usually rounded.

The bottom of the communication trenches never appeared to be below water level and probably varied from 3ft. to 4ft. below ground level.

It is reported that in some cases the walls consisted of cut-up, and re-made packing cases without tops or bottoms, filled with earth, &c., about 4ft. square and shallow. These seemed to be used to support and carry the earth on each side of the communication trenches, being piled one on top of the other to the necessary height.

The outer sides were very well masked, being hidden by earth, grass, thistles, &c.

In one communication trench running back to the German second line there was a large S.A.A. store, occupying an emplacement which looked as if it had been made for a field gun.

All ditches were cleaned and apparently could be utilised as communication trenches.

The German trench in front (West) of the Moulin du Piètre is quite 9ft. deep. In consolidating this trench, steps had to be cut half-way up in order to form a standing fire platform. It does not appear to be used as a fire trench.

DRAINAGE OF TRENCHES.

The trenches are kept dry under foot by wooden gratings or ladder work which rest on a shelf of solid wood or bricks on each side of the trench. Underneath the grating is a trough about 1½ft. wide and 1ft. deep.

There are a certain number of pumps (N.B.—Prisoners say that there were more of these during last winter and that more will doubtless be ordered for the coming winter).

Communication trenches are drained in a similar fashion ; lateral transverse drainage cuts run out of these at right angles into ditches or low ground.

The deciding factor in the depth of the bottom of the communication trenches below ground level appeared to be that they should be dug down to a depth enabling the drainage to be carried off by lateral cuts into the ditches.

DUG-OUTS.

The dug-outs for the men, both in the firing line and rear lines, were weather-proof and, as far as could be ascertained, waterproof from below, with good doors, and wooden floors.

These dug-outs were almost cylindrical in shape, made of corrugated iron sheeting in pieces 2½ft. or 3ft. wide. One dug-out was reported to have a dome-shaped corrugated steel roof about ¼in. thick.

There were bunks, tables and benches in them for about 10 or 12 men.

Some dug-outs were formed by widening and closing in the communication trenches between the firing line and support line. These were high enough to stand up in and had bunks like ship's cabins with wire mattresses. They had a door towards the firing line and also towards the support trenches.

In the trench in front of the Moulin du Piètrie there were a number of very deep dug-outs quite untouched by our shell fire. There were bunks, tables, coffee making and grinding machines, &c.

The Germans seem to have left this trench in a great hurry, as helmets, packs, &c., were strewn all over the place.

One officer saw electric light in the dug-outs further North, also a thick cable laid. Another officer reports a lot of electric light in use in hospitals and officers' dug-outs.

A place for a stove chimney appeared to be provided in the dug-outs, but no stoves were seen.

Machine Guns and Emplacements.

Emplacements were seen, both in the front line and behind the support line, and they all appear to be concreted.

An emplacement in the front line is described as follows :—

It was built in a sort of bay off the fire trench, and consisted of an arch, about 5ft. high and 8ft. or 10ft. across, made of concrete, quite 3ft. thick at the crown of the arch, and in the form of a square monolith.

The inside of the arch was lined with corrugated iron. The depth of the arch was estimated to be about 8ft. from the entrance (there was no door) to the end wall. It was rather dark inside, but there was apparently no sort of loophole in the emplacement, which contained boxes of ammunition and the men's kits.

The tripod was left mounted on the roof of the emplacement in a position to fire over the top of the parapet.

It had four legs, the rear ones fixed, the front adjustable, and a very small lateral traverse for the gun.

The emplacement also contained one oxygen breathing apparatus.

In another emplacement the gun was on an entirely different mounting, consisting of a small platform on two wooden wheels of about 18in. diameter.

On the centre of the platform was a table rotating on a verticle axis and marked off in degrees and minutes. The gun was carried on this table on a sort of cross-head with an elevating screw also marked off in degrees and minutes. In addition to the wheels, the platform had two short handles at each end.

The mounting appeared to be new and of very good workmanship, the elevating gear having some form of fine adjustment.

Two of the emplacements, both high command, built behind the support line, had vaulted roofs with iron arches, and had three chambers, one for the gun, one for the ammunition, of which there was a large store (evidently permanently kept there), and the third forming a sleeping chamber for the officer in charge. There was telephone communication from these emplacements direct.

The emplacements themselves were covered with earth and sods, and were built so that the guns in them could fire over the front line trenches if required.

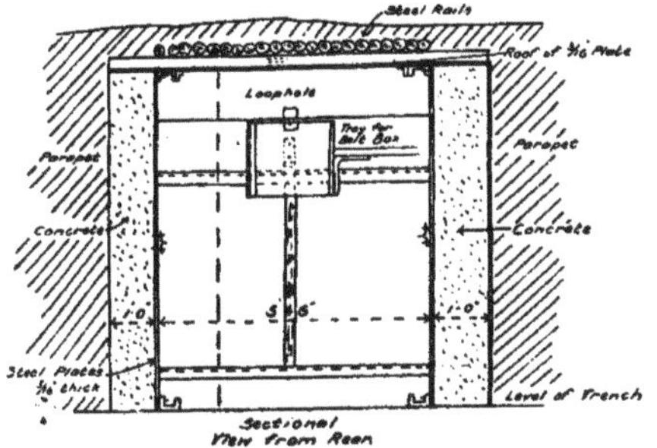

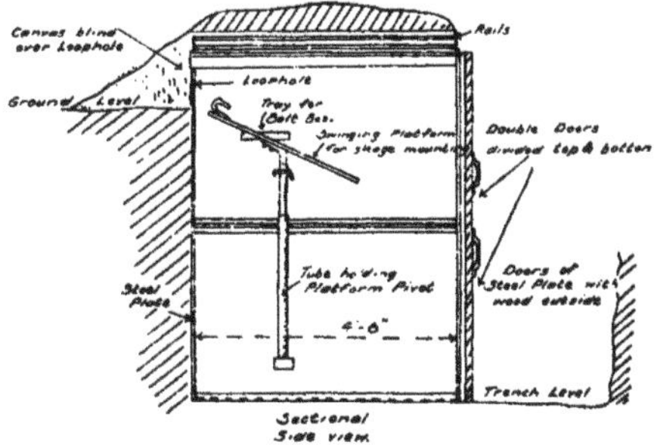

SKETCH OF GERMAN MACHINE GUN EMPLACEMENT.

Made of steel plates, concrete sides, framework of channel iron. Dimensions shown approximately.

HAND GRENADES.

A large number of hand grenades, nearly all with a short wooden handle, were seen in different parts of the trenches. Bombs were kept in large wooden boxes in recesses in the walls of trenches at regular intervals along the trench and clearly labelled BOMBS.

Evidence appears unanimous that not more than two different kinds of grenades were seen in use against us; that generally seen was the handle-grenade, but officers also state that, in the German counter-attack, grenades of a cricket ball type were employed, apparently working with percussion action.

MEDICAL.

There was an aid post situated about 300 yards from the fire trench, on a loop trench running off the main communication trench and close to the trolley line, with which it was connected by a wide trench with shallow steps leading up to the trolley level (probably about M.30.c.9.8.).

It consisted of two concrete dug-outs with arched roofs (shaped like a cellar), with curved corrugated iron lining and a central iron girder.

The floor was at the same level as the communication trench.

Opposite the doors the communication trench was widened so as to admit of stretchers being turned completely round. There was a red cross painted over the door of each dug-out.

There was a large amount of surgical equipment, and the dug-outs were fitted with electric light and a telephone.

Each dug-out would take about eight of our stretchers easily.

Compared with a British Aid Post its chief advantages appeared to be :—

(*a*) The telephone;
(*b*) Proximity to the firing line;
(*c*) Proximity to tram line.

On account of (*b*) and (*c*) very little communication trench would necessarily be used by the wounded.

TROLLEY LINES.

These were well screened, but were not sunk in trenches. All rails appeared to be of steel.

There is a tramway running down the Piètre road as far as the barricade at M.30.c.6.o. This barricade is very low.

MISCELLANEOUS.

(*a*). In one place a large number of things like short iron screw piles had been driven in rows into the ground to form a square about 20ft. by 20ft. These piles resemble giant corkscrews, made of about 1½in. bar iron, the outside diameter of the screw being about 10in. to 1ft.—length about 2ft. 6in. to 3ft.

In many parts of the front trenches similar piles were seen.

(These are probably earth drilling machines for sinking mine shafts).

(*b*). There was barbed wire on the ground level between the firing line and supports, as well as in front of the front line.

(*c*). The Moulin du Piètre was reported to be apparently full of snipers and strongly held. Examination of it by periscope from the trench just in front (West) of it appeared to show the snipers to be well concealed in very rough and natural looking brick emplacements.

[TRANSLATION OF A GERMAN DOCUMENT.]

MACHINE GUNS.

Experience gained during the past weeks has shown that the method of employing our machine guns in trench warfare is in need of improvement. We have only succeeded in a comparatively limited number of cases in stopping the enemy's attacks by fire from our machine guns. As a rule, when the moment came for the assault, our machine guns had already been put out of action by the fire of the enemy's artillery or else their emplacements were constructed in such a manner that we were not able to make use of all the possibilities of this weapon from the point of view of flanking fire.

The following points should be kept in mind as regards the employment of machine guns :—

The employment of machine guns for firing perpendicularly to the front is outside the scope of the proper use of these weapons. It should be avoided on principle. Whenever possible, *machine guns should be used for flanking fire and placed a little to the rear in commanding positions.*

Above all, machine guns should be placed where they can enfilade those portions of the enemy's advanced trenches, which our artillery cannot reach or can only reach with difficulty. At points where the enemy is continually pushing forward his works, and where an attack may be made at any moment, it is important to bring cross-fire to bear on his works.

It is particularly important to provide good cover for machine guns.

Every machine gun should be entirely concealed from the enemy's view, or else so well masked that it remains undiscovered. It is often necessary to strengthen very considerably the roofs of machine gun emplacements.

It is advisable during the day, in places which are very much exposed to the enemy's artillery fire, to remove machine guns from the fire trench and place them in shelters which are well protected against artillery fire. At the same time, when this is done, it must be possible to move the machine gun to its firing position immediately.

It is advantageous frequently to change the firing position of machine guns. Above all, a machine gun which has fired during the night should not remain in the same position during the following day.

When there is a shortage of machine guns, machine gun emplacements should be constructed so that the gun can be fired in two different directions.

It is particularly important for sector commanders and commanders of machine gun companies not to remain satisfied with the emplacements originally selected for machine guns, but constantly to search for positions allowing of a more advantageous use of their guns. It is always possible to find new emplacements, even in positions which have been occupied by the troops for many months.

[TRANSLATION OF A GERMAN DOCUMENT.]

IMPROVEMENT OF THE POSITION NEAR MESSINES.

1. The parapets must be strengthened by earth obtained from in front of the parapet and by earth obtained from behind the trenches. (Thickness of earth at top —1 metre).

2. In Sector E (L.3 in future), it should not be forgotten to make the traverses hollow, in order to provide fire from them to flank the trench.

3. Company Commanders will gradually build up a reserve of 100 cartridges for illuminating pistols for use in special circumstances: these will be properly handed over when the company is relieved.

4. Medical officers will inspect the trenches daily and see that they are kept in a perfectly sanitary condition.

5. The best safeguard against surprise *is a strong obstacle in front* of the position. The greatest attention must always be paid to maintaining and increasing this obstacle.

6. As planks and boards can no longer be issued in sufficient quantities, it is essential that all available material in the evacuated dug-outs in rear of our position, and in houses, should be collected by special detachments and utilized in the defences. Commanders of sub-sectors will issue the necessary orders for this.

7. Rifle racks and order boards for companies, platoons and groups are not yet available in sufficient numbers. In each platoon or group sector, lists will be posted up on which will be entered the names of all group commanders and men on duty for every period of the day: these lists will be protected against rain.

8. In case of an attack by the enemy, *fire must be delivered over the top of the parapet.* For this purpose, steps, benches and ladders, which can also be used for climbing over the parapet, are to be procured at once by each company. They can be constructed even by day in the first line trenches: the most suitable type should be ascertained at once.

9. Company Commanders will decide each day at what time day and night duties are to commence.

10. All commanders and men must know the enemy's position in their front and the enemy's approaches to this position, and must be instructed in the names of localities situated to the front. Every Company Commander must be in possession of plans of the enemy's position, with the trenches numbered.

11. The shutters of many of the steel loopholes cannot be moved: they must be properly oiled.

APPENDIX V.

TRANSLATION FROM "LILLE WAR GAZETTE," 3RD MARCH, 1915.

(This is a weekly newspaper, issued by the Germans in LILLE, in German).

FIRE.

(BY LIEUT.-COLONEL KADEN).

As children many of us have played with it: some of us have seen an outbreak of fire. First a small tongue-like flame appears: it grows into a devastating fury of heat. We out here in the field have seen more than enough of it.

But there is also the fire of joy, of sacred enthusiasm! It arose from sacrificial altars, from mountain heights of Germany, and lit up the heavens at the time of solstice and whenever the home countries were in danger. This year fires of joy shall flare from the Bismarck Columns throughout the length and breadth of Germany, for on 1st April, just one hundred years ago, our country's greatest son was born. Let us celebrate this event in a manner deep, far-reaching and mighty! BLOOD AND IRON.

Let every German, man or woman, young or old, find in his heart a Bismarck Column, a pillar of fire now in these days of storm and stress. Let this fire, enkindled in every German breast, be a fire of joy, of holiest enthusiasm. But let it be terrible, unfettered, let it carry horror and destruction! Call it HATE! Let no one come to you with "Love thine enemy!" We all have but one enemy, *England*: How long have we wooed her almost to the point of our own self-abasement. She would none of us, so leave to her the apostles of peace, the "No War" disciples. The time has passed when we would do homage to everything English—our cousins that were!

"God punish England!" "May he punish her!" This is the greeting that now passes when Germans meet. The fire of this righteous hate is all aglow!

You men of Germany, from East and West, forced to shed your blood in the defence of your home-land through England's infamous envy and hatred of Germany's progress, feed the flame that burns in your souls. We have but one war-cry, "GOD PUNISH ENGLAND!" Hiss this to one another in the trenches, in the charge; hiss as it were the sound of licking flames.

Behold in every dead comrade a sacrifice forced from you by this accursed people. Take tenfold vengeance for each hero's death.

You German people at home, feed this fire of hate!

You mothers, engrave this in the heart of the babe at your breast!

You thousands of teachers, to whom millions of German children look up with eyes and hearts, teach HATE! unquenchable HATE!

You homes of German learning, pile up the fuel on this fire! Tell the nation that this hate is not un-German, that it is not poison for our people. Write in letters of fire the name of our bitterest enemy. You guardians of the truth, feed this sacred HATE!

You German fathers, lead your children up to the high hills of our home-land, at their feet our dear country bathed in sunshine. Your women and children shall starve; bestial, devilish conception. England wills it! Surely, all that is in you rises against such infamy.

Listen to the ceaseless song of the German forest, behold the fruitful fields like rolling seas, then will your love for this wondrous land find the right words, HATE, unquenchable HATE. Germany, Germany above all !

Let it be inculcated in your children and it will grow like a land-slide, irresistible, from generation to generation.

You fathers, proclaim it aloud over the billowing fields, that the toiling peasant below may hear you, that the birds of the forest may fly away with the message: into all the land, that echoes from German cliffs send it reverberating like the clanging of bells from tower to tower throughout the countryside: " HATE, HATE, the accursed English, HATE ! "

You masters, carry the flame to your workshops; axe and hammer will fall the heavier when arms are nerved by this HATE.

You peasants, guard this flame, fan it anew in the hearts of your toilers, that the hand may rest heavy on the plough that throws up the soil of our home-land.

What CARTHAGE was to ROME, ENGLAND is to GERMANY. For ROME as for us it is a question of " to be or not to be." May our people find a faithful mentor like Cato. His " ceterum censeo, Carthaginem esse delendam " for us Germans means :—

" GOD PUNISH ENGLAND."

N.B.—A copy of this newspaper was found on a German prisoner captured during the recent fighting at NEUVE CHAPELLE. *It is of interest as showing the hatred for Great Britain which is being sedulously cultivated in Germany. This hatred is being encouraged and fostered officially by every possible means.*

APPENDIX VI.

MISCELLANEOUS REPORTS AND ORDERS.

STANDING ORDERS FOR TROOPS ON THE HIRED TROOPSHIP S.S. "COCONADA" SEPTEMBER-OCTOBER, 1914, by Lieut.-Colonel D. H. Drake-Brockman, 2/39th Garhwal Rifles, Comdg. Troops.

DUTIES.—I.

(1). A British Officer from the Wing 2/3rd (Q.A.O.) G.R., and the 2/39th G. will be detailed daily for duty from 5 p.m. to 5 p.m. He will visit all guards and sentries once by day and once by night, and report verbally on relief daily at 5 p.m. to O.C. Troops.

(2). Guards and Sentries will be posted as under :—

(*a*) Quarter Guard, 1 N.C.O. and 3 men over the Magazine on the Main Troop Deck, aft. (Furnished by the 2/39th G.).

(*b*) 1 Sentry on each Troop deck furnished by each Company occupying that portion of the Deck.

(*c*) 2 Sentries on the Followers' quarters. (Furnished by the 2/39th G.).

(3). *Cooking Places*, *Latrines* and *Fresh Water Taps* will be picketed by men of the Sanitary Squad. The Forward Taps on Upper Deck by 2/3rd G.R. and the after ones by the 2/39th G.

(4). *The following will be the Orders for the Sentries :—*

(*a*) No smoking, striking of matches, or the use of naked lights is allowed on troop decks on any pretence whatever. Only Ship's lights are to be used.

(*b*) Smoking is only allowed on the Upper Deck.

(*c*) To see that the Decks are kept clean and not fouled in any way and to give the "Alarm" in case of fire.

(5). Every morning at 5 a.m. all kits should be rolled up and hung up on hooks to allow Decks to be cleaned. The Lower Deck will be only dry holystoned daily and the other Decks cleaned with water as well. The rubbing with sand, &c., will be done by the men and the swabbing down with water by the Ship's crew. When the Decks are dry, bedding may be put down again.

DAILY INSPECTION.—II.

The O.C. Troops and Ship's Captain, accompanied by the S.M.O., will make his daily inspection of the Ship at 10.30 a.m. Officers commanding Units on board will be present with their Units at this Inspection.

RATIONS.—III.

Rations will be drawn daily at 3 p.m. Units will make their own arrangements for drawing them. Indents should be submitted the day before so that everything may be ready for issue.

FIRE ALARM.—IV.

On the "Alarm" sounding for Fire or any other reason, *i.e.*, the Ship's bell being rung violently, the following precautions will be taken :—

(*a*) All Men and Followers will fall in on their respective Troop Decks and await orders. British Officers will at once repair to their respective commands.

(*b*) One Sentry furnished by the 2/3rd G.R. will fall in at all forward Gangways leading to Upper, Saloon and Boat Decks, with fixed bayonets, and one Sentry furnished by the 2/39th G. at each after Gangway leading to Upper, Saloon and Boat Decks, to prevent anyone leaving their Decks without Orders.

LIGHTS OUT.—V.

A whistle will be sounded at 9 p.m. for "Lights Out," when all men will keep quiet.

BUGLES.—VI.

No bugles will be sounded on board, except for "Man overboard," when the "Alarm" will be sounded. For this purpose a Bugler detailed by the 2/39th G. will always be on duty on the Forward Well Deck.

WATER.—VII.

Water will be pumped up daily as under : —6-9 a.m. 11.30 a.m.-1.30 p.m. 5-6.30 p.m.

The drawing of water to be regulated accordingly.

MISCELLANEOUS.—VIII.

(*a*) The use of hurricane lamps is strictly forbidden, and all lamps with any oil in them are to be emptied immediately.

(*b*) Men are strictly prohibited from sitting on or leaning too far over the railings or bulwarks.

COOKING RATION.

	ozs.
Atta	16
Rice	12
Garlic	1-6th
Ghee	2
Ginger	1-3rd
Potatoes	6
Salt	1-3rd
Sugar	1
Tamarind	½
Tea	1-3rd
Turmeric	1-6th
Chillies	1-6th

NON-COOKING RATION.

	ozs.
Parched gram ...	12
Dried fruits... ...	16
Garlic	1-16th
Ghee	3
Salt	1-3rd
Sugar	6
Tamarind	2

ORDERS FOR CARE OF RIFLES, &c., IN THE TRENCHES.

The attention of all officers is drawn to the following points to which very special attention should be given while in the trenches :—

1. A careful cleaning of rifles daily ; a time should be appointed for this, and then an inspection held of all daily.

2. The cloth cover for the bolt should be always kept over it, except by the actual men on sentry duty, till it is necessary to use the rifle.

3. It is strictly forbidden for men to wear the Balaclava cap pulled down over the ears when on sentry duty at any time. The cap should, in fact, not be worn at all by men on duty.

4. Careful attention is to be paid to the attached typed instructions regarding the number, posting, relieving and visiting of sentries while in the trenches.

5. British Officers commanding companies should carefully examine with periscope the enemy's trenches and ground to their front and note any additions to wire entanglements, machine guns and other points.

INSTRUCTIONS FOR POSTING AND RELIEVING OF SENTRIES IN THE TRENCHES.

1. In future when units are occupying trenches in the firing line, sentries are to be relieved at least *once per hour*.

2. At night in cold and inclement weather they should be relieved every half-hour.

3. They should be regularly posted by an N.C.O.

4. The N.C.O.s in each section or platoon should be divided into watches to extend over all the hours of darkness.

5. The N.C.O. on watch to be on duty just as the sentries are ; he should patrol his length of trench during his watch, constantly visiting all sentries.

6. The trench should also be continually patrolled by a British officer.

7. Before dusk, when all stand to arms, every loophole should be examined by an officer to see that it is perfectly clear for observation or to fire through.

E. R. P. BERRYMAN,

1.11.14. Capt. Adjt. 2/39th G.

INSTRUCTIONS FOR PICQUETS IN THE FRONT LINE

Held by the 2nd Battalion 39th Garhwal Rifles.

1. The following instructions are issued for the guidance of British and Garhwali Officers for the Picquets placed by them in the front line from their respective Companies.

2. There are 5 Picquets in our Centre Sub-Section. Each will consist of 1 N.C.O. and 3 or 6 Riflemen, *i.e.*, Nos. 1, 4 and 5 of 6 Riflemen and Nos. 2 and 3 of 3 Riflemen.

3. One man from each Picquet should patrol by night along the line of parapet towards the Picquet on his right and left. One man in each Picquet should be on sentry in the Picquet post on the look-out. The sentry will fire occasional aimed shots at the enemy's loopholes. Also the men patrolling along the front should fire occasional shots from different places along the parapet as they are patrolling. Any enemy showing themselves or enemy's patrols should be fired on at once.

The idea in firing occasional shots from different places along the front parapet is to give the enemy the idea that the whole length is still held in strength.

4. One Picquet only in the front line will have a Garhwali Officer in command, in addition to the N.C.O. This duty will be taken in turn by each Company, commencing from the right, *i.e.*, the British Officer concerned will detail one of his Garhwali Officers to command one of the Picquets furnished by his Company. He will be relieved 5 a.m. and 5 p.m.

5. Picquets will be relieved at 5 p.m., 12 midnight, and at 5 a.m. Those going out in relief at 5 a.m. will remain out for the 12 hours, *i.e.*, from 5 a.m. till 5 p.m.

6. All Picquets are to hold on to their positions in case of attack till the last possible moment and demonstrate by fire as much as possible, and then retire, if necessary, on to the main line of Defence in front of the RUE DU BOIS, clearing the Battalion Front as much as possible by retiring by either flank, but without encroaching on the front of Sections on our right and left.

7. A Garhwali Officer will be told off by each Company Commander (*i.e.*, British Officer Commanding the Company) to visit the Picquets furnished by his Company once between 8 p.m. and 12 midnight, and once again between 12 midnight and 5 a.m.

8. British Officers Commanding Companies will themselves visit the Picquets furnished by their respective Companies the first day they are placed out in relief of the relieved Battalion, and so get acquainted with their position and the ground to their immediate front.

9. These instructions are to be kept by British and Garhwali Officers. The latter have been issued with a vernacular copy each.

10. The Garhwali Officer in the Picquet line will remain with that Picquet which has the telephone instrument, so as to be in communication with his Company Commander at Sub-Sect. Hd. Qrs.

E. R. P. Berryman,
26.1.15. Capt. Adjt. 2/39th G.

Note.—*The above Picquets had to be placed out to occupy the original Front Line which had to be temporarily abandoned owing to its water-logged condition. A breastwork* 30-40 *yards in front of the Rue du Bois was held in lieu during the winter of* 1914.

D. H. Drake-Brockman,
26*th January*, 1915. Lieut.-Col 2/39th G.

Headquarters Garhwal Brigade.
16*th October*, 1915.

INSTRUCTIONS
FOR COUNTER-ATTACK

(From Trenches, right resting on the La Bassée Canal, covering Givenchy).

In the event of a hostile attack the most probable situation with which we should have to deal would be the breaking of the line between the outside limits of the junction of COVENTRY STREET with the front line and NEW TRENCH.

In the event of such a situation arising action is to be immediately taken in the following lines :—

Right Counter-attack.

The Garhwal Rifles will attack up the front trench with one grenadier platoon, making at the same time a defensive flank towards the enemy from the front to the local reserve line.

2nd Leicesters will attack up the support line, if necessary, with three bombing parties, from GLASGOW STREET, CAMBRIDGE TERRACE and KING'S ROAD.

2/3rd Gurkhas will support Garhwal Rifles grenadier platoon with one company, grenadier platoon in front, *via* ORCHARD ROAD.

One company with grenadier platoon in front *via* WOLFE ROAD to support Leicesters.

Two grenadier platoons to block QUEEN'S ROAD at junction of LAVENDER STREET and HERTS AVENUE at junction of CALEDONIAN ROAD.

The remainder of the Battalion will move to WINDY CORNER.

Left Counter-attack.

1st Seaforths will attack up NEW TRENCH from GALLOW GATE, and up support line from SCOTTISH TRENCH with two grenadier platoons, they will at the same time make a defensive flank and front of NEW TRENCH and WARE ROAD.

2/8th Gurkhas will support 1st Seaforths in front line with one company, grenadier platoon leading, *via* HITCHEN and CAMBRIN ROADS.

One company, with grenadier platoon leading, to support 1st Seaforths in support line *via* COLDSTREAM LANE and NEW CUT.

Remainder of the Battalion will attack up NEW CUT and THE AVENUE.

The object of the above is to regain possession of our front and support lines, thus cutting off any of the enemy who may have penetrated our front.

The Brigade Grenade Company will move to WINDY CORNER. In order to ensure success it is imperative that all grenadier parties and bombs are always ready to start the attack.

Sd., W. A. S. CASSON, Major.
Brigade Major Garhwal Brigade.

Copy to: Officer Commanding Garhwal Rifles.

STANDING ORDERS
BY
LT.-COLONEL D. H. DRAKE-BROCKMAN, C.M.G.,
Commanding Troops on Hired Troopship, S.S. "Aronda."

1. The following appointments are made: —Ship's Adjutant, Captain G. R. Mainwaring, The Garhwal Rifles. Ship's Quartermaster, Lieut. F. N. Fox, The Garhwal Rifles.

2. The daily inspection of the ship by the captain will be made at 10 a.m.

He will be accompanied by the O.C. Troops, O.C. 107th Pioneers, Medical Officers, Adjutants, 1 Bugler (to be detailed by O.C. 107th Pioneers).

3. Companies will fall in on the bugle sounding the "Fall in" at the stations detailed for them in para 9 and stand at ease, being called to attention when the Inspecting Officers pass. As soon as the inspection is over the "Dismiss" will be sounded.

4. "Reveille" will be at 5 a.m. "Lights out" at 9 p.m.

5. The Indian Officer of the day on duty of the 107th Pioneers and Garhwal Rifles will report to the Ship's Adjutant in addition to the usual report furnished to their own Regiments, that lights are out and all is correct or otherwise during his tour of duty. He will visit the sentries twice by day and twice by night. Tour of duty 5 p.m. to 5 p.m.

6. A British Officer of the day will be appointed daily in rotation from both Battalions.

His tour of duty will be from 5 p.m to 5 p.m. His duty will be to turn out both Quarter Guards and visit all sentries once by day and once by night, reporting verbally to O.C. Troops on relief at 5 p.m., as well as to his own C.O.

7. Kits will be tied up at "Reveille" to enable decks to be cleaned. They will remain tied up until after the daily inspection, when they will be put down immediately after.

8. In addition to the Quarter Guard sentry, other sentries without rifles and with side arms only will be placed on each side of each deck occupied by troops detailed from the Company occupying that portion of deck. Their duties are:—

(1). To see that no smoking is allowed between decks.
(2). To see that no naked lights are used.
(3). To give the alarm on fire being observed.
(4). To see that the decks are kept clean.

9. Stations for the daily inspection and on the "Alarm" sounding are detailed as under:—

107TH PIONEERS. Strength—843.

Aft Rafts (7 at 25 each)	175
Aft Boats (7 at 50 each)	350
Port Side Promenade Deck Boats (4 at 50)	200
Starboard Side Promenade Deck Boats (1 at 50)	50
	775

THE GARHWAL RIFLES. Strength—398.

Forward Rafts (6 at 25, 1 at 60, 1 at 35)	245
Starboard Side Promenade Deck Boats (2 at 50)	100
	345

BRIGADE HEADQUARTERS AND SIGNALLING UNIT. Strength—British 50, Indian 27—77.

Starboard Side Promenade Deck Boats (1 at 50)	50

10. Rations will be issued daily after morning inspection at 10.30 a.m.

11. The machine guns of the 107th Pioneers and The Garhwal Rifles will be placed ready for action as follows:—

Two on small roof of hatchway by foremast and four on the small deck by bridge, and all will be under the Machine Gun Officer of the 107th Pioneers.

12. On arrival in port a sentry will be placed by each unit on the gangway.

13. The time for drawing water is as follows: From 6 a.m. to 9 a.m. and from 4 p.m. to 6 p.m.

14. Men should be practised under regimental arrangements in putting on the lifebelts issued to them, also in falling in on their stations as laid down in para. 9.

N.B.—On the return journey there was a much greater danger from hostile submarines. It will be seen from above orders in para. 9 that there was insufficient boat and raft accommodation for the numbers on board.

APPENDIX VII.

OPERATION ORDERS

ISSUED FOR THE VARIOUS BATTLES WITH REPORTS THEREON.

REPORT ON ACTION OF 9TH NOVEMBER, 1914.

From the Brigade Major, 20th Brigade.

To the Officer Commanding 2nd Battalion 39th Garhwal Rifles.

No. B.M. 186, dated 8th November, 1914.

Reference your sketch. The Major-General Commanding Division thinks trenches are too close and perpendicular to our trenches at cross-roads and that they probably run more from North-East to South-West. Please verify. aaa. He also requires some estimate of numbers of German Infantry attacking Seaforths yesterday and numbers of casualties sustained by enemy. Please send if possible. aaa. G.O.C. Brigade also asks me to thank you for the excellent report and the work done by the Battalion.

No. B.M.194, dated 9th November, 1914. 9.50 a.m.

Officer Comdg. 1/39th G. reports enemy have occupied a trench 50 yards in front of your right. This trench seems to threaten to enfilade 1/39th left trench. I consider enemy should be driven out of this close proximity. Please concert measures in conjunction with O.C. 1/39th G. to make combined attack on this trench rendering it ineffective for enemy's further occupation. No Sappers available to mine it, being withdrawn by Division. Repeated to O.C. 1/39th G.

Endorsement by the Adjutant 2/39th Garhwal Rifles.

To O.C. No. 2 Company.

For information and compliance and return please. Do as you suggest and in consultation with Capt. Lane make a combined attack on this trench.

Reply by Major Taylor, Comdg. No. 2 Company 2/39th G. 9.11.14.

Noted. I have been waiting for the C.O. to come and see the trench. I think there should be a party of at least 100 men (say 50 from us). But as No. 2 Coy. knows the ground by both day and night it would be (in my opinion) inadvisable to use either half-company in full—particularly Nos. 7-8 Platoons should chiefly remain in their trench to give support by fire (if necessary) on other trenches, or to repel a counter-attack. The same applies in a slightly less degree to Nos. 5 and 6 Platoons Company. The party should be under a B.O. Please inform me if the C.O. is coming—or any more orders. I will wait to go and meet Captain Lane until I hear whether the C.O. is coming now or not.

Report by Major Taylor, Comdg. No. 2 Company 2/39th Garhwal Rifles on the night attack on the German trenches facing Richebourg L'Avoué on the night of 9th November, 1914. Dated 10/11/14.

The enemy had been making a trench parallel to ours for 3 or 4 days and I received orders to seize it and fill it in, no explosives being available. I asked for 50 men, and for a similar number from the 1/39th G. to co-operate. I arranged for 10 men behind each party to carry several shovels each and to follow when we had taken the trench. There being a shallow drain leading up to centre of enemy's trench, I took this as my directing mark on my right, and the 1/39th G. were to keep in touch with it, keeping it on their left. The ground we had to move over was open, with no concealment but a few turnips. The ground on the right of the drain (where the 1/39th were) had more cover from view, being covered with high cabbages and other vegetables. The night was clear, moonless, and the distance to be traversed in the open about 50 yards. The advance was slow as we crawled along on our stomachs, the 1/39th men keeping more upright, but losing connection several times. I had ordered a man to snipe up the drain (between the two parties) towards the enemy to make him think nothing unusual was occurring. There was no wire or other entanglement, and eventually we crawled on to the enemy's parapet itself or just below it and lay waiting for the 1/39th party to join up. During our advance several rounds had been fired from their loopholes, but was evidently the usual sniping, and their sentries could not have been very alert, as though we lay on the parapet some time no alarm was raised. I could hear the Germans talking, and on being scolded by an officer or N.C.O. they kept quieter. At length, judging the 1/39th party to have had time to get near the trench, I fired my revolver at a German who appeared in the passage of the trench and shouted "Charge." The men charged and moved further on to the parapet. Many of the enemy fired at us at close range, one round or so, and then bolted. We fired a few rounds after them, and I fired at six men who appeared in the trench below me in turn with my revolver.

We then entered the trench and my party (2/39th G.) captured at once three prisoners. On our charge the 1/39th party also cheered and advanced to the trench. I heard firing and shouting on their part. I went out of the trench to see what they were doing and was fired at twice from a loophole close to the ground. I thought at first it was a 2/39th man, but soon saw it was a loophole from which firing was going on towards our own trench. I went back to the trench, which was more of a field work than a trench. It was seven or eight feet deep, revetted, roofed, loopholed and quite shrapnel proof. Also it was at least 150 yards long, and there was a deep, roofed communication trench leading to the rear.

All this time the din was terrific; rifle and machine-gun fire, and now shells devoted their energies to us. Luckily, the ground being low and by keeping down and in the enemy's trenches, few casualties occurred to the 2/39th G. party. Those that occurred were chiefly suffered, I think, from the fire from the trench at our rush. We had four wounded, but the 1/39th G. loss was, I believe, heavier, but I am not sure of exact details.

Seeing that to fill in the trench with the few men with me would be a task of days, not of hours, also seeing that even if we filled it in, it would be a task of no difficulty and danger for the enemy to sap again from their communication trench and make the trench as good as before in a very short time, and also the fact that the fire was getting heavy, and the Germans attacking on our trenches (although at the time I did not understand what was going on, I feared a counter attack from the fire and movement there), induced me to give the order to both parties to retire. I sent the prisoners off and collected some men to carry Naik Lal Sing Bisht, who was badly wounded. We brought in one German rifle, three Pickle Haubes, six prisoners and one pair of shoulder straps. The 1/39th G. party acted independently of me and I can give no report of their actions. I only gave general orders, as commanding the whole party. The following behaved extremely well and were of great assistance to me :—

Jemadar Khusal Sing Danu, D Coy.,
Havaldar Ranjor Sing Pundir, C Coy.,
Havaldar Diwan Sing Padhiyar, A Coy.

In conclusion, I would mention that the trench seemed to be full of men; I presume nearly 100, if not more, and had they kept efficient watch or had any obstacles or warning apparatus, we must have suffered a severe loss. Now that the Germans have been warned it is not likely that a similar proceeding could be carried out again in the same way.

The chief danger from this trench to us is mining, as we could not tell from which point they would start. They might also try to rush our trenches from it, but if we could have some more barbed wire I think we could secure ourselves against any such attempt.

The Germans were again at work in the trench at an early hour this morning.

G. H. Taylor,
Major, 2/39th G.

REPORT ON THE PART TAKEN IN THE ACTION OF 9th NOVEMBER, 1914, BY 2/39th GARHWAL RIFLES.

To the Brigade Major, 20th Brigade.

Dated 10.11.1914.

I append herewith my report on the attack carried out by Major Taylor on the enemy's trench 50 yards in front of our right flank.

As the enemy's trench had now got rather close, it was deemed advisable to make an attack on it with the object of filling it in and making it useless to the enemy, at any rate for a time.

After an inspection of the hostile trench and receipt of reports from my Company Commander as to the probable strength of the enemy, I suggested a party of 50 men all told, including 25 from the 1/39th G., who had been asked to co-operate, and that the assault should be carried out at 6 p.m., and Major Taylor to be in command.

Later in the afternoon, however, Major Taylor thought he would like a few more men, 100 all told, including those from 1/39th G. I acquiesced.

The assault did not take place at six o'clock owing to unforeseen delay.

When the 1/39th G. arrived the whole detachment was lined up in the irrigation ditch which runs along the front of my position and the "gap" to the 1/39th G. trench.

A portion of them were told off with picks and shovels to fill in the trench after it had been captured.

The whole party, under Major Taylor, got the order to advance, but apparently the order was not passed quickly enough down the line, and the 2/39th G. started by themselves. They crept forward on their stomachs and arrived unchallenged and unseen on the parapet of the enemy's trench and lay waiting for the 1/39th G. party to join, which had delayed in starting. There was no British Officer with this party after all.

No firing took place during the advance except the usual sniping which goes on nightly from the main trench.

The enemy could be heard talking. When Major Taylor judged that the 1/39th G. had arrived at the trench, he fired his revolver at one or two of the enemy passing by as the signal to charge. The men cheered and jumped over the parapet. The enemy fired a round or two and bolted.

Our men entered the trench and at once made three prisoners.

On the 2/39th G. charge taking place, the 1/39th G. also charged, and firing and shouting was heard from their direction.

Three more prisoners were rounded up in the trench.

An attempt was then made to fill in the trench which was about 7 or 8 feet deep, revetted and loopholed, and shrapnel proof, and appeared to be about 150 yards long, and there was a deep, roofed communicating trench to the rear.

Meantime the enemy from their support trench kept up a terrific fire on our main trenches, aided by shrapnel.

It was seen that to fill in the trench was an impossible task, and would have taken days, not hours, and that even if filled in, it would not have been very difficult to have dug it out again.

Meantime a terrific din of rifle fire from the enemy's main trench was going on, and was replied to by us. Owing to it being impossible to fill in the trench, Major Taylor ordered both parties to retire back to the ditch.

The prisoners were sent off and some men collected to bring in a Naik who had been badly wounded.

All the above remarks refer solely to the 2/39th G. The 1/39th G. party, though nominally under his command, acted somewhat independently, Major Taylor only having given the general orders to advance and keep touch. The details regarding their casualties, &c., are therefore not known.

The casualties were as follows :—Indian Ranks : Wounded 4 (one very severely), and the fewness of the casualties was due to the excellent way in which the men kept low while creeping forward, and keeping perfect silence till the actual moment of assault, and also to being safe from fire when in the captured trench.

I think Major Taylor carried out the operation extremely well. I would also like to bring the following to notice for having done well and acted coolly :—

Jemadar Khusal Sing Danu, No. 2 Coy., 2/39th G.,

Havr. Ranjor Sing Pundir, No. 2 Coy., 2/39th G.,

Havr. Diwan Sing Padhiyar, No. 1 Coy., 2/39th G.

In addition to the above I would like to bring the following to the favourable notice of the G.O.C. :—

Yesterday morning, the 9th instant, a patrol of Scouts was sent out in the early morning, one of whom was mortally wounded. No. 1342, Rifleman Ganesh Sing Sajwan, No. 2 Coy., 2/39th Garhwal Rifles, carried him back to the trenches under the enemy's fire—it being light enough to see. The enemy appear to be in the trench at work again this morning, and it is a pity we did not have some Sappers to come and mine it.

I would add here that a bit more wire entanglement is necessary along the front, particularly on the right, and it would be a very useful adjunct if we had some system of flares, as the enemy employ these themselves, which light up our trenches considerably.

Enemy's casualties :—*Known :* 2 killed, 6 prisoners (1 wounded). Difficult to say how many more were wounded.

D. H. Drake-Brockman,
Lieut.-Colonel,
Commandant, 2nd Batt. 39th Garhwal Rifles.

REPORT ON THE PART TAKEN IN THE ACTION OF 13th NOVEMBER, 1914, BY 2nd BATT. 39th GARHWAL RIFLES.

To the Brigade Major, Garhwal Brigade.

Dated 14.11.1914.

I append herewith report on the assault on enemy's trench which took place last night in accordance with operation orders.

By 9 p.m. everything was ready as prearranged, the assaulting party of 2/3rd G.R. being lined up in the ditch with the detachment of 50 of my Battalion under Major Taylor on their left.

I met Colonel Ormsby, who was in command of the operation, in the ditch on the right of my flank company. After seeing him I went and took up a position in the centre between my two flank companies, approximately behind that portion of the ditch where Major Taylor and his party were lined up.

Before leaving the ditch I heard Lieut.-Colonel Brakspear tell Major Taylor that the first gun would be the signal to move forward.

It was a short time after the first gun firing that I heard a cheer raised on the extreme right of the line, followed by heavy firing on the enemy's part.

I then sent my Adjutant to call up the Poona Horse (dismounted) from the supporting trench into the communicating trench, so as to be handier.

After waiting a minute or two I proceeded to the right of my flank Company to see Colonel Ormsby, and also saw Colonel Brakspear in the ditch, which was lined for some distance on both sides of my right flank by men of the 2/3rd G.R.

After listening to what Colonel Brakspear was saying I told Colonel Ormsby that I would go up the ditch to my left to see if I could find any of my party.

I left him and proceeded up the ditch, and after going some considerable distance could see no sign of them.

I turned off into No. 2 Company's trench, where I found some dozen wounded men of Major Taylor's party, with some others who had come back with them.

Meantime the enemy's searchlight began to play along our line.

I then returned back to where Colonel Ormsby was in the ditch on the right of my flank company, and told him of the situation, namely, that I had only come across some wounded men and a few others who had retired with them, but there was no sign of Major Taylor or the Garhwali Officer and the others.

He was at the time arranging for another advance, and asked me to get out another party on the left.

I went back to No. 2 Company's trench and got Captain Robertson-Glasgow and 22 of his men, and told him to extend along the ditch and advance from the same spot and in the same direction as Major Taylor had, and in conjunction with the 2/3rd G.R.

When he had started I went back to where Colonel Ormsby was and informed him.

The searchlight was now playing all along the line of the ditch, which made an advance extremely costly, although the men tried to get up through the fence when the searchlight was on another portion.

I then returned to my position in the centre between my two companies and found a bit of a block in the trench owing to the number of wounded, and got the block relieved by sending the wounded that could walk back to the aid post by Battalion Headquarters, and getting the rest off in stretchers.

I then sent a couple of men to creep out and forward to see if they could see any signs of the officers or party. I sent out two other parties, who all reported that there were no signs of them, and that they could not get very far ahead owing to the searchlight and intensity of fire.

While waiting for the party last sent out to come in, Colonel Widdicombe, of the 9th G.R., passed through my trenches, enquiring for me. I told him Colonel Ormsby was in command and passed him on to him.

It was just previous to this that I had been again round to Colonel Ormsby, where I met Captain Forster, Staff Captain.

After many attempts had been made to advance, the conclusion was arrived at that it was useless to try and advance any more with that searchlight playing all along the ditch and ground they had to advance over.

With the exception of such wounded as lay comparatively near and which it might be possible to get in, it would be better to leave the others out and get them in under the protection of the Red Cross Flag, if possible, was the conclusion we came to.

I forgot to add above that on despatching Captain Robertson-Glasgow and his party I called up half the Poona Horse to occupy the entrenchments vacated by the party.

I returned to my place between the two flank companies and waited there, as nothing more could then be done.

At 5 a.m. I went again to see Colonel Ormsby on my right and found he had gone towards the 1/39th G. Finding it difficult to get down owing to the crush of men in the trench, I wrote him a memo suggesting the advisability of clearing the trench a bit, as if the enemy started howitzer fire at daylight on the ditch, of which they know the range exactly, the loss would be very considerable.

I then returned to Battalion Headquarters and telephoned in to you a brief report.

Casualties.	K.	W.	M.
British Officers	–	—	2
Indian Officers	–	—	1
Rank and File	1	26	9
	1	26	12

The names of the missing Officers are :—

Major G. H. Taylor
Captain A. W. Robertson-Glasgow
Jemr. Khusal Sing Danu

D. H. DRAKE-BROCKMAN,
Lieut.-Colonel,
Commandant, 2nd Batt. 39th Garhwal Rifles.

MESSAGE No. B.M. 654,

DATED 9TH MARCH, 1915.

2nd Leicesters.
3rd Londons.
2/3rd Gurkhas.
1/39th G.
2/39th G.
No. 3 Co. S. & M.

All units will make up numbers of sandbags in possession to 2 per man of fighting strength, the number required being drawn to-day from R.E. Depot, No. 3 Co. S. & M. aaa. Units will also draw and place in advanced ammunition depots the following numbers of sandbags prepared in bundles for carrying. aaa. 2nd Leicesters, 400. aaa. 2/3rd Gurkhas, 400. aaa. 1/39th G., 1,000. aaa. 2/39th G., 800. aaa. The following stores will also be with each unit except Londons. aaa. 12 loophole shields. aaa. 16 boxes of rifle grenades for distribution to companies and 16 boxes for placing in reserve at advanced ammunition depots. aaa. The balance of grenades available for the brigade will be taken over by and retained with the ammunition reserve. AAA.

Addressed to all units of the Garhwal Brigade, and repeated to 3rd Co. S. & M.

From Garhwal Brigade 9 a.m.

(Sd.) J. K. STEWART, Major,
Bde. Major.

BATTLE OF NEUVE CHAPELLE.

OPERATION ORDER No. 21, BY LIEUT.-GENERAL SIR C. ANDERSON, K.C.B., COMMANDING MEERUT DIVISION. DATED 9TH MARCH, 1915.

Reference Map: — France — Bethunc 1—40,000, also General Headquarters No. 589b, issued herewith.

INFORMATION.

1. The 4th and Indian Corps are to attack Neuve Chapelle on March 10th with the immediate object of capturing the enemy's trenches west of the village and the occupation of a line to the east of the eastern boundary of the "diamond" round Neuve Chapelle. The general object of the attack is to enable the 4th and Indian Corps to establish themselves on a more forward line to the east, the eventual objective being the high ground from Aubers to Ligny Le Grand, with the object of cutting off the enemy's troops now holding the front between Neuve Chapelle and La Bassée.

The 8th and Meerut Divisions, reinforced by the Artillery of the Lahore Division and heavy guns, are to carry out the attack. The Lahore Division will be in the Indian Corps Reserve. The dividing line between the 4th and Indian Corps is a point where the dividing line between the squares "M" and "S" cuts Neuve Chapelle cross-roads in S.6 a. 6.9.—cross-roads at La Cliqueterie Farm. The 1st Corps is assaulting the enemy's lines at north-east of Givenchy.

INTENTION.

2. The Meerut Division will as its first objective attack the German trenches extending from the front of Port Arthur to opposite the left of the line held by the Meerut Division (C to H) and push on to the north side of the cross-roads F.D. forming the base of the triangle with its apex at Neuve Chapelle village till the line C.O.G.H. is reached.

Subsequent objectives will be :—

(*a*) The best available line on the east side of Port Arthur–Neuve Chapelle Road.

(*b*) The Eastern Edge of the Bois du Biez.

(*c*) Line through Le Hur and Ligny Le Grand to La Cliqueterie Farm exclusive.

During these various advances all Commanders must bear in mind the necessity for being prepared to specially protect the right flank of the movement.

3. The Artillery, reinforced by that of the Lahore Division and Heavy Artillery, 1st Army, will carry out preliminary bombardment for thirty-five minutes, commencing at 7.30 a.m., to destroy obstacles, defences and machine guns on front to be assaulted, to render hostile observing stations untenable, and prevent arrival of reinforcements. Batteries have also been detailed to demonstrate against the enemy's trenches on the Rue du Bois front. The range and fuse will then be increased to cover the Infantry assault at 8.5 a.m. on the enemy's trenches.

Artillery fire will be maintained on Neuve Chapelle village M.35, a and c from 8.5 a.m., when the village will be assaulted.

GARHWAL BRIGADE.

4. The Garhwal Brigade will assault the enemy's trenches as in paragraph 2. The Assault will be delivered at 8.5 a.m. The Assault by the 8th Division on the village of Neuve Chapelle will commence at 8.35 a.m. and the Garhwal Brigade will advance to the Eastern boundary of the Neuve Chapelle diamond in conjunction with the advance of the 8th Division on its left. It will form for the assault in Port Arthur, advanced post No. 2, in the trenches along the Estaires-La Bassée road and in the two new lines of breastwork immediately in rear of them.

Blocking parties to close all enemy trenches and bombing parties to work outwards and clear enemy's trenches on both flanks will be organised by General Officer Commanding, Garhwal Brigade, and will accompany the assault. Report Centre S.3 b 5-2.

DEHRA DUN BRIGADE.

5. The Dehra Dun Brigade will be in support and will be formed up in positions of readiness in work A.1, works D.6 and D.7 and the breastwork connecting them E.7 and E.8 and E.9 and 10 and work about cross-roads at St. Vaast. It will move into position of assembly in rear of the Garhwal Brigade and the parties of sappers and miners and pioneers mentioned in paragraph 7, and will be careful not to block any of those units. As the attack progresses the Brigade will be closed up to the position occupied by the Garhwal Brigade prior to the attack. Report Centre —House M.32 d 8-4.

BAREILLY BRIGADE.

6. The Bareilly Brigade will continue to hold the present line of trenches. During the artillery bombardment a heavy rifle fire will be maintained in the enemy's trenches and the assault by the Garhwal Brigade will be assisted by heavy fire on both flanks. The progress of the attack by the 8th Division must be watched to avoid fire from our left flank striking it. Troops holding the line from Port Arthur exclusive to the extreme left of the front held by the Meerut Division will be prepared to move forward to take over a portion of such new line as may be established by the action of the attack. Port Arthur will remain garrisoned as a keep.

Garrison of Port Arthur and advanced post No. 2 will be withdrawn before the artillery bombardment commences and will re-occupy their posts after the first ten minutes of the bombardment has been completed. The garrison of the isolated advanced posts of Sub-sections A and B on the Rue du Bois front will be withdrawn just before daylight, the line of resistance along this front being the Guard trenches, Orchard and Crescent. The houses on the Rue du Bois should be vacated by all ranks during the operations, as they will be liable to very heavy artillery fire. Report Centre S.2 d 10.0.

SAPPERS AND MINERS.

7. The following parties will be formed under detailed orders of the Commanding Royal Engineers :—

(*a*) Half Company Sappers and Miners and two Companies 107th Pioneers to assemble in the southern of the three lots of small breastworks "Z" close in rear of "D" Sub-section of the Bareilly Brigade front.

(*b*) Half company Sappers and Miners and one company 107th Pioneers to assemble in two northern lots of breastwork referred to above "X" and "Y." These parties, each under a Royal Engineer Officer and equipped with the necessary tools and materials, will follow the Garhwal Brigade into their position of assembly and will be ready to advance when ordered, to put localities "C" and "D" respectively in a state of defence.

TRENCH GUNS.

8. All trench guns will be disposed under instructions already issued to the Divisional Trench Gun Officer. He will hold eight of these guns at disposal of General Officer Commanding, Garhwal Brigade.

DIVISIONAL RESERVE.

9. 4th Indian Cav. Bde., 1 Coy. S. and M., H.Q. 1 Coy. 107th Pioneers, 2/8th Gurkha Rifles (less 1 Coy. to be detailed for work under C.R.E.)

The troops as above will be formed up under cover in vicinity of bridge over Loisne River S.7b and will form the Divisional Reserve under Lieut.-Colonel H. F. Stainforth, 4th Indian Cavalry. One Coy. 2/8th Gurkhas will be sent forward to Bareilly Brigade Report Centre to take over prisoners, when called for by the General Officer Commanding, Bareilly Brigade.

HOUR OF ASSEMBLY.

10. All troops will be in position by 4.30 a.m. on 10th March.

OBSTACLES.

11. Wire in front of our trenches will be cut and necessary bridges placed over ditches in front of our trenches under orders of the General Officer Commanding, Bareilly Brigade, under cover of darkness during night 9th-10th March.

MEDICAL.

12. The wounded will be collected at the existing regimental aid posts in Rue des Berceaux (S.8b and S.3c). Ambulance will be at Vielle Chapelle and Zelobes. Line of evacuation along the Northern Richebourg Road and from Richebourg St. Vaast to Vielle Chapelle, thence *via* Fosse on the Locon-Lestrem Road.

S.A. AMMUNITION DEPOT.

13. Depots will be formed as under :—

Garhwal Brigade close in rear of front line in sub-section " D."

Dehra Dun Brigade in breastworks north-east from work A.1.

PRISONERS.

14. Prisoners will, in first instance, be passed back to troops of the Bareilly Brigade, who will hand them over to one Coy. 2/8th Gurkha Rifles at the Bareilly Brigade Report Centre at S.2 d 10.0. Prisoners will be marched to Locon from this point.

AEROPLANE REPORT CENTRES.

15. A station for receiving aeroplane signals will be established near Bareilly Brigade Report Centre at S.2 d 8.2.A. A station for receiving messages from aeroplanes will be established at R.34 a 3-8 head Divisional Report Centre.

General Officer Commanding, Bareilly Brigade, will detail six men from 4th Royal Hussars as observers for this station, to be in position by daylight on 10th March.

TRAFFIC.

16. The Assistant Provost Marshal will stop all civilian traffic in the Meerut Divisional Area east of Locon-Lestrem Road from 6 a.m. on 10th March. Ammunition supply vehicles from Artillery Brigade Ammunition Column will leave the Locon-Lestrem Road at X.1 b 7-0 and move *via* trestle bridge at X.8 a 10-5 road junctions X.8 b 8-6, X.4 a and X.4 d 4-7, then immediately west of La Couture Church through R.34 b over Pont Levis at Vielle Chapelle, thence *via* R.33 b, rejoining the Locon Lestrem Road at R.32 d 1-8. Ordinary military traffic will leave the Locon-Lestrem Road at Zelobes and move south-east to La Couture and Richebourg St. Vaast by the road south of the Loisne River. It will move north-west by the road east of La Couture and Vielle Chapelle to Fosse, where it will rejoin the Locon-Lestrem Road.

REPORTS.

17. To be addressed " Meerut Report Centre," which is established at the White Chateau at Road Junction west of Hog-backed bridge over canal on southern La Couture Road (R.34 a 3-8).

SUPPLIES.

18. Supply depôts for use in emergency have been established at Richebourg St. Vaast and La Couture for 6,000 British and 10,000 Indian Rations, half at each place.

(Sd.) C. NORIE, Colonel,
General Staff, Meerut Division.

Issued at 1 p.m. by Signal Company.

APPENDIX E.

No. 327-20-G. Copy No. 1.

INSTRUCTIONS BY LIEUT.-GENERAL SIR C. A. ANDERSON, K.C.B., COMMANDING MEERUT DIVISION.

Reference Operation Order No. 21.

1. In the event of the attack being postponed on account of the weather :—

(*a*) The Dehra Dun Brigade must march at once to its billets in La Couture and Vielle Chapelle so as to clear the roads for the withdrawal of the Garhwal Brigade.

(*b*) The Garhwal Brigade must file back from the trenches into Richebourg St. Vaast and La Couture, and re-occupy the billets they occupied to-day, 9th March. The G.O.C. Garhwal Brigade, in framing his orders for this evacuation, must include the details of Sappers and Miners and of Pioneers who are in the area and trenches occupied by his Brigade. He will time the commencement of his move from the time the last man of the 1/9th Gurkhas passes Post A.1.

(*c*) The G.O.C. Bareilly Brigade will discontinue wire cutting and bridge placing on his front.

(*d*) The Commanding Royal Artillery will notify any batteries in the close vicinity of the roads between the left of our front and Richebourg St. Vaast, of the movement of our infantry, in case they should fire at these as they are crossing their front.

All the above will take place in the event of a postponement of the attack.

(Sd.) C. NORIE, Colonel,
General Staff, Meerut Division.

8 p.m. 9th March, 1915.

Copy No. 1 Indian Corps.
" No. 2 Lahore Division.
" No. 3 Dehra Dun Brigade.
" No. 4 Garhwal Brigade.
" No. 5 Bareilly Brigade.
" No. 6 Royal Artillery, Meerut Div.
" No. 7 Royal Engineers, Meerut Div.
" No. 8 107th Pioneers.
Copies Nos. 9 and 10 File.
Copy No. 11 War Diary.
Copies Nos. 12 and 13 General Staff.

APPENDIX F.

Copy No. 1.

INSTRUCTIONS BY LIEUT.-GENERAL SIR CHARLES ANDERSON, K.C.B., 9TH MARCH, 1915.

Reference Map France—Bethune 1-40,000 and Operation Order No. 21.

1. There may—indeed will—be some artillery fire before the hour named for the bombardment to commence, but the hours of the artillery bombardment itself are absolute.

2. Attacks are not to hang up all along the line on account of one or two small localities holding out (*e.g.*, a house, &c.). These should be contained and engaged. The rest of the line will push forward.

3. When the Dehra Dun Bde. commences its advance against the Bois du Biez the G.O.C. Garhwal Brigade will send on at least two Battalions, prolonging the right of Dehra Dun Brigade's advance.

4. As soon as the Garhwal Brigade has established itself on a line east of Port Arthur-Neuve Chapelle Road, the G.O.C. Bareilly Brigade will move up all his troops holding the line north of Port Arthur to take over and occupy a new line from Port Arthur to north-eastwards and including the defences which will be under construction in the orchard by the cross-roads in S.5a 0.1.

(Sd.) C. NORIE, Colonel,
General Staff, Meerut Division.

EH/

Issued by Signal Company at 6 p.m.

Copy No. 1 to Indian Corps.
„ 2 to 8th Division.
„ 3 to Lahore Division.
„ 4 to Dehra Dun Brigade.
„ 5 Garhwal Brigade.
„ 6 Bareilly Brigade.
„ 7 Commanding Royal Artillery, Meerut.
„ 8 Commanding Royal Artillery, Lahore.
„ 9 File.
„ 10, 11 } War Diary.
„ 12, 13, 14 } General Staff.

SECRET.

OPERATION ORDER No. 25

BY

BRIG.-GENERAL C. G. BLACKADER, D.S.O.,
Commanding Garhwal Brigade.

Ref. $\frac{1}{40000}$ Bethune Sheet.

$\frac{1}{50000}$ Sketch Map No. 589b.

Garhwal Brigade Headquarters.
9th March, 1915.

INFORMATION.

1. (*a*) No further information has been received regarding the enemy.

(*b*) The Indian and 4th Corps are to co-operate in an attack on Neuve Chapelle on the 10th March. The 8th Division is to attack from the 4th Corps front, and the Meerut Division from that of the Indian Corps.

The Artillery of the two Corps will bombard the area to be attacked for 35 minutes before the assault.

This bombardment will commence at 7.30 a.m. and cease at 8.5. a.m., artillery fire continuing with increased fuse and range.

INTENTION.

2. The Garhwal Brigade (simultaneously with 8th Division attack) will assault the enemy's trenches east of the Estaires-La Bassée road at 8.5 a.m., as follows, assembling beforehand as detailed in Table A (issued with addition to O.O. No. 25).

3. DISTRIBUTION OF ATTACKING TROOPS.

Unit.	Objective.	Limits of Zone of Attack.	Lines to be occupied and immediately consolidated.	Special Point to be made good and occupied.
1/39th G.	C.	*Left:* Line from N.E. exit of RUE DU BOIS from PORT ARTHUR to Road D-N where it crosses the RIV. DES LAYES.	S.E. corner of PORT ARTHUR thro' C to road D-N at crossing of R. DES LAYES.	Junction of enemy trenches at B.
2nd Leicesters	Groups of houses around cross-roads at D.	*Right:* As for left of 1/30th G. *Left:* Natural ditch running towards enemy's lines from ESTAIRES-LA BASSEE road 300 yards from PORT ARTHUR cross-roads.	Road D-N at crossing of R. DES LAYES to O and then to road (inclusive) 100 yards N.E. of cross-roads at D.	
2/3rd G.R.	Group of houses at road junction at F.	*Right:* As for left of Leicesters. *Left:* Road S.4. b. 3.2. to NEUVE CHAPELLE (inclusive).	From road (exclusive) 100 yards N.E. of cross-roads at D, through G to road (inclusive).	200 yards from G in enemy trench which runs parallel to road to NEUVE CHAPELLE.
2/39th G.	Line G-H.	*Right:* As for left of 2/3rd G.R., but road exclusive.	From left of 2/3rd G.R. (road exclusive) to H.	To join hands with 8th Division.

On the objective (column 2 above) being attained, all trenches leading towards the enemy will be double blocked beyond bombing distance and then cleared beyond the barricades made.

BRIGADE RESERVE.

4. 1/3rd London Regiment in the more westerly breastwork parallel to and 200 yards from ESTAIRES LA BASSEE road.to move forward to the breastwork 100 yards east when it is cleared after the bombardment.

MACHINE GUNS.

5. Each assaulting Battalion will have two machine guns. The remaining machine guns will be disposed under the orders of the Brigade M.G. Officer to support and guard the left flank of the attack.

Right Flank Protection.

6. Bomb guns will be disposed to support and guard in co-operation with artillery and with rifle and machine-gun fire of the BAREILLY Brigade, the right flank of the attack.

Ammunition, &c., to be Carried.

7. Each man will carry 150 rounds of S.A. ammunition, two sandbags, emergency ration, and unexpended portion of the day's ration. Each assaulting unit will carry 192 bombs.

Reserve of Ammunition and Bombs.

8. Magazines of Reserve S.A.A. and bombs have been formed with 100 boxes S.A.A. and 192 bombs in each of the following points :—Southern portion of PORT ARTHUR, northern portion of PORT ARTHUR, southern portion of advanced post S.4.b.3.2 and northern portion of advanced post at S.4.b.2.2. Twenty boxes S.A.A. are also stored for Brigade Machine Guns at S.4.a.8.7.

The Brigade ammunition reserve will be at Brigade Headquarters (with some additional bombs).

Company ammunition mules with ammunition will be at Brigade ammunition reserve.

Battalion ammunition carts will be with the 1st line transport, animals ready to hook in.

9. In order to indicate to artillery and to units supporting the attack by fire the locality reached by attacking troops coloured flags (pink for flank battalions and light and dark blue for centre battalions) will be placed by leading bodies of troops on our side of enemy trenches or buildings captured.

Regarding Communication.

10. Telephone and visual signalling will be maintained between Brigade Headquarters and headquarters of units.

First Line Transport.

11. First line transport (less ammunition mules and medical equipment) at LA COUTURE.

Dressing Station.

12. At existing Aid Post in RUE DE BERCEAUX (S.8.b and S.3.c.).

Reports.

13. Reports to farm at S.3.a.5.2, where Brigade Headquarters have been established.

(Sd.) J. H. K. Stewart, Major,
Brigade Major Garhwal Brigade.

Issued through Signal Section at 6.30 p.m.

Copy No. 5—2/39th Garhwal Rifles.

ADDITION TO OPERATION ORDER No. 25

BY

Brig.-General C. G. BLACKADER, D.S.O.,
Commanding Garhwal Brigade.

Information.

1. The general object of the attack is to enable the 4th and Indian Corps to establish themselves on a more forward line to the east, the eventual objective being the high ground from AUBERS to LIGNY LE GRAND.

The dividing line between the 4th and Indian Corps is point where dividing line between squares M. and S. cuts the NEUVE CHAPELLE — cross-roads in S.6.a.6.9 — cross-roads at LA CLIQUETERIE Farm.

The 1st Corps is assaulting the enemy's line N.E. of GIVENCHY. The subsequent objective to the line C.O.G.H. which the Brigade is to assault will be :—

(*a*) The best available line in the east side of PORT ARTHUR-NEUVE CHAPELLE road.

(*b*) The eastern edge of the Bois du Biez.

(*c*) Line through LE HUR and LIGNY LE GRAND to LA CLIQUETERIE farm (exclusive).

During these several advances all commanders must bear in mind the necessity for being prepared to specially protect the right flank of the movement.

The 8th Division assault on the village of NEUVE CHAPELLE will commence at 8.35 a.m.

The Dehra Dun Brigade will be in close support of the Garhwal Brigade.

The Bareilly Brigade will continue to hold the present line of trenches.

Parties of Sappers and Miners and Pioneers have been ordered to put localities in a state of defence.

Assembly.

2. All battalions will be in position by 4.30 a.m.

Prisoners.

3. Any prisoners will be sent back in parties under escorts to be specially detailed (and not by individuals on their own initiative) to the front line of the Bareilly Brigade, to whom the prisoners will be handed over, escorts returning to their units immediately.

(Sd.) J. K. Stewart, Major,
Brigade Major, Garhwal Brigade.

TABLE A.
(with O.O. No. 25 dated 9.3.1915).

Unit.	Place of Assembly.	Route.	Time of passing starting point road junction at S.2.c.2.2.
2nd Leicesters	Trenches from PORT ARTHUR road junction to 300 yards N.N.W. along LA BASSEE road, and southern half of front breastwork parallel to and 100 yards west of ESTAIRES-LA BASSEE road.	EDWARD road, RUE DU BOIS, ROOME's trench.	11.30 p.m. night 9th-10th.
2/3rd G.R.	Trenches on line of ESTAIRES-LA BASSEE road from left of LEICESTERS to road junction S.4.b.3.2 and northern half of front breastwork parallel to and 100 yards west of ESTAIRES-LA BASSEE road.	S.3.c.4.2 RUE DES BERCEAUX to S.4.a.0.4 thence across country.	12.30 a.m.
1/39th G. ...	Part of PORT ARTHUR south of RUE DU BOIS and in ROOME's trench.	As for 2nd Leicesters.	1 a.m.
2/39th G. ...	In trenches on line of ESTAIRES-LA BASSEE road N.N.W. of road junction S.4.b.3.2.	As for 2/3rd G.R. to S. 4. a. 0. 4, thence continue along RUE DES BERCEAUX to destination.	1.30 a.m.
1/3rd London.	Second breastwork parallel to and 200 yards from the ESTAIRES-LA BASSEE road, leaving 60 yards at southern end clear for Pioneers.	EDWARD road and thence across country.	1.15 a.m.
Brigade Machine Guns	Trenches at S.4.a.8.9.	As for 2/39th G.	Verbally communicated to Brigade M.G.O.

NOTE.—A conference was held by G.O.C. at his Headquarters the day before to explain his plan and see that each C.O. thoroughly understood his orders.—D.B.

OPERATION ORDER No. 1

BY

LT.-COLONEL D. H. DRAKE-BROCKMAN,
Commandant 2nd Battalion 39th Garhwal Rifles.

Ref. Map $\frac{1}{40000}$ Bethune. Copy No. 1.

Battalion Headquarters.

9th March, 1915.

1. The Garhwal Brigade will attack the German trenches covering NEUVE CHAPELLE on the W., to-morrow, commencing at 8.5 a.m., after an intense bombardment of 35 minutes by the Divisional Artillery.

The 8th Division is also attacking in combination on our left.

2. The G.O.C. Brigade intends attacking that portion from H to PORT ARTHUR. The 2/39th G. will attack the front from and exclusive of the road running E., through the small centre salient at S.4.b., on a front of 4 Platoons, up to and inclusive of the communication trench at H., and establish itself on the line H-G., and protect the left flank of the Brigade.

3. Nos. 1 and 2 Companies will form the Firing Line and Supports, Nos. 3 and 4 Reserve.

4. The Battalion will fall in at 1 a.m. (as per para. 5), and march *via* southern exit to village near the church and *via* cross-roads in square S.3.c. On arrival at Brigade Headquarters in the fortified house in square S.3.b.6.3 the Battalion will form single rank and proceed up to the next barricade on the road, where it will turn in to the right up the communication breastwork and file into the trenches held by the 6th Jats along the Estaires-La Bassée road.

The head of the leading Company will halt on arrival at the small bridge over the ditch near N.W. end of centre salient in square S.4.b., and the remainder close up.

Each platoon of each Company will then form two deep and close up to its front platoon and Companies will close up on the leading Company.

5. Companies will fall in and march as follows :—No. 2, No. 1, left leading ; then No. 3, No. 4, right leading.

6. Further orders will be issued when the Battalion has formed up in above order in the fire trench.

7. 200 rounds per man will be carried.

8. The trained bomb throwers of Nos. 1 and 2 Companies will carry the 8 boxes of bombs, 4 each Company.

9. Nos. 9 and 10 Platoons will carry the spare sand bags.

10. Nos. 15 and 16 Platoons will carry the entrenching tools.

11. The Machine Guns will concentrate by the salient in the place pointed out to the M.G. officer and await orders for the advance.

12. First Line ammunition mules will be at Brigade Headquarters at 5 p.m. to-day. First Line ammunition carts will remain with 1st Line, with animals saddled ready to be hooked in, at LA COUTURE.

13. Machine Gun mules will remain at cross-roads in Square S.3.c.

14. Some men in the leading platoons in firing line whose kukris fit easily in scabbards will be told off ready before advancing and reaching the hedge, to draw kukris to cut hedge if necessary to clear passage through.

15. The assaulting line must advance punctually at 8.5 a.m. and press forward with the greatest energy to the objective, H-G., and the nearer trenches passed on the right opposite No. 1 Coy. are not to be entered by the firing line, but will be attended to by the Companies pushed up in support.

No. 2 Company will press forward to the point H, its right on the hedge of small orchard running N.E. and S.W., and No. 1 Company to the point G, with its left on this hedge.

16. On arrival in the hostile trenches any wires seen should be cut at once.

17. Immediately the objective H-G is reached, blocking and bombing parties must go up communication trenches at once and link up with the Brigade on our left and the reverse parapet got ready for firing over.

18. No man on any pretence is to fall out to attend wounded men, who must remain where they are till taken in by the stretcher bearers.

19. All stretcher bearers with stretchers will fall in and march separately behind No. 4 Company.

20. The depôt for S.A.A. reserve and bombs is situated in the salient in Square S.4.b.

21. The Aid Post will be in the house in road at Square 3.c.

22. One Signaller from No. 1 Company will be detailed to remain with C.O., to run out a wire when ordered to.

The Signallers of No. 4 Company will also remain with C.O. at Battalion Headquarters in fire trench. Remainder with their respective Companies.

23. Strict silence must be observed and men kept well down under cover till the moment to advance.

24. On any flares going up when marching and close up to the front line men should momentarily halt and crouch down.

25. Company Commanders will take their periscopes and the pink coloured cloth for placing on captured trenches as they advance to indicate their position to our Artillery.

26. C.O. will be in fire trench near salient, Square S.4.b., where a telephone station will be established with Brigade Headquarters.

E. R. P. Berryman,
Captain,
Adjutant 2nd Batt. 39th Garhwal Rifles.

Issued verbally to
assembled British and
Garhwali Officers at
8 p.m.

REPORT ON THE PART TAKEN BY 2/39th GARHWAL RIFLES IN THE BATTLE OF NEUVE CHAPELLE, 10th-12th MARCH, 1915.

From the Officer Commanding,
2nd Batt. 39th Garhwal Rifles.

To the Brigade Major,
Garhwal Brigade.

No. 218/W.A. *Dated 16th March*, 1915.

I have the honour to submit the following report on the part played by my Battalion in the attack of NEUVE CHAPELLE on the 10th instant and in subsequent operations.

The Battalion left billets at RICHEBOURG ST. VAAST at 1.30 a.m. to proceed to the rendezvous in the entrenchments held by the 6th Jats of Bareilly Brigade. The Battalion arrived and was formed up in the entrenchment ready by 4.30 a.m., the appointed time, opposite that portion of the enemy's entrenchment which the Battalion had to attack.

When reconnoitring the front given me on the previous days, *i.e.*, from the road on centre salient (square S.4.b.) exclusive up to N. end of entrenchment in square S.4.a. along the main ESTAIRES-LA BASSEE road, I found that, owing to the conformation of the ground which sloped very slightly from the German trenches down to the ditch along the La Bassée road, I could get my two assaulting lines out without being seen in front of, and to the E. of, our line of entrenchments and ditch, and that this would be greatly facilitated if a portion, say three feet, of the N. end of the hedge and parapet of the salient joining the road were cut down or a passage made through it, and in addition a 2ft. deep trench were dug along the E. edge of the ditch which runs alongside of the further side of the main road.

Accordingly I arranged with the Officer of the 6th Jats on the spot for this to be done at night and also officially through the Brigade. By this they were enabled, lying down, to keep under better cover during the bombardment and out of sight of the enemy, and at the same time have a very much better " take off," and so get off more quickly and make the attack a much greater surprise, which was very essential to the success of the undertaking, than if the assaulting lines had had to climb up the ladders supplied for getting out of our main trench, which would have delayed them considerably.

At 5.15 a.m. I directed the first two assaulting lines to file outside the trench through the gap in single file into and line the small trench and edge of the ditch and lie down close together and wait till the moment came to deliver the assault, which was to be at 8.5 a.m.

This was done very well, quietly and quickly, and without the enemy getting any idea of its taking place.

In the meantime the other two Companies closed up to their right in the main entrenchment immediately behind the assaulting lines.

I took great coats with me, carried open by the men on the arms, with waterproof sheets strapped on the back, and the coats they threw over themselves while lying down in the trench waiting, as it was very cold. When the assault took place these were thrown off and left lying in the trench, and so the men were very much lighter for the actual assault. (These great coats were left in charge of the regiment holding main trench and collected after the battle).

Punctually at 7.30 a.m. the bombardment began, a perfect tornado of shells, and was most accurate. The salient (S.4.b.), of course, was vacated, as it was impossible for reasons of safety to occupy it during the bombardment.

During the bombardment one German high explosive shell hit the interior of the parapet close by where my Adjutant and I were sitting, with my orderly and one man of the 6th Jats between us, killing the two men and wounding two others of my men but leaving us both unhurt, beyond a shaking and concussion, and covering us with green mud and a mouthful of green sulphurous smoke. Two men also were killed and six wounded either by our own or German shells of the two assaulting Companies while lying down in the shallow trench outside awaiting the moment to advance.

I had given the portion of the front (V-V) along which ran the hedge of the orchard covering the nearest German trench to one Company (No. 1) and the other portion (V-Y-H), where the trench ran through the hedge across the open, to the other Company (No. 2), *vide* map of Battle, the whole under command of Captain Burton, the senior Company Commander.

Punctually at 8.5 a.m., when the artillery lengthened fuse and range, my leading lines advanced at a steady double across the open towards the objective, followed at 30 yards distance by the second line, which was reached before the enemy was fully aware of the fact and could open as hot a fire as he might have done had he been aware of our advance from the commencement.

I had directed the right Company (No. 1), whose final objective was the S.E. portion of the long trench marked H-G, not to stop at the first trenches, V-V, W-W, V^1-V^1, met with, but to press right on to the final objective H-G, as these could be looked after by the Companies I would push up in support, as I considered it very essential that the objective should be reached as soon as possible and the task given me accomplished, *i.e.*, to get to this trench H-G, establish myself there and work up from it, gain touch with the British Brigade on my left and double block any communication trenches.

The advance was extremely well carried out by Nos. 1 and 2 Companies, under Captains Burton and Blair, in line of platoons, *i.e.*, on a front of four platoons, the front rank of each platoon supported by its rear rank as second line.

The right Company on reaching the trench running along and behind the hedge V-V found it empty and pressed on to the next trench, W-W, where a machine gun was captured with some prisoners. The advance was then continued to the third trench, V^1-V^1, and finally to the objective, H-G. It was during the passage across this open space between V^1-V^1 and H-G that most casualties occurred from fire in direction of H from a party of the enemy and a machine gun, whom the other Company on the left eventually engaged. This trench H-G, having been reached, was about to be reversed for firing, but it was found to be 2ft. deep in water and mud, and so a fresh one was commenced on the same alignment. Parties were sent out to the village to scout and link up with the Brigade on our left, and also up the communication trench running out of H-G. In the meantime No. 2 Company on the left had advanced at the same time and went straight on to Y-W, clear of the hedge and ditch V-W-V^1, and some on into that portion of the main trench Y-H, and began working up this trench, bombing and rounding up prisoners, towards H, and capturing a machine gun, and further beyond towards J ; also a party was sent up the communication trench Z-Z and up H-G. Shortly afterwards connection was made with the Berkshires in the main trench.

The enemy in main fire trench, finding themselves taken under fire from two directions, soon began to surrender, but great care had to be exercised, as they might have been up to any dirty trick. For instance, when surrendering, a party of the enemy in the main fire trench Y-H began beckoning to our men to come on. It was found that probably their intention was to get our men to come on towards them, and as they passed a short piece of trench (not marked on the official map) marked Z^1, they would have come under machine-gun fire. Fortunately they were not to be taken in so. This machine gun was captured.*

The Companies were now reorganized, the objective having been reached and prisoners collected and sent back. No 3 Company, under Captain Wilcox, had been sent up in support before, when I thought it was needed, and I kept No. 4 Company, under Major MacTier, still in hand for emergencies. Shortly after this I sent up two more platoons under Major MacTier, with tools, to dig a line on the first objective H-G if necessary, and very shortly afterwards I went up myself with the remaining two platoons. On arrival at H-G I saw that this line was unnecessary, so had parties sent out into the village to search for snipers in the houses and followed on after them. I saw the Rifle Brigade and Berkshires on our left going into the village.

Nos. 1 and 2 Companies, under Captain Burton, followed by No. 3 under Captain Wilcox, had before this on arrival at H-G pushed on into the village, helped to clear the houses and then swung round to the S.E. and commenced digging the trench ordered by me in rear of the 2/3rd Gurkhas, approximately on the line S-Q as a support and second line to the Brigade Front. The 2/3rd and Leicesters of our Brigade and those of the British Brigade on our left with whom we had linked up, had by now occupied the " Old Smith Dorrien " line of trench marked L-P and were strengthening it. I also received an order from the Brigade to dig the line I had commenced, S-Q, shortly after.

Here on the left or N.E. of S-Q I linked up with the Rifle Brigade in the trench that they were constructing. I consolidated my support trench S-Q and was fortunate in finding in a ruined house (marked W3 on the map) on the road west of S-Q, a lot of sandbags and spades which considerably facilitated my task.

It was now about 9.30 a.m. The whole village was in our hands and that of the Brigade on our left, and work was continued on the trench S-Q which by the evening was made quite strong. I established my telephone station in communication with Brigade Headquarters in the house W2 on the road west of S-Q.

About 6 p.m. I was sent for from my trench S-Q to the telephone station as the G.O.C. wished, I was informed, to speak to me. As it was difficult to hear I asked that a message might be sent by an orderly. This I subsequently received, directing me to proceed to Port Arthur and personally consult with Colonel Swiney of the 1/39th Garhwalis, who had been wounded, and to take measures to consolidate the right flank and use both battalions of the 39th Garhwalis. Accordingly I set out, but after having gone some distance fell into a " Black Johnson " hole in the dark and hurt my knee temporarily so that I could not get on immediately. I therefore sent up my Second-in-Command, Major MacTier, to go on ahead and see Colonel Swiney and tell him that I would follow shortly. This I reported to the Brigade. About 12 midnight orders were received for the Battalion to proceed. Meanwhile I had gone on ahead, while the Battalion later was brought up by Captain Burton to Port Arthur. After wandering about in a maze of trenches in the pitch dark I eventually found the 1st Battalion Headquarters and that Colonel Swiney had been evacuated to the Field Ambulance. I did not meet Major MacTier,

* See Aerial Map, page 49.

but on my starting to return to the telephone station at W2 (where I found on arrival that the Dehra Dun Brigade had also established their headquarters) I received a note from Major MacTier saying that he had seen the G.O.C. Garhwal Brigade, who had directed him to take over the command of the 1/39th Garhwalis.

It was now about 1 a.m., and on the way back I met the Battalion coming up under Captain Burton at the first German trench where it crosses the road just in front of Port Arthur and brought it back with me. On arrival at " D," where the road leads to the houses at " F," and where I understood that Brigade Headquarters was to be established, I halted the Battalion while I proceeded to those houses in order to see the G.O.C. However, I only found Captain Lodwick, who informed me that the Headquarters had not yet arrived. So I returned and took my Battalion back to its trench S-Q and sent a message to that effect to the Brigade Headquarters. I also saw the G.O.C. Dehra Dun Brigade in the house W2 and shortly afterwards received orders for my Battalion to be attached to that Brigade and to guard its right flank during the contemplated attack on the Bois du Biez this day, the 11th March.

Accordingly at 5 a.m. (11th March, a damp, misty and raw morning) I took my Battalion over *via* road " D-N " to a position on the open ground in front of our entrenchments held by the 2nd Leicestershire Regiment and Seaforths, that is, in front of and S.E. of " C-L " and to the E. of road " D-N " leading to the Ferme du Biez, covered by my scouts with my right on the road. Here I formed it up in two lines, three companies in front line and supports and one company in second line as reserve with the machine guns and lay out in the open in shell holes and such slight folds of the ground as there were waiting for the advance to commence.

As, however, when we were in position and it became lighter, a heavy fire was opened on us by the enemy from the Bois du Biez and many casualties took place and as no attack was taking place, it having been countermanded, I withdrew the Battalion back to the line held by the 2nd Leicestershire Regiment to a small orchard in rear where the companies entrenched themselves on the line " O-K." Here we waited all day while a bombardment of the Bois du Biez took place and of the houses along its northern edge and along the road " D-N " to the Ferme du Biez.

No advance took place this day, 11th March, and eventually about 11 p.m. I received orders to go back to La Couture to bivouac there, where we arrived at 3 a.m. on 12th March. In accordance with orders received I marched this morning, 12th March, at 7 a.m., for the vicinity of Les Lobes, where billets were apportioned off to us, arriving there during the forenoon.

During the afternoon, at 4.40 p.m., I received urgent orders through the Dehra Dun Brigade to march back forthwith to Richebourg St. Vaast, where we arrived at 9 p.m. and occupied some of the ruined houses there. We remained here all day, 13th March, till the evening, when orders came at 5 p.m. to proceed to billets in the vicinity of Zelobes, where the Battalion is now at the time of writing this report.

The work of the Battalion throughout the operations has been excellent, and the actual attack was carried out splendidly and with great dash. The comparatively few losses are due to the assaulting lines rising without hesitation to the attack precisely at the moment ordered and to their pressing forward with dash and determination so that they were on the hostile trenches before the enemy (the majority of whom had undoubtedly withdrawn to trenches close in rear and dug-outs during the bombardment) could return and man their main fire trench. The result was most satisfactory. We suffered comparatively few casualties, and captured 3 officers, 187 men and 3 machine guns. Two machine guns only were sent in; one, I understand, is being sent in by the Berkshire Regiment, who, with the Rifle Brigade, linked up with us on our left, covering the village.

I send in on separate report a list of those whom I consider especially deserving of recognition during the operations.

D. H. Drake-Brockman,
Lt.-Colonel,
Commandant 2nd Battalion 39th Garhwal Rifles.

Note.—It may be of interest to record that among the prisoners taken by the Battalion on 10th March, 1915, were the identical men who fraternised with us in the " informal Armistice " held on Christmas Day, 1914, and who belonged to the 16th Regiment.

BATTLE OF AUBERS.

COPY No. 11.

OPERATION ORDER No. 40

BY

BRIG.-GENERAL C. G. BLACKADER, D.S.O.,
Commanding Garhwal Brigade.

Reference Maps. 7th May, 1915.
Trench Map, 1/10,000.
Map of France and Belgium, Sheet 36 (3rd edition) 1/40,000.
Map of France, Bethune Sheet, 1/40,000.

INFORMATION.

1. The 1st Army is attacking on the 8th May with the object of breaking through the enemy's line and gaining the LA BASSEE-LILLE road between LA BASSEE and FOURNES and then advancing on DON.

The 1st Corps, retaining its right at GIVENCHY advances on the RUE DU MARAIS, LORGIES and ILLIES.

The Indian Corps will operate to cover the left of the 1st Corps, capture the FERME DU BIEZ, and subsequently advance to the line LIGNY LE GRAND—LA CLIQUETERIE FERME.

The 4th Corps operate through AUBERS with a view to effecting a junction with the Indian Corps at LA CLIQUETERIE FERME.

LAHORE Division holds the front except that portion from which the attack is to be delivered.

MEERUT Division is to deliver the attack.

ARTILLERY of the MEERUT Division, reinforced by that of LAHORE Division, one section HOTCHKISS motor battery, one section mountain artillery and some heavy batteries will prepare and support the attack.

The DEHRA DUN Brigade is to assault the enemy's front line trenches from the point V6 to the vicinity of the port 56 and push on against further objectives, leaving garrisons at SOUTHERN end of LA TOURELLE, DISTILLERY, road junction S.11.a (points 52 and 53), houses near point 50 and the FERME DU BIEZ.

BAREILLY Brigade (less one Battalion) in trenches north of RUE DU BOIS, and in and east of LANSDOWNE Post is to occupy the assembly positions of DEHRA DUN Brigade as they are vacated and to support that Brigade.

One Battalion BAREILLY Brigade (less two Companies with S and M) will remain in LANSDOWNE Post and follow the Garhwal Brigade into the assembly trenches just north of the RUE DU BOIS.

INTENTION.

2. Garhwal Brigade (less two battalions) will be Divisional reserve.

DETACHMENT.

3. Lieut.-Colonel Drake-Brockman commanding, Capt. Etherton, Staff Offr., GARHWAL Rifles, 2/8th GURKHA Rifles, Machine guns of the above, two trench guns. Will pass road junction M.27.d at 10 p.m., and march *via* PONT LOGY and the area between the main drain on the west and the ESTAIRES-LA BASSEE road on the east to the two eastern blocks of assembly trenches north of the RUE DU BOIS, to be in position by 1 a.m., reporting arrival to G.O.s C. DEHRA DUN and GARHWAL Brigades.

INFANTRY MOVEMENTS.

4. The Garhwal Brigade (less two Battalions, machine gun sections and trench gun battery) will occupy trenches pointed out to O.s C., moving as under :—

Unit.	Position of assembly.	To march off at
2/3rd Gurkhas	North and clear of cross-roads in CROIX BARBEE	2.30 a.m.
2nd Leicesters	CROIX BARBEE - RICHEBOURG ST. VAAST track	2.15 a.m.
3rd Londons	East and clear of cross roads in CROIX BARBEE	2.15 a.m.

Main roads are not to be blocked ; troops will form up off the roads for filing into their trenches.

All units will report by 3 a.m. that they are in their allotted positions.

MACHINE AND TRENCH GUNS.

5. The Brigade machine gun detachments (less 6 guns) and the brigade trench gun battery (less 2 guns) will march at 2 a.m., *via* RUE DES PUITS and ESTAIRES-LA BASSEE road to trenches at S.4.a.8.7, and will report when in position.

S.A. AMMUNITION.

6. Two hundred rounds per man will be carried.

S.A.A. depôts have been established at R.E. depôt, RUE DU BOIS, and dug-outs in rear of front trench, as shown on sketch of RUE DU BOIS in vicinity of PORT ARTHUR, which have been sent to O.s C. Battalions.

The 3rd Londons, when ordered to advance will carry up one box of S.A.Ammn. per two men from breastwork east of LANSDOWNE Post to the front line trenches and on from thence.

R.E. DEPOTS.

7. Advanced R.E. depôts will be at RUE DU BOIS and FARM at M.32.d.7.7.

HAND GRENADES AND BOMBS.

8. Each Battalion has been provided with approximately 150 hand grenades in carrying boxes. An advanced base for bombs (trench gun) and hand grenades has been established 100 yards in rear of the right of the assembly position of the BAREILLY Brigade.

RATIONS.

9. The unexpended portion of the day's ration and the emergency ration will be carried by each man.

MEDICAL.

10. A collecting station will be established between LANSDOWNE Post and where the tramway line crosses the RUE DES BERCEAUX. The route for wounded returning from the front will be by the "Orchard" communication trench, which runs from the RUE DU BOIS to the RUE DES BERCEAUX along the north-east side of the tramway line and some 100 yards from it. This trench will be reserved for the return of the wounded only, after fighting has commenced.

SANDBAGS.

11. Every man will carry two sandbags.

MASKS.

12. All masks will be kept in readiness and soaked in soda solution.

FLAGS.

13. All ranks should know the distinguishing flags for marking the positions of advanced troops of the various divisions.

PRISONERS.

14. Prisoners will be handed over to the LAHORE Division at DEHRA DUN report centre on the RUE DU BOIS.

TIME.

15. An officer from Brigade Headquarters will give the official time to all units about 8 p.m.

FIRST LINE.

16. First line transport will march *via* WELLINGTON Road in accordance with orders issued separately, and will be parked at R.35.b.2.2. It will be ready to move at half-an-hour's notice from 10 a.m. to-morrow onwards.

REPORT CENTRE.

17. Brigade headquarters will be at LANSDOWNE Post from 9 p.m. to-night.

J. H. K. STEWART, Major,
Brigade Major, GARHWAL Brigade.

Issued through signal section at 3 p.m.

Copy No. 1 ..... 2nd Leicesters.
2 ..... 3rd Londons
3 ..... 2/3rd G.R.
4 ..... Garhwal Rifles.
5 ..... 2/8th G.R.
6 ..... Bde. M.G.O.
7 ..... Bde. TRENCH GUN Offr.
8 ..... MEERUT Division.
9 ..... DEHRA DUN Bde.
10 ..... BAREILLY Bde.
11 ..... Col. Drake-Brockman.
12 ..... War Diary.
13 to 15 Staff.

NOTE.—Operation Orders by Lieut.-Colonel Drake-Brockman for his Detachment were issued on receipt of above and Divisional orders. They consisted of March orders to get to the Place of Assembly and action to be taken after advancing to the capture of the Bois du Biez and La Russie. Actual orders to advance from place of Assembly depended on the success or otherwise of the attack of the Dehra Dun Brigade and would have been issued on the ground.

BATTLE OF FESTUBERT.

Copy No. 4.

OPERATION ORDER No. 41

BY

BRIG.-GENERAL C. G. BLACKADER, D.S.O.,
Commanding Garhwal Brigade.

Reference Maps :—
France—Bethune Sheet, 1/40,000.
Trench Map 1/10,000.

Dated 15th May, 1915.

INFORMATION.

1. The 1st Corps and Indian Corps are to attack and to establish a line FESTUBERT-LA QUINQUE RUE-TOURELLE cross-roads—PORT ARTHUR, and are then to push on towards VIOLAINES and BEAUPUITS.

The 2nd Division is to assault on the right of and simultaneously with the Meerut Division, and the 7th Division on the right of the 2nd.

The SIRHIND Brigade is to support the Garhwal Brigade; Bareilly Brigade in Divisional Reserve; DEHRA DUN Brigade in Corps reserve.

ARTILLERY.

(*b*) A deliberate artillery bombardment is to precede the assault and is to cease on the front to be assaulted at 11.25 p.m. to-day.

The bombardment will continue on points 59 and 60 and on points east of a line 59-V6E-V5E.

INTENTION.

2. The GARHWAL Brigade with maxim guns of BAREILLY, trench guns of BAREILLY and DEHRA DUN Brigades and No. 4 Trench Mortar Battery will hold the present front of the Brigade and will attack the enemy's line between the ditches which run from S-S-E to N-N-W, through the points V.5 and V.6.

ASSAULTING BATTALIONS.

3. The 2nd Leicestershire Regiment with six machine guns will assault with its right on the ditch which runs through V.5, having as objective the enemy's trenches marked in the tracing given to the O.C. and will get into touch with the 2nd Division on the right, clearing and double blocking beyond bombing distance any trenches leading to the front.

The Garhwal Rifles with six machine guns will assault with left on the ditch which runs through V.6, having as objective the redoubt S.E. of V.6, marked on the tracing given to the C.O., and will form a defensive flank to the left, clearing and double blocking beyond bombing distance all trenches leading to front or flank.

TIME OF ASSAULT.

4. The assault will be delivered from the enemy's side of the ditch at 11.30 p.m. on the night of the 15th-16th May.

SUPPORTING BATTALIONS.

5. The 3rd LONDONS in the eastern half of assembly trenches B.1 and B.2 will support the Garhwal Rifles.

Two Companies 2/3rd GURKHAS, under Major Tillard, in the W. half of assembly trenches B.1 and B.2 will support the 2nd Leicesters.

These supports will keep fileing up the trenches to the front as they are vacated.

The rear company of each body of supports will carry up ammunition from the depôt in the RUE DU BOIS and form advanced depôts for the Officers Commanding assaulting battalions.

CONSOLIDATION OF POSITION.

6. The objectives given for the attack will be consolidated before daylight.

BRIGADE RESERVE.

7. The 2/3rd GURKHA RIFLES (less two Companies) in B.1 and B.2 assembly trenches in rear of the supporting companies of the 2/3rd G.R.

DEFENCE OF THE LINE.

8. Lt.-Col. Morris, 2/8th, commanding, 8th GURKHA Rifles, Machine guns of GARHWAL and BAREILLY Brigades (Less 12 guns), No. 4 Trench Mortar Batty. bomb guns of BAREILLY, Garhwal and Dehra Dun Brigades,	will hold the line from the LA BASSEE - ESTAIRES ROAD (exclusive) to but excluding the centre communication trench from the ORCHARD to the front line.

THE MACHINE GUNS AND BOMB GUNS will be disposed in accordance with instructions given to machine and bomb gun officers, so as to cover the left flank of the attack.

BOMBING PARTIES, &c.

9. Assaulting Battalions will organise bombing, blocking, sandbag and tool parties. These will be provided with flags to mark the position reached by them.

SANDBAGS AND RATIONS.

10. Every man will carry two sandbags and one day's rations in addition to emergency ration.

DEPOTS FOR AMMUNITION, &c.

11. Two depôts in the front line, containing in each case :—
100 Boxes S.A. Ammunition.
200 Bombs.
2,000 Sandbags.
2 Boxes Very Pistol Ammunition.

The bombs are not in carrying boxes; it is therefore imperative that units send back their boxes when sending for more bombs.

There is also an ammunition depôt at the R.E. Store in the RUE DU BOIS.

MASKS.

12. Masks will be kept in readiness soaked in solution prepared under directions of Medical Officers, and will be worn by assaulting troops.

COMMUNICATION TRENCHES.

13. The 2nd LEICESTERS will have the use of the new HAZARA communication trench and the right Orchard communication trench.

The GARHWAL RIFLES will use the centre and left Orchard communication trenches.

The wounded will return by the communication trench which leaves the front line 50 yards to the east of the ditch which passes the east side of the Orchard, to the RUE DU BOIS and thence by the Orchard communication trench parallel to and 100 yards east of the tramline, to the DUE DES BERCEAUX.

MEDICAL.

14. A collecting station will be established between LANSDOWNE POST and the point where the tramline crosses the RUE DES BERCEAUX.

DISTINGUISHING MARKS.

15. The 2nd Division troops are wearing at night a white bit of cloth showing both to front and rear.

The position of advanced or flank bombing parties of the 2nd DIVISION will be marked by yellow screens, 6 feet x 28 inches in the case of battalions and yellow flags 28 inches by 28 inches for companies.

The 1st DIVISION red flags 3 feet x 3 feet, with white perpendicular stripe.

LONDON DIVISION sandbag cloth disc, 2 feet in diameter with black cross in centre.

LAHORE DIVISION yellow flag 16 inches square.

COMMUNICATION TRENCHES TO BE OPENED.

16. As soon as it is practicable communication trenches will be opened up to the captured position.

REPORTS.

17. To report centre on north side of RUE DU BOIS close to and east of the R.E. DEPOT.

WATCHWORD.

18. GARHWAL.

J. H. K. STEWART, Major,
Brigade Major, Garhwal Brigade.

Issued at 2 p.m. through Signal Section.

Copy No. 1—2nd Leicesters.
" 2—3rd Londons.
" 3—2/3rd Gurkhas.
" 4—Garhwal Rifles.
" 5—2/8th Gurkhas.
" 6—Brigade M.G.O.
" 7 " Bomb Gun Officer.
" 8—Meerut Division.
" 9—Sirhind Brigade.
" 10—6th Inf. Brigade.
" 11—War Diary.
" 12—Retained.

COPY OF MESSAGE No. B.M.161, DATED 15TH MAY, 1915, FROM THE GARHWAL BRIGADE, TO THE OFFICERS COMMANDING, 2ND LEICESTERS & THE GARHWAL RIFLES.

The following instructions have been received :—

1. If your night attack succeeds you will hold on to V.6, at all costs, even if the Division on your right fails.

2. If your night attack fails do not persist in it, but if 2nd Division on your right succeeds, then use every endeavour to connect up with its left.

3. If both your and the 2nd Division night attacks fail, you will make a fresh attack at 3.15 a.m., to synchronise with the 7th Division attack. This attack will be preceded by an artillery bombardment from 2.45 to 3.15 a.m.

4. If attack fails again another attack will be delivered, probably six hours later, and will be carried through by the Sirhind Brigade.

BATTLE OF FESTUBERT.

Copy No. 1.

OPERATION ORDER No. 2
BY
LT.-COLONEL D. H. DRAKE-BROCKMAN, C.M.G., Commanding The Garhwal Rifles.

Ref. Tracing and French Map.
Map Bethune. 1/40,000.

15-5-1915.

1. The enemy are entrenched strongly across our front, and his breastworks covered with barbed wire. His breastworks are distant approx. 50 yards to 200 yards on our extreme left by the LA BASSEE road.

His entrenchments consist of a front line breastwork in our immediate front with a second line approx. 100 yards in rear, with a redoubt marked V.6 in the centre of it.

The whole of the hostile front to be attacked, V.1 to V.6, has been subjected to a continual bombardment, with object of damaging his parapet and obstacles.

The 2nd Division, and 7th Division on the right of the 2nd, is co-operating on our right, and the left of our line is held by the 2/8th Gurkhas with the Lahore Division, prolonging the line to NEUVE CHAPELLE. The Sirhind Brigade is in our support.

2. The object of the attack by the Garhwal Brigade is to capture the front line trenches and work V.6, and form a defensive flank along the left or east communication trench which runs along the small ditch on our left flank and along E. edge of the work V.6, to guard the left flank of the 1st Division which is attacking on our right in co-operation.

3. The Garhwal Brigade less 2/8th Gurkhas, will attack that portion of the enemy's entrenchments to its immediate front, the left resting on a small ditch running out from the main ditch along our front down to the redoubt V.6, and the right of a similar small ditch running parallel to this ditch in front of the old "Gap" to V.5.

4. The Brigade will attack on a two-Battalion front. The 2nd Leicesters on the right and the Garhwal Rifles on the left, supported by the 2/3rd Gurkhas and 3rd London, respectively.

The Garhwal Rifles will have as frontage from the small ditch mentioned in para 2 above on the left to the ditch running down to the W. edge of the orchard on the right and the 2nd Leicesters from that ditch onwards to the small ditch on the right above mentioned running down to V.5.

5. Nos. 2 and 3 Companies will form the assaulting Lines, on a front of a platoon, supported by Nos. 4 and 1 Companies, in above order.

6. Each platoon will be formed in single rank and follow each other in the assault at 30 yards distance.

7. To enable the assaulting lines to advance simultaneously the first two platoons will file quietly out at 10.30 p.m.. beyond the parapet by the exits made by the S. & M. last night and also by the exit by the listening post and line up beyond the ditch, using the bridges which will have been placed out before hand. It is most essential that this be done in absolute silence. They will lie down beyond the ditch and remain quiet till the signal to advance, which will be given at 11.30 p.m. Touch must be made with and kept up with the 2nd Leicesters on our right. The ditch on our left should be left 6 yards to 8 yards clear on our left owing to a possible M.G. being in place to fire down it.

8. Immediately the first two Platoons of No. 2 Coy. have filed out, the other two Platoons will in like manner file up along into the trench vacated by them and file out through the same exits and lie down beyond the ditch.

9. Two Platoons of No. 3 Coy., in single rank, will then immediately occupy the fire trench vacated by No. 2 Coy. and file out and lie down between the trench and the ditch, and await their opportunity to advance over the ditch when those in front start, and continue without any hesitation the advance at the distance of 30 yards.

The other two Platoons of No. 3 Coy. will then in like manner at once move up to the place vacated by the other two Platoons of No. 3 Coy., and act unhesitatingly in like manner.

10. The remaining two Coys., No 4 and 1, will be pushed forward in like manner, the principle being that platoons should advance successively one behind the other, in depth at a distance of 30 yards between each.

11. The 3rd London Regiment will in like manner at once keep progressing forward gradually and occupy successively the places vacated by the Companies of the Garhwal Rifles, and push forward in like manner on the assault commencing, in support of the Garhwal Rifles.

12. The communicating trenches should not be used for this purpose in front of the orchard, but platoons in single rank should advance across the open to the fire trench and into and over it to the assault.

13. The chief objective of this left attack is the redoubt V.6. The leading platoons of the assault will pass over the first trench and press on vigorously to the objective V.6.

14. The bomb throwers of the leading platoons of No. 2 Company should be dropped on arrival at the first trench reached in order to bomb up the two parallel communication trenches which run straight up to V.6., one on each flank. For this purpose the bomb throwers of No. 2 Company will follow the rear platoon of the Company, half being on either flank. in order to at once commence working up the two parallel communication trenches running up to the work V.6.

The remaining Bomb Throwers of assaulting Companies will accompany the rear platoon of their respective Companies, all on the left flank, in order to at once commence bombing up the main fire trench and communication trenches running out eastwards from the E. communicating trench which runs up to V.6, and out of this work. The 2nd Leicesters taking those communication trenches running to the W.

15. The following will be carried as under :—

By Companies.

Very Pistols and ammunition for them.
Bombs.
Masks ready soaked, by each man, to be worn by assaulting troops.
Distinguishing flags.

By Signallers.

Flags, helios and lamps.
Telephone wire.
M.S. Books

16. The spare ammunition boxes at present carried by certain Companies will not be taken but stored in the ammunition depôt at head of communication which runs along W. edge of ORCHARD to the fire trench. Each man should be made up to 200 rounds at evening alarm posts, in case any had been expended while in occupation of the fire trench.

17. A signalling station for visual signalling will be established as soon as the objective V.6 is reached, to communicate with Regimental and Brigade Headquarters till a telephone wire is run out.

18. The bridges taken over from Brigade Headquarters will be put out by Captain Etherton at 9 p.m. precisely and marked by luminous boards to facilitate recognition by night.

The utmost secrecy is essential, and men taking them out must be impressed upon to keep absolute silence.

19. Spare entrenching tools will be left collected in one place in the centre communication trench.

The rear Platoon only of each Company will take six Shovels and two Picks.

20. The Bomb Throwers of No. 1 Company will accompany the rear platoon of No. 1 Company in order to be available to bomb up the communication trench which runs S. out of V.6 to V.5.E.

21. The two rear Platoons of No. 1 Company will carry six extra sandbags per man.

Captain Harbord will arrange to take these over from R.E. Depot by Brigade Headquarters near RUE DU BOIS tonight as he goes up. He will also complete up with the necessary number of bombs short from the Ammunition Depôt at head of centre communication trench.

22. The Machine Guns, under Captain Lyell, will remain in fire trench and stand by ready to advance on order being given.

23. The objective when reached will be consolidated before daylight.

24. Bombing parties will each carry flags to mark the portion reached by them.

25. One day's cooked rations will be carried by each man, in addition to the emergency ration, and water bottles filled.

26. An Ammunition Depôt has been established in front line where the right communication trench meets the fire trench. When sending for more bombs, empty boxes should be sent.

27. Wounded will be returned by the trench which leaves the front line 50 yards east of the ditch which passes to the E. of the Orchard to the RUE DU BOIS, and then down the Orchard communication trench.

28. A collecting station will be established between LANSDOWNE POST and the point where the tramway crosses the RUE DU BERCEAUX.

29. Watchword : GARHWAL.

30. Reports to O.C. in fire trench at bridge over ditch running along W. edge of ORCHARD.

P. T. Etherton, Captain,
Acting Adjutant The Garhwal Rifles.

Issued at 5 p.m.

Copies Nos. 2-5 issued
to all Company Commanders.

REPORT ON THE PART TAKEN BY THE GARHWAL RIFLES IN THE NIGHT ATTACK OF THE 15TH/16TH MAY, 1915, ON THE GERMAN TRENCHES FACING RICHEBOURG L'AVOUE DURING BATTLE OF FESTUBERT.

On May 15th the Regiment was occupying bivouac trenches along the RUE DE BERCEAUX between LANSDOWNE POST and WINDY CORNER. In accordance with Operation Orders, Regiment left bivouac at 8 p.m., and proceeded across country S. of Lansdowne Post to the CRESCENT communication trench, up which it filed and through Assembly trenches N. of RUE DU BOIS and by centre communication trench through ORCHARD to the fire trench in front of the ORCHARD. The front from which the battalion was to attack was from the ditch along the right ORCHARD communication trench on the right to a small ditch running at right angles to our front up to V.6 on the left, a front of approximately 60 yards. In order to cross the ditch full of water running along the front of our entrenchments, bridges had to be put out for the attacking troops to get over. On arrival at the front line trenches, where I had previously had bridges collected, I immediately commenced the operation of having these laid out. I detailed Captain Etherton, who was assisted by one man of the 3rd Londons, to do this, to save delay, as my leading Company had not arrived. This was successfully completed by 10.45 p.m. It was attended with a certain amount of difficulty owing to the fact of heavy firing occurring on the left in front of NEUVE CHAPELLE, which made the Germans send up a great number of flares and increased sniping. It would have been far better if fire had not opened until our attack commenced, as it only caused the Germans to be more on the "qui vive" and anticipate an attack. On arrival of the leading Company it was at once filed out by the openings made previously by the S. & M. in the parapet and over the bridges to other side of ditch, and formed up lying down. Two more platoons of the next Company were formed up in like manner on our side of the ditch.

Two other platoons were drawn up in fire trench, and two others in rear of the parados, with the rest of the Battalion in rear of these. These preparations were finally completed by 11.20 p.m.

Punctually at 11.30 p.m. the leading platoons, together with 2nd Leicesters on the right, advanced, and simultaneously with our advance a heavy rifle fire broke out from the German line. After the space of about two minutes this was augmented by the fire of two machine guns, in addition to those firing from the flanks. The two platoons in the fire trench at once pushed forward in support and their places were taken by two more from the rear.

The ORCHARD and the open space between the latter and fire trench were being swept by sharpnel fire and bombs.

It was soon evident that the attack had been stopped and after 2½ Companies altogether had been sent forward I saw it was useless prosecuting the attack any further and reported matters to Brigade Headquarters.

Orders were then received to prepare for another attack at 3.15 a.m. The 3rd Londons were ordered to relieve the Regiment in fire trench, which was ordered to withdraw to the ORCHARD and remain in close support. I sent out word to the attacking platoons, and those beyond the ditch, to withdraw, and those wounded and unwounded who were able to do so were eventually got back to the fire trench and withdrawn to the ORCHARD and reorganized.

The second attack was not pressed nor was I called upon to send up any platoons in support. The Regiment was subsequently withdrawn to assembly trenches just N. of RUE DE BOIS.

D. H. DRAKE-BROCKMAN,
Lieut.-Colonel,
Commanding the Garhwal Rifles.

D/- 16th May, 1915.

See Map in illustration of the part taken at the Battle of FESTUBERT).

ACTION OF PIETRE

(BATTLE OF LOOS).

SECRET. Copy No. 4.

OPERATION ORDER No. 88

BY

BRIG.-GENERAL C. G. BLACKADER, D.S.O.,
Commanding Garhwal Brigade.

Reference Trench Map. Sept. 23rd, 1915.

INFORMATION.

1. The 1st Army is resuming the offensive. Indian Corps will

(*a*) Attack enemy's line between SUNKEN and WINCHESTER Roads and establish our line along MAUQUISSART—DUCK'S BILL road.

(*b*) Press on with its left in front, until its left gains the high ground between HAUTE POMMEREAU and LA CLIQUETERIE FERME.

(*c*) Continue its advance from there in a South-Easterly direction. The Garhwal Brigade and Bareilly Brigade will carry out the assault with the Dehra Dun Brigade in Divisional reserve.

The assault will be preceded by

(i.) Four days' deliberate bombardment by Artillery and Trench Mortars: rifle, rifle grenade and machine gun fire being employed to prevent the enemy repairing the damage done to his obstacles and defences by this bombardment.

(ii.) The explosion of a mine under the enemy's parapet at M 30 a 3.4 to take place two minutes before the gas and smoke attack commences.

(iii.) A gas and smoke attack immediately before the assault.

(iv.) Formation of thick smoke barrages on each flank of the assaulting troops.

The immediate objective of the assault is the general line of the road from M 36 a 3.4 to M 30 c 7.9 and thence due North to the enemy's front parapet at M 30 a 7.6, and is to include the capture of all enemy's front and supporting lines. The 19th and Lahore Divisions will hold the front of the Indian Corps less that allotted to the assaulting Brigades. The 20th and Lahore Divisions will cover the flanks of the attack by fire and will advance and maintain touch with the Meerut Division when the latter advances beyond the enemy's front and supporting line trenches. The dividing line between the assaulting Brigades runs from centre of salient M 30 c 0.4 on a true bearing of 98 degrees 26 minutes (magnetic bearing 112 degrees) and passes between two solitary dead trees. They are about four feet apart and about 100 yards from our trenches. The line is also marked by sandbags for a few yards from our trenches.

INTENTION.

2. The Garhwal Brigade is to capture that part of the enemy's line between M 36 a 3.4. and the dividing line (*vide* map). The troops are not to delay in the enemy's front line trenches but will push on and capture the supporting lines. They will not halt if portions of the line are held up but will push on towards their objective. Should the enemy's opposition be unshaken they will consolidate the position gained, pushing forward covering parties and patrols. All trenches on the right flank or forward will be double blocked and vigorous bomb attacks continued along them to maintain touch with the enemy and to find out whether he shows any sign of weakening. Should the enemy's opposition be slight the subsequent advance will be on HAUTE POMMEREAU and LA CLIQUETERIE FARM.

3. **Distribution for assault** (*vide* **map**)—

UNIT.	OBJECTIVE.	DIVIDING LINE.	PATROLS TO
2/3rd Gurkhas 2 M.G.'s 2 parties Grenadier Coy.	M36 a 4.4. to M36 a 6.5 inclusive to house M36 a 6.5. exclusive (in yellow)	Right on Ditch, "3ft. wide, dry" Left on Ditch "4ft. wide, 4ft. deep," both bearing 145 degs. mag.	(1) Road M36 d S of Pietre cross-roads. (2) In direction of LA RUSSIE.
2nd Leicesters 2 M.G.'s	House M36 a 6.5. incl. by house M36 a 9.8 incl. to road M30 c 6.0. incl. (in green)	Right on Ditch "4ft. wide, 4ft. deep," 145 degs. mag. Left from point 100yds. of S salient M30 c 0.4. on bearing 129 degs. mag. to old German communication trench bearing 140 degs. thence along above trench	(1) PIETRE cross-roads.
2/8th Gurkhas 2 M.G.'s 1 Party Grenade Coy. (British)	Road M30 c 6.0 exclusive through M30 c 8.3. to road at M30 c 6.5. incl. (in brown)	Right on Leicesters Left Left on Brigade dividing line	(1) Road N31 a.

Each Battalion will be responsible that there is no gap on its left flank, keeping a strong platoon in hand for this purpose. Battalion bombing parties will be ready to operate on the inner flanks of flank battalions and on both flanks of centre battalions. Brigade Grenade parties will be on the outer flanks of battalions they accompany.

3rd Londons, as soon as position is captured, will continue and occupy trench along North side of the MAUQUISSART road from the DUCK'S BILL to the German Trench still holding the DUCK'S BILL and its Neck.

GARHWAL RIFLES.

Brigade Reserve; moving up to front trenches as they empty, keeping their bombing parties in the centre of the Battalion.

MACHINE GUNS.

Eight in Brigade reserve move to head of COLVIN Street as trenches empty.

No. 13 TRENCH MORTAR BATTERY AND BRIGADE BOMB GUNS.

As soon as position is captured an officer from each unit will go forward to reconnoitre suitable positions.

BRIGADE GRENADE COMPANY RESERVE

will move to the head of S. TILLELOY Street as the trenches empty.

AMMUNITION.

4. 200 rounds S.A.A. on the man and 150 Grenades will be carried per Battalion.

DEPOTS OF S.A.A. AND GRENADES.

5. In front line near heads of SUNKEN and SOUTH TILLELOY Streets and at salient M 30 c 0.4, 18 boxes S.A.A. and 160 grenades, 1 box Very Pistol and 1 box illuminating pistol in each

LAFONE POST COLVIN POST	100 boxes D.A.A. 500 hand grenades 120 rifle grenades in each
Junction of LAFONE St. & RUE TILLELOY	250 boxes S.A.A. 300 rounds Very Pistol ammunition.
M 29 c 0.6 where tramline crosses RUE TILLELOY	1,000 hand grenades.

The above are marked by notice boards, and direction arrows have been erected in front line to point out way to nearest ammunition or hand grenade depot.

The position of these dug-outs are to be explained to all ranks.

WIRE CUTTING.

6. *The last wire* in front of our trenches will be cut on the night previous to the assault by the assaulting Battalions concerned.

ARRANGEMENTS FOR ASSAULT.

7. All timings on the day of assault are from ZERO, which will be the hour at which the gas attack commences. Zero will be marked by the simultaneous discharge of a bunch of red, blue and yellow daylight rockets from a point close to Bareilly Brigade report centre.

Assaulting Battalions will cross our parapet at 0.9 hours counting from Zero, and will form up in front of our wire. They will advance to the assault of the enemy's front trenches at 0.10 hours.

SALLY PORTS.

8. *Sally ports* are not to be used between 0.0 hours and 0.20 hours on the day of assault.

DISTINGUISHING FLAGS.

9. *Distinguishing flags* will be carried to assist in showing localities reached by our own troops. There will be 2 with each Grenade party and 10 per Battalion. A coloured diagram of flags used by our and other units is attached.

SANDBAGS.

10. Each man will carry 2 sandbags. Depots have been established on S. TILLELOY, COLVIN and S. MOATED GRANGE Streets in front of the support line. Brigade reserve of 5,000 is at Brigade report centre.

VERMOREL SPRAYERS.

11. Four filled Vermorel Sprayers and 2 refills will be carried per assaulting Battalion; remaining Battalions carry 3 each and 2 refills.

PACKS.

12. Packs will not be carried.

SMOKE HELMETS.

13. All ranks will wear Balaclava Caps and not ordinary caps. On the day of the assault ten minutes before the emission of gas they will wear the old pattern smoke helmet rolled up and so arranged as to be able to be pulled down into position over the head and face at a moment's notice. Tube helmets will also be carried by all ranks in the usual way.

TRENCH TRAFFIC.

14. *Traffic* in long communication trenches must move in accordance with direction arrows.

Following are "UP":

SUNKEN STREET
S. TILLELOY STREET
COLVIN STREET.

Following are "DOWN":

EBENEZER STREET
LAFONE STREET
S. MOATED GRANGE STREET
MOATED GRANGE STREET

Traffic rules may be broken for urgent tactical reasons only.

SAPPERS AND MINERS AND PIONEERS.

15. Sappers and Pioneers will make strong points at

(*a*) Group of houses M36 a 5.3.
(*b*) Road junction M36 a 8.8.

and will open communication trenches.

No. 1. M36 c 1.9 to M36 a 4.4. (assisting 3rd Londons) to be converted to fire trench.
No. 2. M35 b 9.8. to M36 a 4.4.
No. 3. M30 c 1.1½ to M36 a 4.8.
No. 4. M29 d 9.7. to M30 a 3.3.

MEDICAL.

16. Regimental Aid Posts are established in SOUTH MOATED GRANGE STREET and LAFONE STREET.

Collecting Stations are established at—

1. M28 d 8.4, near junction of LAFONE STREET and RUE TILLELOY.
2. M28 d 6.2.
3. EBENEZER FARM.

Wounded will reach collecting stations by LAFONE STREET or SOUTH MOATED GRANGE STREET.

PRISONERS.

17. Prisoners will be escorted to RUE BACQUEROT *via* MIN STREET and handed over to 4th Cavalry, when escort will return immediately to its unit. Prisoners to be searched immediately for documents and other articles as soon as possible after being captured. These must accompany prisoners and be handed over with them.

REPORT CENTRE.

18. Garhwal Brigade M35 a 6.5 (junction of LAFONE STREET and old German line).

Bareilly Brigade M29 d 4.2.

Hour of opening will be notified later.

REPORTS.

19. Reports to M14 d 10.9.

W. F. S. CASSON, Major,
Brigade Major,
Garhwal Brigade.

Issued to Signals at
Copy No.

1	to 2nd Leicesters, with map and flags plate
2	1/3 Londons „
3	2/3rd Gurkhas „
4	Garhwal Rifles „
5	2/8th Gurkhas „
6	Bde. M.G.O. „
7	Bde. B.G.O., with flags
8	Bde. Grenade Coy, with map and flags plate
9	Bde. Signals „
10	Meerut Division, with map
11	4th Bde. R.F.A. „
12	C.R.A. „
13	C.R.E.
14	Bareilly Brigade
15	Jullundur Brigade
16	Dehra Dun Brigade
17	War Diary, with map and flag
18	File, with map and flag

SECRET. Copy No. 3.

ORDERS FOR THE SMOKE AND GAS ATTACK AND SMOKE BARRAGES.

Referred to in Operation Order No. 88, para. 7.

1. The Smoke and Gas Detachments will be in their allotted places in the front Line by 6.0 p.m. on the 24th inst.

2. From 6.0 p.m. on the 24th inst. until 0.8 hours, counting from Zero, No Troops except One Sentry per Two Bays are to be in the bays in which groups of Smoke and Gas Detachments are stationed.

3. The programme between the explosion of the mine and the assault is as follows :—

–0.2	(*i.e.*, 2 minutes before Zero) Mine fired.
0.0	Daylight Rocket Signal sent up from Bareilly Bde. Report Centre to mark Zero.
0.0	Commencement of Gas.
0.0	Artillery commences bombardment of enemy's fire trenches.
0.5	Smoke screens on flanks commence.
0.5	Smoke commences along entire front concurrently with the gas.
0.8	Gas to be cut off.
0.8	Infantry fill up all bays of the fire trench and get into position to cross parapet.
0.9	Infantry cross parapet and form up.
0.9	Artillery lifts 100 yards.
0.10	Assault commences.
0.11	Artillery lifts another 100 yards.
0.14	Artillery lifts to German second position, about 500 yards in rear of their front trench.
0.15	Smoke screen on flank stops, but the smoke has still to disperse.

4. Gas cylinders are to be exhausted during the first six minutes if possible; if not, the gas may run concurrently with the smoke until 0.8, when all gas must be turned off punctually.

5. The FIRST Smoke Candle will be lit at 0.5
The SECOND 0.7
The THIRD 0.8

Candles are to be held so that the top projects slightly over the parapet to enable the smoke to drift over the parapet. They are NOT to be thrown forward out of the trenches.

6. The smoke barrage on our right will be made by the Lahore Division and will fill the area between the DUCK'S BILL and the German trenches, no bombs falling North or West of a line between the DUCK'S BILL and the German communication trench at M36 a 7.1. This smoke barrage will also extend between our line and the German line South of the Duck's Bill.

7. The fumes of all smoke appliances are innocuous.

No infantry, including right and left flank bombing parties, are to go beyond the line between M36a and M36c on our right flank, until the smoke has cleared sufficiently to ensure that our artillery are able to see our flank troops.

8. Men of the smoke Detachment will wear YELLOW arm bands on the right arm. Men of the Gas Detachment will wear RED, WHITE and GREEN arm bands on the right arm.

W. F. S. CASSON, Major,
Brigade Major,
Garhwal Brigade.

Issued to Signals at

Copy No.	1	2nd Leicesters.
	2	2/3rd Gurkhas.
	3	39th Garhwal Rifles.
	4	2/8th Gurkhas.
	5	3rd Londons.
	6	B.M.G.O.
	7	B.B.G.O.
	9	Bde. Grenade Coy.
	10	File.

SECRET. Copy No. 4.

OPERATION ORDER No. 89
BY
BRIG.-GENERAL C. G. BLACKADER, D.S.O.,

September 23rd, 1915.

INFORMATION.

1. In case the wind should be unfavourable for gas attack, the Garhwal Brigade will

attack as follows :—

0.0 No. 88 being " A " Attack.
0.0 No. 89 being " B " attack.

Except as hereinafter detailed all arrangements laid down in 0.0.88 hold good.

DISTRIBUTION.

2. The same Battalions as in "A" attack will assault with the same objective, each with 1/2 Battalion in 2 lines and 1/2 Battalion in Regimental Reserve. The assaulting 1/2 Battalion will be formed up by 4.20 a.m. in the long grass outside our present wire, using the sally-ports.

TIME TABLE OF ASSAULT.

3. Time Table of assault is as follows :—

4.20 a.m. Assaulting 1/2 Battalions to be formed up lying down outside our wire.
4.25 a.m. Intense artillery bombardment by whole of the artillery.
4.27 a.m. Mine explodes.
4.30 a.m. Artillery lifts 100 yards.
4.31 a.m. Artillery lifts another 100 yards
4.34 a.m. Artillery lifts on enemy's reserve trenches.

4. Special instructions have been issued for Field Guns and Maxims in parapet.

5. Grenade parties in reserve and Bombing parties of Garhwal Rifles will move up to the front line trenches at head of cut just south of COLVIN STREET in front of Garhwal Rifles.

6. Balaclava Caps will be worn and two Smoke Helmets carried as usual. The old pattern Smoke Helmet will be immediately put on in case of necessity.

W. F. S. CASSON, Major,
Brigade Major,
Garhwal Brigade.

Issued to Signals at 11.15 p.m.

Copy No. 1 to 2nd Leicesters.
2 3rd Londons.
3 2/3rd Gurkhas.
4 Garhwal Rifles.
5 2/8th Gurkhas.
6 B.M.G.O.
7 B.B.G.O.
8 Grenade Coy.
9 Signals (Garhwal Bde.)
10 Meerut Division.
11 4th Bde. R.F.A.
12 C.R.A.
13 C.R.E.
14 Bareilly Bde.
15 Jullundur Bde.
16 Dehra Dun Bde.
17 War Diary.
18 File.

SECRET.

NOT TO BE CARRIED FORWARD BEYOND OUR FRONT PARAPET UNDER ANY CIRCUMSTANCES.

PROGRAMME "A."

TIME TABLE IF GAS AND SMOKE ARE EMPLOYED.

−0. 2 (*i.e.*, 2 minutes before ZERO). Mine fired.
0. 0 Daylight rocket signal sent up from Bareilly Brigade Hdqrs. (near junction of COLVIN St. and HOME COUNTIES TRENCH).
0. 0 Commencement of GAS.
0. 0 Artillery, except guns in our parapet, opens shrapnel fire on the enemy's front trenches, and H.E. fire on enemy's defences further in rear.
0. 4 Two field guns and Hotchkiss gun in our front parapet open fire.
0. 5 Smoke screens on flanks commence.
0. 5 Smoke commences along entire front concurrently with the Gas.
0. 8 Gas to be cut off.
0. 8 Infantry fill up all bays of the fire trench and get into position to cross our parapet.
0. 9 Infantry cross our parapet and form up.
0. 9 Artillery lifts 100 yards.
0. 9 Field gun in our front trench near the BIRDCAGE ceases fire.
0.10 Assault commences.
0.10 Field gun in our front trench near DUCK'S BILL ceases fire.
0.11 Artillery lifts another 100 yards.
0.14 Artillery lifts to German 2nd position about 500 yards in rear of their front trench.
0.15 Smoke screens on flanks stop, but the smoke has still to disperse.
0.20 Hotchkiss gun in our front parapet ceases fire.

PROGRAMME "B."

TIME TABLE IF GAS AND SMOKE ARE NOT EMPLOYED.

4.20 a.m. By this time the assaulting infantry are to be lying in position outside our parapet.
4.25 a.m. Artillery bombardment commences, including guns in our front parapet.
4.27 a.m. MINE explodes.
4.30 a.m. Assault.
4.30 a.m. Artillery lifts 100 yards.

4.30 a.m. Field guns in our front trenches cease fire, but Hotchkiss gun continues to fire.
4.31 a.m. Artillery lifts another 100 yards.
4.34 a.m. Artillery lifts to German 2nd position about 500 yards in rear of their front line.

SECRET. Copy No. 7.

OPERATION ORDER No. 3,
BY
LT.-COLONEL D. H. DRAKE-BROCKMAN,
C.M.G., Comdg. The Garhwal Rifles.

Reference Trench Map
Sheet S.W.1, Scale 1/10000.
and BETHUNE Sheet 36a.S.E.
Scale 1/40000. Regimental Hdqrs.
24.9.15.

INFORMATION.

1. The INDIAN CORPS is to capture the enemy's trenches between SUNKEN and WINCHESTER Roads, and to establish our Line along the road running through MAUQUISSART to the DUCK'S BILL.

The MEERUT Division will carry out the attack allotted to the INDIAN CORPS.

The GARHWAL and BAREILLY Brigades will carry out the Infantry attack.

The Assault will be preceded by a bombardment lasting 4 days. Prior to the Infantry assault there will be a preparation with gas and smoke.

The gas and smoke cloud will extend well beyond the flanks of the enemy's position to be attacked.

Just before the attack a mine will be sprung under the German parapet and Salient on WINCHESTER Road.

The assault will be delivered under cover of the gas and smoke cloud and will be supported by Trench Mortars and Rifle Grenade fire on the enemy's trenches and indirect fire by Machine Guns on selected portions in rear of his position.

The dividing line between the GARHWAL and BAREILLY Brigades will be the centre of the Salient just N. of S. MOATED GRANGE St. at M.30.c.15.30. Thence through the Salient in the enemy's line at M.30.c.4.5. which will be inclusive to the BAREILLY Brigade. Magnetic bearing 112 degrees from the point of the Salient.

INTENTION.

2. The attack will be carried out by 3 Battalions in the front line and one in Reserve.

The OBJECTIVE of the Brigade is to consolidate a line from M.36.a.4.4 — M.36.a.6.5—M.30.c.8.3.—M.30.c.6.5.

The 2/3rd GURKHAS will take the Line from M.36.a.4.4. — M.36.a.6.5 inclusive to the house M.36.a.6.5. exclusive.

The 2nd LEICESTERS will take from the house M.36.a.6.5 inclusive by house M.36.a.9.8 inclusive to the road M.30.c.6.0 inclusive.

The 2/8th GURKHAS will take from the road M.30.c.6.0 exclusive through M.30.c.8.3 to road M.30.c.6.5 inclusive.

O.C.s are responsible that there are no gaps in the left flanks of their Battalions.

The Assaulting Line will not delay at the enemy's First Line of trenches, but press on and capture the objectives.

3. The Brigade will be formed up in the front and support Line of our trenches as follows :—

The 3rd LONDONS on the right from SUNKEN Road inclusive to SUNKEN St. exclusive and DUCK'S BILL and NECK.

The 2/3rd GURKHAS from the ditch marked "3ft. wide dry" to ditch "4ft. wide 4ft. deep."

The 2nd LEICESTERS from ditch "4ft. wide 4ft. deep" to ditch "3ft. wide 3ft. deep."

The 2/8th GURKHAS next from ditch "3ft. wide 3ft. deep" to S. MOATED GRANGE St.

The GARHWAL RIFLES will be in the HOME COUNTIES TRENCH from LAFONE St. to COLVIN St. in Reserve.

AMMUNITION.

4. There will be Depôts of S.A.A. at the following places :—

LAFONE POST, COLVIN POST	100 boxes S.A.A., 500 grenades	each
Junction of LAFONE St. and RUE DU TILLELOY in Dug-out of H.Q.IND.5.B.	200 boxes S.A.A.	
Junction of New Tramway and RUE DU TILLELOY	1,000 grenades	

These are marked by notice boards.

All ranks must be made acquainted with their position.

Trench Ammunition in "B" Line is being collected at junction of

Communication Trenches in the places marked in the sketch issued.

Regimental Reserve Ammunition of 50 rounds per man in full boxes will be at Battalion Headquarters at junction of SUNKEN St. and HOME COUNTIES Trench.

MEDICAL.

5. Collecting Stations will be located at :—

(i.) Junction of SUNKEN St. and RUE DU TILLELOY.

(ii.) Junction of LAFONE St. and RUE DU TILLELOY.

(iii.) EBENEZER FARM.

(iv.) Regimental AID POST on LAFONE St. between fire trench and LAFONE Post.

ROUTES for wounded will be by :—

(i.) S. MOATED GRANGE St.

(ii.) MOATED GRANGE St.

(iii.) LAFONE St.

FLAGS.

6. The distinguishing Flags are :—

GARHWAL BRIGADE — BLUE with RED bar.

BAREILLY BRIGADE — BLACK with YELLOW bar.

DEHRA DUN BRIGADE—YELLOW.

LAHORE DIVISION—YELLOW with BLACK vertical bar.

20TH DIVISION—GREEN and PINK.

The leading Troops will carry these and place them in the trenches reached so as to be seen by our Artillery.

TIME OF MARCH.

7. The Regiment will parade at 7.45 p.m. and march *via* HARROW ROAD and ROUGE CROIX to the RUE DU BACQUEROT and thence by SUNKEN St. Communication trench to its place of assembly in the HOME COUNTIES Trench, following the 3rd LONDONS.

Companies will march in the following order :—

No. 1 Company—3, 1, 4, 2 }
No. 4 Company—15, 13, 16, 14 } Platoons in this order.
No. 3 Company—10, 12, 9, 11 }

On arrival at the junction of SUNKEN St. and HOME COUNTIES Trench No. 1 Company will file to its right and occupy the right portion of the trench with its right on LAFONE St., leaving LAFONE St. clear.

Nos. 4 and 3 Companies will follow No. 1 Coy. and file to the left, and No. 4 Coy. will proceed on till it comes to S. TILLELOY St., where its left will rest. No. 3 Company will fill up the interval between No. 1 Coy. and No. 4 Coy.

A portion of the HOME COUNTIES Trench 30 yards in length must be left clear for the Detachment of the Brigade Grenadier Coy., which has to occupy that portion nearest S. TILLELOY St.

This Detachment will march with the Battalion at the head of No. 4 Coy.

EQUIPMENT TO BE CARRIED.

8. Each Company will carry the following :—

1 W.P. Sheet }
2 Sandbags }
2 Smoke Helmets in Satchel }
1 Emergency Ration } each man
Cooked portion of the day's ration in the haversack }
200 rounds of S.A.A. }
Filled Waterbottles }
1 VERMOREL Sprayer
6 Bottles with Solution
53 Shovels
16 Picks
1 Illuminating Pistol (by Nos. 1 and 3 Coys. only). Bomb boxes.

SMOKE HELMETS.

9. The second Smoke Helmet (old pattern) will be worn on the head rolled up ready to be pulled down at a moment's notice, when the gas has been turned on. F.S. Hats will be packed in kits and left behind. The Balaclava Cap only will be worn.

This Smoke Helmet will be put down as soon as necessity arises. Coy. and Platoon Commanders must keep a watchful eye on this and give the order when necessary.

BOMBING PARTIES.

10. FOUR special bombing parties will be detailed as per annexed table. Bayonet men to accompany these will all be told off by O.C. No. 3 Coy. Each party will carry 2 of the special flags mentioned in para. 6 above.

They will be attached to No. 3 Coy. and be placed in the centre of the Coy. when in position in the fire trench. They should therefore march between Nos. 12 and 9 Platoons.

The remaining Bomb Throwers of each Company will be on the outer flanks of their Companies.

ROLE OF THE BATTALION.

11. The Role of the Battalion is at first to occupy the HOME COUNTIES Trench. Watch carefully the assaulting Battalions in front and move forward and successively occupy the support and fire trenches as vacated by them and hold the line from SUNKEN Road to the Salient

M.30.c.15.30, which is the left of the 2/8th GURKHAS, and be prepared to carry up ammunition, tools and bombs, and if orders are received, to reinforce.

Company Commanders must then carefully watch the Battalions to their front and move up at once without waiting for direct orders to do so. They should post an Officer at the Support Line to give timely notice.

SIGNALLERS.

12.—A party of 3 Signallers and 1 Linesman will be told off to Battalion Headquarters and each Company.

The following will be carried :—

1 Telephone }
1 Lamp } by each party.
Large and small flags }

The Headquarters Party will in addition carry 1 Helio.

Each Linesman will carry 1 Drum of Wire.

In case of wires getting cut visual signalling will have to be resorted to.

ORDERLIES.

13. Each Company Commander will detail 1 intelligent man to act as orderly. They will remain with Battalion Headquarters.

DISCIPLINE.

14. When marching to take up position in the position of assembly strict silence must be maintained and no smoking or striking of lights be allowed.

Companies must go slowly and keep closed up.

REGIMENTAL RESERVE S.A.A.

15. The 20 boxes of S.A.A. stored at Battalion Headquarters in the HOME COUNTIES Trench will be carried up to the fire trench by No. 3 Company.

REGIMENTAL RESERVE S.A.A. TRAFFIC.

TRAFFIC.

16. The following routes from and to the front Line will be observed :—

From REAR to FRONT :

SUNKEN STREET
S. TILLELOY STREET
COLVIN STREET

From FRONT to REAR.

EBENEZER STREET
S. MOATED GRANGE STREET
MOATED GRANGE STREET
LAFONE STREET

17. Each Company will tell off from one complete platoon, under a Garhwali Officer, 30 men and keep them ready when the fire trench has been reached to carry up S.A.A. and Bombs, which are stored in the Depots at the head of the Communication Trenches. This party should be detailed from the support.

If Ammunition is sent up the men must return at once on completion of the duty.

18. Immediately these depôts have been emptied the Company Commander concerned will at once send a written message to the Officer of Dehra Dun Brigade, at the junction of the Support Trench and Communication Trench to send up more and complete re-filling of Depôts.

19. Orderlies sent with messages may use any Communication Trench.

20. Officers will set their watches with that of the Commanding Officer. The times for the various operations are given in a separate secret memorandum issued to officers.

21. Garhwal Brigade Report Centre is situated at Square M.35.a.8.5, *i.e.*, at the junction of LAFONE Street with the old German Line on the west or left-hand side coming down the trench.

22. REPORTS to Battalion Headquarters at junction of SUNKEN Street and HOME COUNTIES TRENCH, and after moving up to the Front Line at the dug-out at junction of Fire parapet and COLVIN Street.

G. R. MAINWARING,
Captain, Acting Adjutant,
The Garhwal Rifles.

Issued at 5 p.m.

No. 1 Copy War Diary.
No. 2 Copy to O.C. No. 1 Company.
No. 3 Copy to O.C. No. 3 Company.
No. 4 Copy to O.C. No. 4 Company.
No. 5 Copy to Medical Officer.
No. 6 Copy for Record.
No. 7 Copy Filed.

N.B.—Owing to casualties the Regiment only consisted of three Companies.

DETAILS OF SPECIAL BOMBING PARTIES.

To be supplied by	Bomb Throwers. Belts filled on arrival in firing line trench. 1 box for both.	Spare Bomb Throwers, with 1 Box each as carriers to leading Throwers.	Balance with 2 boxes each.
No. 1 Company			
1st Party	2	2	1 N.C.O. and 4
No. 3 Company			
2nd Party	2	2	1 N.C.O. and 4
No. 4 Company			
3rd Party (G. Coy.)	2	2	1 N.C.O. and 4
4th Party (H. Coy.)	2	2	1 N.C.O. and 4
Total	8	8	4 N.C.O.s and 16

Note.—All the Bayonet men for these parties will be supplied by No. 3 Coy., *i.e.*, a total of 32 men for the 4 Bombing parties. All should be detailed from one Platoon and the whole party be kept in the centre of the Company, *i.e.*, between Nos. 12 and 9 Platoons. Each party will carry 2 of the special flags issued.

SECRET MEMORANDUM issued to each Officer Commanding Companies.

Programme "A" (If Gas and Smoke are employed).

- −0. 2 EXPLOSION of mine (Bareilly Brigade Front).
- 0. 0 Daylight Rocket to give the time to Gas and Candle men, to mark zero.
- 0. 0 Commencement of Gas.
- 0. 0 Artillery bombardment of Trenches.
- 0. 5 Smoke screen on Flanks begins.
- 0. 5 Smoke along entire Front.
- 0. 8 Gas cut off. Infantry file up actual bays of trench.
- 0. 9 Infantry cross parapet and form up.
- 0. 9 Artillery lifts 100 yards. Field Gun near DUCK'S BILL ceases fire.
- 0.10 Assault commences.
- 0.11 Artillery lifts 100 yards.
- 0.14 Artillery lifts to German Second Line, about 500 yards in rear of front trenches.
- 0.15 Smoke screen on Flanks finishes, but has now to disperse.
- 0.20 Hotchkiss gun in our front parapet ceases fire.

Programme "B" (If Gas and Smoke are NOT employed).

- 4.20 a.m. Assaulting Infantry to be lying in position outside parapet.
- 4.25 a.m. Artillery Bombardment commences.
- 4.27 a.m. Mine explodes.
- 4.30 a.m. Assault.
- 4.30 a.m. Artillery lifts 100 yards.
- 4.30 a.m. Field Gun in parapet ceases fire. Hotchkiss Gun continues firing.
- 4.31 a.m. Artillery lifts another 100 yards.
- 4.34 a.m. Artillery lifts to German second position, about 500 yards in rear of front line.

REPORT ON THE PART TAKEN BY THE GARHWAL RIFLES IN THE OPERATIONS OF 25th SEPTEMBER, 1915, AGAINST THE GERMAN TRENCHES COVERING MAUQUISSART (Action of PIETRE during Battle of LOOS).

24/9/15.

1. The Regiment which was bivouacked at junction of ETON and OXFORD roads marched at 7.45 p.m., to take up its position in the place of assembly assigned to it in the HOME COUNTIES trench, marching *via* ROUGE CROIX and Rue du BACQUEROT and SUNKEN Street communication trench.

The Regiment was in position by 10.30 p.m.

The night passed quietly.

25/9/15.

2. At the time appointed, *i.e.*, 5.48 a.m., when the mine was sprung, my three Companies commenced immediately to file out of the HOME COUNTIES trench by SUNKEN Street, S. TILLELOY Street, and COLVIN Street communication trenches in order to get up to and occupy the fire trench and the old Support Line.

In spite of shelling and bombs from Minenwerfer they managed to reach the top of communication trenches in good time.

My right Company was able to get into its position in the fire and support trench quickly, but my centre and left Companies were delayed, as some of the Assaulting Companies had not all advanced at that moment. Also, owing to the Gas on account of the wind not acting as anticipated, a party of 2nd Leicesters was met coming down the trench apparently to escape the Gas, so these two Companies had to file into the support line, from whence they were eventually able to get up and occupy the fire trench. Immediately on arrival of my left Company (No. 4 Company) in fire trench, 30 men with boxes of ammunition were sent up to the 2/8th G.R., and succeeded in reaching them safely with only a few casualties. This platoon on arrival did not return, but was kept by order of a Major of the 33rd P.I., and so has not rejoined me, which accounts for the number under the head " Missing."

After giving the Companies what I considered sufficient time to be clear of the communication trenches I went up to the 2/3rd G.R. Headquarters, where I had a brief talk with the O.C. 2/3rd, and then proceeded on to what was to be my Headquarters near junction of COLVIN Street and fire trench, and found it still occupied by the O.C. 2nd Leicesters. My left Company in the firing line was subjected to a heavy bombardment, the parapet being broken in one or two places.

It was now about 7.30 a.m.

After a brief conversation with O.C. 2nd Leicesters and from such reports as he had received he dispatched a telegram explaining the situation and that we were both of opinion that a fresh attack should be organised.

I then despatched a message asking if I should send up reinforcements to the Leicesters, to which I received a reply : " Be ready to do so, but not until I tell you," in B.M.19, time 8.47 a.m.

Meantime a message B.M.23 time 8.21 a.m. was eventually received ordering me to send up two Bombing parties and half a Battalion to reinforce Leicesters left.

The numbers of these messages and the time of each made it very doubtful as to which was the later message.

I left Leicesters Headquarters in the fire trench to get in touch with my Company Commanders, but found that the Dehra Dun Brigade, *i.e.*, 1st Seaforths and 2nd Gurkhas, had commenced filing in, and this, coupled with a certain amount of congestion which had already begun owing to wounded and others returning back from the fire trench, made communication extremely difficult and also delayed the receipt and despatch of messages by hand, or being able to get to the telephone. On receipt of your B.M.45, I sent word to O.C. No 3 Company in the centre to close down as quickly as he could to his left behind No. 4 Company, preparatory to launching the attack ordered.

I sent a message at 12.20 p.m., pointing out the crowded state of the trenches and that quick movement was impossible.

Fortunately, I met G.O.C. Dehra Dun Brigade and pointed out the congested state of the trenches owing to his Brigade filing in and that I had been ordered to organise an attack to reinforce 2/8th G.R., and he told me he had given orders for that portion to be cleared. This was eventually done and I was enabled to get my Companies in position by 2.30 p.m.

In course of conversation with the G.O.C. Dehra Dun Brigade he informed me he was also making an attack, the right of which was contiguous to my left, so I suggested that as the dispositions for both would be ready at the same time, both should be made simultaneously, to which he agreed. While the Companies and two Bombing parties were getting into position and preparations were being made I reconnoitred the portion to be attacked, and it appeared from what I could see that the Germans were in possession of the trench again, as a small German flag, red, white and black, was visible on a portion of the parapet. Also I received a report from two of my men who had attempted to take up bombs that they had been unable to reach the 2/8th, as they had seen Germans bombing down the trench to the left.

In the meantime, too, the Germans had opened fire from that trench which had been originally occupied by the 2/8th, on our parapet opposite to them.

The Companies were ready for the advance by 2.30 p.m. Also the Companies of the 2nd Gurkhas which had been ordered to advance on our left. The whole advanced on a given signal over the parapet, and immediately a heavy fire broke out from the Germans, bullets striking all along the top of the parapet and some men falling in the act of getting over.

Owing to the casualties suffered I did not order the next two platoons to advance, and the G.O.C. Dehra Dun Brigade, who was standing on the right flank of my Company, also stopped any more men advancing.

The two Platoons that had advanced had got about 30 or 40 yards and were obliged to take cover and advance by crawling up in the grass and folds in the ground. Some of them eventually got to within about 20 yards of the German wire, but could get no further and eventually retired back to our line under cover of darkness.

Before this attack was launched I had also received messages to organise a right attack to aid the 2/3rd, who were supposed to have got in, but before anything could be done I had received a verbal message delivered by Captain Stone in person from

O.C. 2/3rd G.R., to the effect that the half Company which he had been ordered to place at my disposal was to stand fast.

As I felt certain that the 2/3rd had not got in on the right and the wire in their front was reported uncut, I did not carry on with launching that right attack. Companies were re-organised and the fire trench from SUNKEN Street, exclusive, to S. MOATED GRANGE Street, exclusive, was occupied by my Regiment.

The remnants of the 2nd Leicesters, 2/3rd and 2/8th were withdrawn to the support line and HOME COUNTIES trench. During the night some wire was put out and parties were sent out to bring in the wounded. A certain number of both officers and men were brought in.

The next day, 26th, the Brigade was relieved by the Dehra Dun Brigade, the Regiment marching to billets in HARROW Road, the last company reaching billets at 6.30 p.m.

The total casualties were :—

	K.	W.	M.	Remarks.
British Officers ...	—	—	—	
Indian Officers ...	—	*2	—	*1 by shell, shrapnel, 1 by rifle fire
O.R.I.				
1/39th G. ...	—	9	21	
2/39th	4	19	11	
B.M.P. ...	—	3	7	
Tihri S. & M. ...	1	5	2	
Total ...	5	*36	41	*Rifle fire 33, shell 3

D. H. Drake-Brockman,
Lieut.-Colonel,
Commanding The Garhwal Rifles.

N.B.—It was after this battle that I sent in a report on the gallantry of a man of the 2/3rd Gurkhas in bringing in a wounded man of the Leicesters under fire, which was brought to my notice by Captain Burton, D.S.O., and which I am glad to say gained him the V.C.

LIST OF MESSAGES RECEIVED AND SENT DURING ACTION OF PIETRE, 25th SEPTEMBER, 1915.

To GARHWAL BRIGADE.

No. 1. Dated 25. In reply to

Shall I send up reinforcements to aid Leicesters.
From Garhwal Rifles.
Time 7.30 a.m.

(Signed) D. H. Drake-Brockman,
Lieut.-Colonel.

To GARHWAL BRIGADE.

No. 2. Dated 25. In reply to No. B.M.7.

Two Companies are in front line and third one coming in now a a a tremendous block in all trenches.

(by hand)
From Garhwal Rifles.
Time 8.50 a.m.

Sd., D. H. Drake-Brockman,
Lieut.-Colonel.

To 2nd Leicesters, Garhwal Rifles, 3rd Londons, 2/8th Gurkhas, 2/3rd Gurkhas

(By orderly)

No. B.M.9. Dated 25. In reply to

Bareilly report 4th B.W. over front parapet at 6.25.

From Garhwal Brigade.
Time 6.40 a.m. (Received 11.45 a.m.)

Sd., W. H. Casson, Major.

To 39th. (By orderly).
Leicesters.

No. B.M.23. Dated 25. In reply to

Send half-Battalion and two of your bombing parties to reinforce Leicesters' left a a a As soon as they have got into German line bombing parties supported by the half-Battalion are to clear the German trenches towards our right thus assisting Leicester's right frontal attack addressed 39th repeated Leicesters.

From Garhwal Brigade.
Time 8.21 a.m. (Received 11.45 a.m.)

Sd., W. H. Casson, Major.

To Garhwal Rifles. (By orderly).

No. B.M. 19. Dated 25. In reply to No. 1.

Be ready to do so, but not till I tell you.

From Garhwal Brigade.
Time 8.47 a.m. (Received 11.45 a.m.)

Sd., W. H. Casson, Major.

To Garhwal Rifles. (By orderly)
Leicesters,

No. B.M.30. Date 25. In reply to

2/8th Gurkhas have reached objective and are holding lines as per sketch attached (to Garhwal Rifles) the half-Battalion ordered to reinforce can get in there and work to their right a a a Will you also see Col. Ormsby, find out where his men have got in, put in your other half-Battalion with two bombing parties there, and work to their left in a similar manner. Addressed Garhwal Rifles repeated Leicesters for information.

From Garhwal Brigade.
Time 8.15 a.m.

Sd., W. H. CASSON, Major.

To All Infantry Units.

No. B.M.34. Date 25. In reply to

20th Division on our left reported advancing without opposition on German third line a a a Dehra Dun Brigade ordered to attack and reach high ground Bas Pommereau-La Cliqueterie.

From Garhwal Brigade.
Time 10 a.m.

To Garhwal Rifles.

No. B.M.38. Date 25. In reply to

Let me know how matters are progressing with you a a a Bareilly Brigade reports that 2/8th Gurkhas appear to be giving way a a a A Company 33rd Punjabis is being sent to fill gap between 2/8th and 4th B.W.

From Garhwal Brigade.
Time 10.25 a.m.

To Garhwal Rifles. (By orderly).

No. B.M.42. Date 25. In reply to

My B.M. 30 begins 2/8th Gurkhas have reached objective and are holding line they were ordered to a a a The half-Battalion ordered to reinforce can get in there and work to their right a a a Will you also see Col. Ormsby and find out where his men have got in a a a Put in your other half-Battalion with two bombing parties and work to their left in similar manner. Addressed Garhwal Rifles repeated Leicesters for information ends.

From Garhwal Brigade.
Time 11.1 a.m.

Sd., W. H. CASSON, Major.

To Advanced Garhwal Brigade Hdqrs.

No. 3. Date 25. In reply to No. B.M.38.

At present am in fire trench holding the line from SUNKEN ROAD to MOATED GRANGE STREET in accordance with original orders a a a Your message regarding attacking with two Platoons 2/3rd and half-Battalion Garhwalis not received a a a Two Companies 2nd GURKHAS have also come up in fire line a a a Shall I reinforce 2/8th GURKHAS or attack salient in front of LEICESTERS.

From Garhwal Rifles.
Time 11.5 a.m.

Sd., D. H. DRAKE-BROCKMAN,
Lieut.-Colonel.

To 39th.

No. B.M. 44. Date 25. In reply to

Have you received B.M.23 timed 8.21 a.m.

From Garhwal Brigade.
Time 11.12 a.m.

To Garhwal Rifles. (By orderly).

No. B.M. 45. Date 25. In reply to No. Nil.

If you have not already advanced you will advance to where the 2/8th have made their lodgement with half a Battalion and two bombing parties a a a with these bombing parties enter towards our right and join hands with Leicesters a a a Support bombing parties with both companies if necessary a a a if not have one company in support of 2/8th a a a A similar procedure is to be carried out on our right with two bombing parties and the other half of your Battalion but extending to our left from where the 2/3rd have made a lodgement a a a acknowledge.

From Garhwal Brigade.
Time 11.35 a.m.

Sd., W. H. CASSON, Major.

To Garhwal Rifles.

No. B.M.46. Date 25. In reply to

Place your last half-Company at Colonel Drake-Brockman's disposal for his right attack acknowledge addressed 2/3rd repeated Garhwal Rifles.

From Garhwal Brigade.
Time 11.45 a.m.

To Garhwal Brigade.

No. 3. Date 25. In reply to

2nd Gurkhas and 4th Seaforths have come into front line and have blocked all trenches a a a impossible to start attack until they are clear.

From Garhwal Rifles.
Time 12.20 p.m.

Sd., D. H. DRAKE-BROCKMAN,
Lieut.-Colonel.

To Garhwal Rifles.

No. B.M.54. Date 25. In reply to No. 3.

If crowded out follow close behind Dehra Dun and carry out your orders for joining 2/8th and Leicesters.

From Garhwal Brigade.
Time 1 p.m.

To Garhwal Rifles.

No. B.M.62. Date 25. In reply to

How are you progressing a a a both 2/8th and Leicesters stand in need of assistance.

From Garhwal Brigade.
Time 3.5 p.m.

To Advance Garhwal Brigade.

No. 5. Date 25. In reply to No. B.M. 45 and 62.

Organised the attack as ordered but Germans had retaken from 2/8th all or greater portion of trench captured and attack was unsuccessful owing to heavy rifle and machine gun fire a a a After putting in one Company and seeing attack a failure I did not put in any more a a a One Company 2nd Gurkhas attacked in combination a a a Am now holding front line with two Companies and half Company in support but rather divided up having Leicesters in between my two Companies a a a attack on right I did not start as I don't think 2/3rd got in and wire in front was uncut; from report of two men who tried to get up bombs I should imagine 2/8th must have been captured as the whole of their trench seemed retaken.

From Garhwal Rifles.

Time 3.45 p.m.

(Sd.) D. H. Drake-Brockman,
Lieut.-Colonel.

To Leicesters, 2/8th, 39th.

No. B.M. 45/26. Date 26. In reply to

Following from a D.O. 1st Army through a D.O. Indian Corps and a D.O. Meerut Division begins, At sunset of the first day of the great battle we have now commenced the Field Marshal Commanding-in-Chief desires to convey to the 1st Army his hearty congratulations and warmest thanks for the splendid work accomplished a a a he feels confident that the fine courage and magnificent spirit which animated all ranks will ensure a speedy victory over the enemy. ends.

From Garhwal Brigade.
Time

le Drumez
LAVENTIE
Rue de Paradis
Riez Bailleul
Ft. d'Esquin
Picantin
Rue du Bois
le Trou
Rue Tilleloy
le Tilleloy
la Flinque
Wangerie
Rue Masselot
Fme l'Epinette
Pont du Hem
Rue Bacquerot
Eglise
Rouge Croix
Rougès Bancs
Fme Delaval
Distillery
Ferme Vaubain
Rue du Puits
Croix-Barbée
Aubers
Bas Pommereau
Ston
St. Vaast
Neuve Chappelle
Richebourg-St. Vaast
Rue des Berceaux
Ligny-le-Petit
Richebourg l'Avoue
Fme du Biez

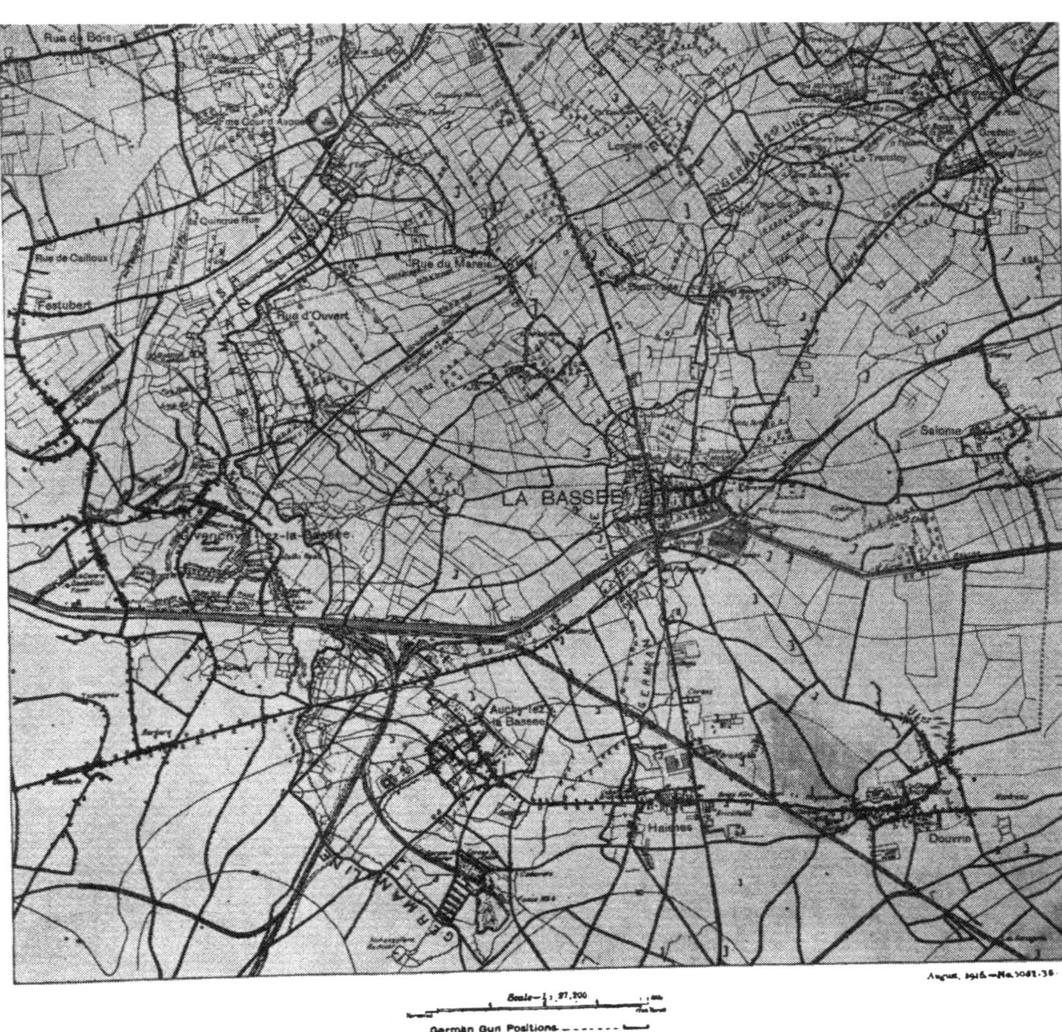
Rue du Bois
Rue de Cailloux
Festubert
Rue d'Ouvert
Rue du Marais
LA BASSEE
Givenchy-lez-la-Bassee
Auchy-lez-la Bassee
Haisnes
Douvrin
Salome
GERMAN LINE
German Gun Positions

www.ingramcontent.com/pod-product-compliance
Ingram Content Group UK Ltd.
Pitfield, Milton Keynes, MK11 3LW, UK
UKHW041645190726
13854UKWH00006B/2702

9 781845 743260